Community Policing

This textbook discusses the role of community-oriented policing, including the police image, public expectations, ethics in law enforcement, community wellness, civilian review boards, and what the community can do to help decrease crime rates. In addition, the author covers basic interpersonal skills and how these might vary according to the race, sex, age, and socioeconomic group with which the officer is interacting. Finally, students learn how to initiate new programs in a community, from the planning process and community involvement to dealing with management and evaluating program success.

Michael J. Palmiotto, Ph.D. is Professor of Criminal Justice at Wichita State University. He is a former police officer in New York State and has experience in establishing and operating a Police Training facility. He has a master's degree from John Jay College (CUNY) and a doctorate from the University of Pittsburgh. Professor Palmiotto has published ten books and numerous articles and book chapters in the criminal justice field.

Criminology and Justice Studies Series

Edited by **Chester Britt**, *Northeastern University*, **Shaun L. Gabbidon**, *Penn State Harrisburg*, and **Nancy Rodriguez**, *Arizona State University*

Criminology and Justice Studies offers works that make both intellectual and stylistic innovations in the study of crime and criminal justice. The goal of the series is to publish works that model the best scholarship and thinking in the criminology and criminal justice field today, but in a style that connects that scholarship to a wider audience including advanced undergraduates, graduate students, and the general public. The works in this series help fill the gap between academic monographs and encyclopedic textbooks by making innovative scholarship accessible to a large audience without the superficiality of many texts.

Books in the Series

Published:

Biosocial Criminology: New Directions in Theory and Research edited by Anthony Walsh and Kevin M. Beaver

Community Policing in America by Jeremy M. Wilson

Criminal Justice Theory: Explaining the Nature and Behavior of Criminal Justice edited by David E. Duffee and Edward R. Maguire

Lifers: Seeking Redemption in Prison by John Irwin

Race, Law and American Society: 1607 to Present by Gloria J. Browne-Marshall

Today's White Collar Crime by Hank J. Brightman

White Collar Crime: An Opportunity Perspective by Michael Benson and Sally Simpson

The New Criminal Justice: American Communities and the Changing World of Crime Control by John Klofas, Natalie Hipple, and Edmund McGarrell

The Policing of Terrorism: Organizational and Global Perspectives by Mathieu Deflem

Criminological Perspectives in Race and Crime, 2/e by Shaun Gabbidon

Corrections by Jeanne Stinchcomb

Forthcoming:

Crime and the Lifecourse by Michael Benson

Structural Equations Modeling for Criminology and Criminal Justice by George Higgins

Crime Emergence: Reducing Uncertainty in Theory and Research by Christopher Sullivan, Jean McGloin, and Les Kennedy

Criminal Justice Research by Brian Withrow

Experiencing Criminal Justice: Practitioners' and Outsiders' Perspectives of Policing, Courts, and Corrections edited by Heith Copes and Mark Pogrebin

Program Evaluation for Criminal and Juvenile Justice by J. Mitchell Miller and Holly Ventura Miller

Race, Racism, and Crime: A Theory of African American Offending by James Unnever and Shaun Gabbidon

Causes of Delinquency Revisited by Chester Britt and Barbara Costello

Community Policing

A Police–Citizen Partnership

Michael J. Palmiotto

Routledge
Taylor & Francis Group

NEW YORK AND LONDON

First published 2011
by Routledge
270 Madison Avenue, New York, NY 10016

Simultaneously published in the UK
by Routledge
2 Park Square, Milton Park, Abingdon, Oxon OX14 4RN

Routledge is an imprint of the Taylor & Francis Group, an informa business

© 2011 Taylor & Francis

The right of Michael J. Palmiotto to be identified as author of this work
has been asserted by him in accordance with sections 77 and 78 of the
Copyright, Designs and Patents Act 1988.

Typeset in Adobe Caslon, Trade Gothic and Copperplate Gothic by
Florence Production Ltd, Stoodleigh, Devon
Printed and bound in the United States of America
on acid-free paper by Walsworth Publishing Company, Marceline, MO

Library of Congress Cataloging in Publication Data
Palmiotto, Michael.
   Community policing: a police-citizen partnership/Michael J. Palmiotto.
      p. cm.— (Criminology and justice studies series)
    Includes bibliographical references and index.
   1. Community policing—United States.   2. Police–community
relations.   3. Crime prevention—Citizen participation.   4. Police
administration.   I. Title.
HV7936.C83P353 2011
363.2′3 – dc22   2010034849

ISBN13: 978-0-415-88974-2 (hbk)
ISBN13: 978-0-415-88975-9 (pbk)
ISBN13: 978-0-203-83050-5 (ebk)

TABLE OF CONTENTS

9   COMMUNITY-ORIENTED POLICING   210

10   PLANNING THE IMPLEMENTATION OF COMMUNITY POLICING   244

SERIES FOREWORD

Criminology and Justice Studies offers works that make both intellectual and stylistic innovations in the study of crime and criminal justice. The goal of the series is to publish works that model the best scholarship and thinking in the field today, but in a style that connects that scholarship to a wider audience including advanced undergraduates and graduate students. The works in the series help fill the gap between academic monographs and encyclopedic textbooks by making innovative scholarship accessible to a large audience without the superficiality of many texts.

Professor Palmiotto's *Community Policing: A Police–Citizen Partnership* provides a comprehensive overview of community policing. Beginning with a detailed history of policing, the author provides readers with an introduction to several aspects of policing that were critical considerations with the move toward the large-scale adoption of community policing (e.g., police culture, police discretion, etc.). The author also provides essential discussions on neighborhoods, multiculturalism, and crime prevention. Each of these topics provides students of community policing with additional insights into this policing philosophy and also the advances in policing that led to the formal development of the strategy. The use of concrete examples from an assortment of police agencies represents a hallmark of the book. Thus, after reading Professor Palmiotto's book, students of community policing will have a clear understanding of the challenges and processes that are required to implement and sustain the strategy.

Shaun L. Gabbidon

PREFACE

This book provides an overview on community policing and fo~~~ ~~~
the needs of students who wish to learn about c~~ ~~~~ policing in our
society. The first chapter covers police history relevant to community
policing. Chapters 2 and 3 cover police culture, police discretion, and police
misconduct, which must be reviewed in any book on community policing.
Concepts, strategies, experiments, and research findings that have influenced community are examined in Chapter 4 while Chapter 5 deals with
communities and neighborhoods. Chapter 6 covers multiculturalism,
diversity, and organizational change. Chapter 7 clarifies crime prevention
as it relates to community policing. Problem-oriented policing is explained
in Chapter 8 while Chapter 9 explains community-oriented policing.
Planning and the implementation of community policing are reviewed in
Chapter 10. Chapter 11 reviews planning and training while Chapter 12
covers various community-policing programs. The final chapter, Chapter
13 looks at the possibilities of the future of community policing.

Pedagogical features of the book include chapter objectives that orient
students to the main objectives of the chapter, a chapter summary that
reinforces the major topics in the chapter, key terms for each chapter to
assist students in reviewing material, and discussion questions to help
students test their knowledge of the chapter.

1

POLICE HISTORY RELEVANT TO COMMUNITY POLICING

CHAPTER OBJECTIVES

1. Understand why knowledge of police history is important for understanding policing today.
2. Be familiar with the crime-fighting image of policing.
3. Be familiar with police issues of the 1960s.
4. Be familiar with governments' influence on policing in the 1960s.
5. Be familiar with the concept of police professionalism.
6. Be familiar with the various eras of policing.

Introduction

The philosophy of community policing is being advanced as the new policing system for the twenty-first century. How can police administrators, leaders, or students of policing support or even understand the value of and need for community policing in our contemporary world if they lack knowledge of where police have been? How can effective decisions and policies be implemented if those politicians and police administrators making decisions have no knowledge or understanding of police history? Formal policing as we know it today is relatively new, being less than two centuries old. Knowledge can be gained from familiarity with the historical role the police have played in society. This holds true even though the history of policing is sketchy and the variety of roles the police have played in the past have not all been documented. There does appear to be sufficient information of value to modern-day police. For example, anyone familiar with policing or police officers often hears the claim that they are not social workers, but in the late nineteenth century and early twentieth century, the police performed tasks that are currently performed by social service agencies, including finding jobs for the unemployed, operating soup kitchens, and using the police station as a night shelter.

Politicians and police administrators, along with police supporters and students of policing, should understand the history of policing, including its various strategies and police methods, if they hope to have an impact on the field. Police decision makers with a knowledge of the various police roles and tactics used throughout history should be in a better position than those with no or limited knowledge of police history to improve policing or at least avoid some of the problems that have occurred in the past.

American Policing

The Metropolitan Police Act of 1829 that established the London police force became the model for American policing. The New York City Police Department is often credited for initiating the modern police department in America in 1845. Before that time, American peacekeeping strategies were similar to those of the English. Boston founded the first night watch in America in 1634; it consisted of six soldiers and an officer. Two years later, a town watch, consisting of townspeople and not military personnel, was initiated to keep the peace. This system lasted until 1712, when Boston voted to pay their watchmen (Bopp and Schultz 1972, 17–18). Charlestown in 1680 and Philadelphia in 1682 appointed constables who had responsibilities similar to those of their English counterparts. As in England, county governments appointed sheriffs as their primary peace officers, and it was an obligation of citizens to serve as watchmen and constables (Johnson 1981, 5).

The American Revolution

During the American Revolutionary War, peacekeeping was maintained by troops, who were English or American, depending upon who occupied the area. After the war, peacekeeping reverted back to civilian control. Providence, in 1791, retained 12 night watchmen to take over the public safety duties performed by the militia. In 1801, Boston became the first city to mandate that permanent night watchmen be employed. That same year, Detroit hired its first civilian police officer. More and more civilian peacekeepers were being employed after the Revolutionary War because of the growth of cities and the increase in crime associated with them (Bopp and Schultz 1972, 25–28).

Traditional peacekeepers—sheriffs, constables, and night watchmen— were unable to control crime occurring in American cities. The crime during this period consisted of violence, riots, and vice. Modern America still has these problems, but today the responsibilities to solve them have been given to community policing officers.

To regulate Philadelphia's crime problem, Stephen Girard, upon his death, left the city of Philadelphia financial resources for public safety. With the Girard money, Philadelphia established a day force of 24 police officers and a night force of 120 night watchmen. Maintaining separate day and night watches created difficulties in peacekeeping. Recognizing this, New York legislature unified the day and night watches of the New York City Police Department in 1845. New York City had the first unified police force in the United States, modeled on the London Metropolitan Police Department. The combining of day and night patrols became the model of American police departments (Bopp and Schultz 1972, 33–38).

Modern policing developed in America during a period marked by disorder and violence. Most American cities experienced mob disorder. A variety of factors appear to have contributed: conflicts of native Americans with Irish and German immigrants; racial conflict, with whites attacking abolitionists and free blacks; economical disasters, which led mobs of financially ruined investors to attack banks and employees to destroy the property of their employers; attempts to solve issues of morality, as when brothels were attacked as a means of cleaning up the city; and political conflicts, as in the case of the frequent mob riots on election days in major cities such as New York, Philadelphia, and Baltimore. It was generally left to the militia to suppress riots. The series of major riots in American cities led to the establishment of the "new police," the forerunner of our contemporary police departments (Walker 1977, 4–5).

The New Police

Unlike our police of today, the "new police," when first formed in New York City in 1845, did not wear uniforms or carry firearms. Not until the mid-1850s did New York City require police officers to wear uniforms. Eventually, the requirement that officers wear uniforms was adopted by other cities. Firearms began to be used in the 1840s. Without formal approval, police officers began carrying them to protect themselves from armed thugs. Eventually, the cities gave formal approval for police officers to carry firearms. Today, we expect police officers to be armed and to wear uniforms.

During the nineteenth century, city populations increased substantially. Cities that were hamlets grew into urban centers. Industrialization increased the demand for workers. Cities grew substantially, with immigrants arriving from foreign countries. There was also a migration from the farms to the cities. This influx of population into cities affected policing in three ways. First, it increased the geographical size of the cities enormously to accommodate this influx and thus the police were unable to maintain a suitable presence on the city streets. Second, the poor crowded into overflowing neighborhoods where they could afford the rents. Overcrowded neighborhoods became slums where violence and tensions commonly occurred. Third, thousands of various ethnic, national, and racial groups were living in close quarters. These included blacks, Irish, Germans, Scandinavians, Italians, Poles, and Jews (Johnson 1981, 36).

Changes in Policing

Policing in American cities during the nineteenth century was primarily decentralized and neighborhood oriented. The major dilemmas of the policing model were corruption, inefficiency, incompetence, and political influence. A number of Americans wanted to see improvements in American policing, and eventually there were attempts to improve the administration of police departments. The first attempt to control city police departments was in New York State in 1857. Based on the claim that New York City was too corrupt to govern itself, the state legislature passed a law—the Metropolitan Police Bill, modeled after Sir Robert Peel's London Metropolitan Police Bill—that placed the New York City Police Department under state control by putting it under the supervision of a board appointed by the governor. State control of police departments spread to other states: Baltimore in 1860, St. Louis and Chicago in 1861, Kansas City in 1862, Detroit in 1865, and Cleveland in 1866. There was some opposition to this development. In addition, there was a lack of uniformity in controlling police agencies throughout the state (Fogelson 1977, 43–44).

Around the turn of the century, the Progressive movement emerged as a voice to improve city government, including policing departments. This movement reflected upper-middle-class concerns to safeguard the honesty of public officials, establish uniform standards, and operate by well-defined regulations and procedures (Johnson 1981, 67). A city police department in which each captain responded to his neighborhood's customs could not expect to possess uniform standards. Disorder and drunkenness were acceptable among some ethic groups, and the police who recruited from these ethnic groups looked the other way when minor offenses were committed. A tolerance toward brothels, public intoxication, and rowdiness was not acceptable to the upper classes of America's cities. Police critics of this period supported scientific management and the hiring of specialists to solve a city's problems. They were disturbed not only by the lack of uniform police standards but also by the lack of discipline and efficiency and the poor quality of police personnel.

The National Prison Association, founded in 1870, championed civil service, police training, and a nonpartisan police department through its Standing Committee on Police. However, changes in policing come slowly. Civil service was adopted by New York City in 1883 and by Chicago in 1895. A major crusader for police change in New York City was the Reverend Charles Parkhurst, president of the Society for the Prevention of Crime. Parkhurst charged that police corruption and vice were rampant in New York City. His campaign led to the New York legislature establishing the Lexow Commission in 1849 to investigate police activities. The commission found political interference with the police process, police connivance with criminals, and police payoffs for appointments and promotions (Johnson 1981, 66–67).

An outcome of the Lexow Commission was the creation of a four-member board of police commissions for New York City. Theodore Roosevelt was appointed president of the board and served a two-year term. Roosevelt worked to improve the quality of police recruits, raise standards of police performance, and curtail corruption. The crime-fighting image of the police was projected under Roosevelt's tutelage through awards of medals and certificates to patrolmen for specific acts of bravery. Roosevelt's purpose was to motivate the rank-and-file patrolmen to be productive (Walker 1977, 46). Although the image of police as crime fighters was not accurate, it persisted and is still with us today. Even today, there are police chiefs who sell policing to politicians and the public by arguing that the police are crime fighters. This myth is even believed by some rank-and-file police officers. However, the community policing philosophy runs counter to the crime-fighting image. Community policing officers are problem solvers who work in partnership with neighborhood residents to solve crime and disorder problems.

The Crime-Fighting Role

Critics of policing in the nineteenth century advocated police training; the elimination of corruption, police brutality, and inefficiency; and the removal of politics from police affairs. Nineteenth-century police officers, as mentioned earlier, were expected to perform activities not normally associated with policing, including charity work, street cleaning, and boiler inspection. Critics believed that such assignments distracted police from their crime-fighting task and diminished the image of the police. Their goal was to professionalize the police, and they felt that this could best be accomplished by giving the police the new image and goal of crime fighting. Police chiefs in America readily accepted that police should be primarily crime fighters. The foremost change agent for improving police departments in the first half of the twentieth century was a strong advocate of the crime-fighting mission. August Vollmer, who began his police career as a town marshal in Berkeley, California in 1905, and ended up being police chief there until 1932, is credited with being the chief spokesman for the professionalization of the police and their training in the science and technology of all aspects of crime-fighting work (Carte and Carte 1975, 2).

With Vollmer and other police chiefs advocating crime fighting as the most important mission of police, it did not take long before this philosophy became ingrained in the police culture. Crime fighting was sold as the primary function of the police, even though crimes such as homicide, rape, and assaults are usually not preventable by the police and are often not even solved. The philosophy of crime fighting is reflected in those departments that still do "bean counting," or counting the number of arrests that each officer makes. In some police departments, officers are rewarded for what are considered "good arrests," or arrests for which there is sufficient evidence to obtain a conviction.

The police have difficulties in implementing their crime-fighting philosophy when the community refuses to cooperate with them in providing information about drugs, gambling, or prostitution and when they are dealing with juvenile gangs. To be successful in fighting crime, they must decide which crime or crimes their resources should be concentrated upon.

While Vollmer was president of the International Association of Chiefs of Police in 1922, he made a number of recommendations. He suggested that police departments began employing clerks, typists, photographers, and other professionals such as identification experts. He also supported lateral entry for police officers, claiming that the system of requiring all police officers to work their way up through the promotional process was inadequate. Vollmer had nine additional recommendations for improving policing and the criminal justice process:

1. Increased use of policewomen, especially in the "vast field of pre-delinquency."
2. Police schools for training purposes, wherein the content "may vary slightly in different communities, but the fundamentals in the police school curriculum should be identical in all departments."
3. Modern equipment, such as signal devices, wireless telephony and telegraphy, automobiles, motorcycles, motorboats, and laboratory apparatus. We must be prepared to meet the criminal with better tools and better brains than he possesses if we hope to command the respect of the community that we serve.
4. Greater emphasis on crime prevention as our principal function.
5. More police contribution toward solving the problem of unnecessary delay and miscarriage of justice in criminal trials.

6. Uniform national and even international laws, uniform classification of crimes, simplified court procedures, better methods of selecting and promoting properly trained jurist and modern requirements.
7. Abandonment of trial-and-error methods of crime solving for more efficient scientific techniques and crime laboratories, enlisting the aid of microscopists, chemicals analysts, medico psychologist, and handwriting experts.
8. Centralized and improved methods of maintaining police records. A bureau of records, if properly organized, is the hub of the police wheel.
9. Petitioning of universities to devote more time to the study of human behavior and its bearing upon political and social problems and to the training of practical criminologists, jurists, prosecutors, policemen, and policewomen.

(Carte and Carte 1975, 56–57)

The crime-fighting model did establish the image of the American police as trained professionals who concentrated on solving crimes and had the skills to control crime in their communities. Crime fighting is associated with the model of traditional policing that contemporary advocates of community policing consider a failure. But I believe that the founders of crime-fighting philosophy deserved credit for bringing the police closer to professionalism. Traditional policing has not been a failure, because it has provided successful services to the public services that people have learned to expect from their local police department. Still, crime-fighting tactics have only been partially successful in solving crimes. Generally, police departments solve only 50–70 percent of the homicides in their cities—a record that can hardly be considered good. Although projection of the crime-fighting image has led the public to believe that police investigate all crimes and will solve all crimes, police officers know that this is not true. Because police administrators recognize that the crime-fighting model has not been a complete success, they are adding the community policing philosophy to those aspects of the crime-fighting model that work.

Crime Prevention

Since the founding of the modern police system in London by Sir Robert Peel, the British police have considered crime prevention as one of their primary responsibilities. But this philosophy did not take root in the United States until much later. The founder of the American police did not consider crime prevention to be a primary objective of the police. The American police were trained to react to the commission of a crime, not to try to prevent the crime. Vollmer's recognition of crime prevention as a crucial police objective was an important step forward. The police and the community, according to Vollmer, should form an alliance to develop strategies to control crime (Carte and Carte 1975, 33–34). This premise is right in line with the philosophy of community policing today.

Raymond Fosdick's book *American Police Systems*, first published in 1920, devoted a chapter to crime prevention. Fosdick asserted that the policeman, like the watchman of an earlier time, had the obligation to forestall and apprehend the law violators and that police work had as its goal the prevention of crime. However, he argued that large numbers of police officials were skeptical about the possibilities of crime prevention, and he reported two of New York City's highest ranking officers as stating that crime prevention had only limited value in crime control. According to Fosdick, many police administrators disclaimed any responsibility for crimes committed in their jurisdiction. They felt that the solution to rising crime was simply to add more policemen, and they lacked vision in that they never considered working with the resources at hand and developing creative strategies to control crime. The emphasis of the typical police department was to function defensively against crime and not to attack the roots of crime by limiting crime opportunities. Law enforcement strategies took precedence over crime prevention strategies.

Fosdick portrayed Commissioner Woods of New York City as a progressive police administrator who supported crime prevention programs. Under Wood's tenure, a system of junior police was established for boys between the ages of 11 and 16. The boys received training in first aid and safety rules and were involved in athletic activities under the supervision of police officers. Woods was instrumental in establishing playgrounds and "play streets" that were closed to traffic for several hours to allow children to play. Also, the New York City police officers went to the schools to talk to children and held Christmas parties for neighborhood children at precinct houses. The goal of these crime prevention programs was to divert youngsters away from the trouble before they became involved with the criminal justice process. Other cities followed New York and established crime prevention programs for children (Fosdick 1920, 354–370).

In the first quarter of the twentieth century, women who had been primarily trained as social workers began to enter the field of policing. The involvement of women in policing had its roots in the protection movement of the period, launched by private organizations, to oversee the welfare rights of women and children. It also developed out of the "white slavery scare" of the 1910s and 1920s. In the early 1900s, there was a major concern, fueled by the entertainment and news media, that women were being abducted and sold into prostitution. Movies and newspapers all had stories about innocent girls being kidnapped and sold into prostitution. Reformers pointed to the failure of police to enforce vice laws and to the culpability of men in fostering prostitution (Appier 1992, 5–7, 11–12).

Women's role in policing was considered to be primarily preventive. Although women police officers had the same arrest powers as their male counterparts, neither they nor the male officers considered male and female assignments to be the same. The expectation was that the female police officer would give counseling and guidance while the male officer would have the duty to make arrest.

Thus, the crime prevention model became, to a large degree, shaped by and associated with women. It had three major principles:

1. The highest form of policing is social work.
2. Crime prevention is the most important function of the police.
3. Women are inherently better than men at preventing crime.

(Appier 1992, 5)

Women police officers of this era readily accepted the crime prevention role. Many of them brought the social service philosophy with them when they entered the police field. They worked with children, helped find missing persons, and interviewed juvenile and woman offenders. They also gave advice to parents about mischievous children and to married couples on how to deal with domestic situations. In Detroit, women police officers were involved in preventing girl delinquency. The steps that they outlined for establishing a delinquency prevention program for girls included the following (Connolly 1944, 19):

1. Creation in the police department of a crime prevention bureau that thoroughly investigated cases of delinquency and potential delinquency and referred them for solutions to the right public and private agencies.
2. Provision of "clean, proper detention places".
3. Provision of a children's court or the equivalent, with competent probation officers and judges who were not political appointees.
4. Financing of public and private agencies so that they could give delinquents and potential delinquents "careful long-term aid" that many of the cases required (including not only rehabilitating delinquent girls and boys but cleaning up the areas that produced them).
5. Punishment of parents for willful neglect.

Such ideas fit in well with today's concepts of community policing. Community police officers are expected to perform the same activities that Commissioner Woods required. They are involved in crime prevention and are expected to work with neighborhood residents to prevent crime.

The 1930s and 1940s were decades of little change for policing. The Great Depression marked the decade of the 1930s whereas World War II consumed the 1940s. During these decades, the influence of the crime prevention model began to wane, and crime control, achieved by making arrests, became the most important function of police departments. This *crime control model* remained dominant until the political upheavals of the 1960s and 1970s began to shake up policing, as well as expose it to scrutiny.

The Decade of Turmoil, Violence, Chaos, and Change

The 1960s was a decade of turmoil, violence, and chaos that resulted in changes in society and policing. Although there were many negative aspects to this decade, also much was positive. First, Congress passed the civil rights law, creating opportunities for minorities. The civil rights movement was followed by the movement against the Vietnam War, the feminist movement, the gay rights movement, and the movement for rights of the disabled. The police, because of their position as law enforcement officers, played a major role during this time and were perhaps more abused than at any other time in American history. They were placed in an awkward position because their duties required them to defend governmental policies and laws that many Americans were against. Police officers are sworn to uphold the U.S. Constitution and the constitution of their state, to enforce the laws of the federal and state government, whether these laws are popular or unpopular, and to protect governmental property and public officials from acts of violence.

The police of the 1960s were placed under more scrutiny than police in any other decade before or since, and the police officers of later generations have reaped the benefits. America might not have had community policing if American policing had not been evaluated and analyzed by various governmental commissions that often found fault with police procedures and behavior. Credit must also be given to progressive-thinking police administrators who were willing to experiment with new strategies of policing. And various experimental strategies of policing instituted in eras before community policing have contributed to the community policing philosophy implemented in the later part of the twentieth century.

The 1960s began with hope, promise, and enthusiasm but ended in darkness and malaise. The decade began with the election of John F. Kennedy, a young and charismatic president who offered hope for a better life to all Americans, regardless of their race, class, or ethnic background. But by the time it ended, five political and civil rights leaders—John F. Kennedy, his brother Robert Kennedy, Martin Luther King, Jr., Medgar Evers, and Malcolm X—had been assassinated. Americans became cynical and mistrustful toward their fellow citizens and their government. The five assassinations were not the only acts of violence occurring in American communities and streets. Others were the bombing of a black church in Birmingham, Alabama, and the attacks on civil rights workers and demonstrators in the South, including the murder of young civil rights workers in Mississippi.

There were also numerous riots in America's urban centers. The nonviolent civil rights movement espoused by Martin Luther King, Jr., which attracted many people in the first part of the 1960s, became unacceptable to a number of civil rights activists for whom "equality" and "desegregation" were occurring too slowly. Some civil rights leaders broke with the nonviolent movement of Reverend King and adopted violence as a solution to obtaining equal opportunity and rights. During the mid-1960s, a number of militant black groups were formed that advocated violence and espoused the ideology that all white people were evil. Leaders such as Stobely Carmichael and H. Rap Brown took to the streets to proclaim that the only way the black man would get his rights would be by taking them through violence. Militant organizations such as the Black Panthers, led by activists like Bobby Seale, had open and at times violent confrontations with the police. Black activists openly advocated disrespecting the police and called them "pigs." This often caused agitation between the police and name callers and at times led to confrontation between the police and the militants. Militants argued that the American government was evil and that the police were the protectors of the American government; therefore, the police were enemies of the people. Black militant acts included arson and shooting down police officers.

Riots in American cities by blacks, similar to the Los Angeles riot of 1995, were common in American cities during the 1960s. Not only large urban centers such as Harlem (New York), Watts (Los Angeles), Newark (New Jersey), and Detroit (Michigan) but also midsized and smaller American cities experienced burning and looting. Often police actions would precipitate a riot because of exaggerated rumors. For example, when the police made a traffic stop and arrested the driver for a crime, rumors might travel through the predominantly black community that the police had unmercifully beaten the driver. Also, riots during this decade seemed to be contagious. For the first time, Americans could watch a riot in progress on the 6.00 p.m. national network news. Individuals prone to rioting observed what rioters were doing in other cities and became copycats in attempting to start a riot in their own neighborhoods. Although the rioters burned and looted the stores and businesses in their own neighborhoods, they did so not only to get something for nothing but to get back at the majority of owners, who did not live in the black community. Anti-Semitism against the white business owners played a role as well.

An investigation of these civil disturbances by the National Advisory Commission on Civil Disorders (1970) found that police behavior toward blacks, particularly aggressive police patrol and harassment in urban communities, was a major factor contributing to riots. According to the commission's report, in Newark, in Detroit, in Watts, in Harlem—in practically every city that had experienced racial disruption since the summer of 1964—abrasive relationships between police and Negroes and other minority groups have been a major source of grievance, tension, and ultimate disorder (8).

Other commissions of the 1960s reported that at times the police had even created potential riot situations. The Walker Report on the major confrontation that occurred between peace demonstrators against the Vietnam war and the police during the 1968 Democratic Convention in Chicago called this disturbance a police riot.

The Vietnam war escalated under the presidency of Lyndon Johnson. This led to demonstrations and violence in American streets. A segment of the American population believed that America had no business being involved in Vietnam. Many of the protesters were college students. They often demonstrated on campuses and took over buildings or departments, such as science departments, that had contacts with the Pentagon or took over the administrative offices of the university. The police were frequently called in to retake university buildings and protect university property. At times, violent confrontations took place between the police and university students. At Columbia University, the Ivy League university in New York City, both students and police officers were seriously injured; one student jumped on a police officer's back, paralyzing him. Demonstrations not only by college students but also by other Americans continued until the war came to an end under the Nixon presidency in the 1970s.

The police in the 1960s found themselves attempting to control disturbances not only by minority citizens but also by university and college students who were predominantly white and middle class and confronting Vietnam war protesters who included entertainment celebrities, business leaders, professionals, and average citizens. Serving as the defenders of an unpopular government policy could only tarnish the police image. The police in the 1960s were severely criticized for their handling of public demonstrations as well as for their poor relations with minority neighborhoods.

In the last decades of the twentieth century, the police have been more respected and treated with more courtesy than they were during the 1960s. The attitude of the public had become more positive toward police, making it possible for community policing to be established in many communities.

The Challenge of Crime in a Free Society

In 1965, President Lyndon Johnson established the President's Commission on Law Enforcement and Administration of Justice, referred to as the President's Crime Commission. Its report *The Challenge of Crime in a Free Society* (President's Commission 1967) contained a number of recommendations to improve policing (Exhibit 1–1). Many of these recommendations were imitated, and some are still in effect. For example, many states have a state agency overseeing police standards.

The 1960s was a decade when crime increased substantially. Between 1960 and 1969, murder increased 62 percent, aggravated assault 102 percent, and robberies 177 percent (Federal Bureau of Investigation (FBI) 1970). The establishment of the commission and the passage of the Law Enforcement Assistance Act in 1965 were the first steps in providing federal grant-in-aid programs for helping state and local government to reduce crime (National Advisory Commission on Intergovernmental Relations 1970, 8). Since the late 1960s, the federal government has continued to provide police agencies with funding to improve policing. Most police departments initiated their community policing strategy with federal funding. Federal grants were available for the hiring of additional police officers and equipment if the police department agreed to establish community policing. The City of Wichita Police Department, Kansas, and the Sedgwick County Sheriff's Department, Kansas are two law enforcement agencies that instituted community policing upon receiving federal monies.

Through federal funding, made available by the Law Enforcement Assistance Act through the Justice Department's Office of Law Enforcement Assistance (OLES), 27 states established new criminal justice planning committees or broadened the activities of existing committees, 17 states began police science and college degree programs, 20 states initiated or expanded police standards and training systems, and 33 large cities developed police and community relations programs. The Safe Streets and Crime Control Act was passed during the Johnson administration in 1967 to implement many of the recommendations of the President's Commission on Law Enforcement and Administration

EXHIBIT 1-1: RECOMMENDATIONS OF THE CHALLENGE OF CRIME IN A FREE SOCIETY

1. Police departments should have community-relations machinery consisting of a headquarters unit that plans and supervises the department's community-relations unit.
2. A minority-group neighborhood should have a citizens' advisory committee that meets regularly with police officials to work out solutions to problems of conflict between the police and the community.
3. Departments in communities with a substantial minority population should have as high priority the recruitment of minority officers and should deploy and promote them fairly.
4. Every jurisdiction should provide adequate procedures for the processing of all citizens' grievances and complaints about the conduct of any police officer.
5. Police departments should develop and enunciate policies that give police personal specific guidance for the common situations requiring exercise of police discretion.
6. Basic police functions should be divided among three types of officers termed the community service officer, police officer, and police agent.
7. Police departments should recruit more actively at college campuses and inner-city neighborhoods.
8. The ultimate aim of all police departments should be that all personnel with general law enforcement powers have baccalaureate degrees.
9. Police departments should take immediate steps to establish a minimum requirements of a baccalaureate degree for all supervisory and executive positions.
10. Background investigations and personal interviews should be used by all departments to determine moral character and intellectual and emotional fitness of police candidates.
11. Primary emphasis for police recruiting should be on education, background, character, and personality of a candidate for police service.
12. To attract college graduates, salaries should be competitive with other professions that seek the same graduates.
13. Police salaries within local government should stand on their own merit and not be tied to other city departments.
14. Promotion eligibility should stress ability over seniority.
15. Police specialists should be selected for their talents and abilities without regard to their prior service.
16. A national police retirement system should be established to encourage lateral movement of police personnel.

Exhibit 1-1 continued

17. All training programs should provide instruction on subjects that prepare recruits to exercise discretion properly, and to understand the community, the role of the police, and what the criminal justice system can and cannot do.
18. Professional educators should teach specialized courses such as law and psychology.
19. Formal police training of recruits should consist of a minimum of 400 hours of classroom work spread over a 4–6 month period so it can be combined with carefully selected and supervised field training.
20. Entering officers should serve probation periods preferably of 18 months but certainly no less than one year.
21. Every police officer should have at least one week of training annually.
22. States should establish a commission on police standards.
23. Police departments should employ a legal advisor.
24. Police departments should implement the organizational principle of central control.
25. Police departments should organize key staff and line personnel into an administrative board similar in function to a corporation's board of directors.
26. Police departments should have a comprehensive program for maintaining integrity and an internal investigative unit only responsible to the chief.
27. Police departments should commence experimentation with a team policing concept that envisions those with patrol and investigative duties combining under unified command with flexible assignments to deal with the crime problems in a defined sector.
28. Police departments should have a firearms policy that firearms can only be used when the officer's life or the life of another person is in imminent danger.
29. States should assume responsibility for assuring that area-wide records and communications needs are provided.
30. Crime laboratories should be provided to police departments by either the city, county, regional area, or state.
31. State agencies should assist smaller agencies in specialized investigations.
32. Consolidation of police services should be considered in metropolitan or county areas to keep down expenses and to provide a service that normally would not be provided.
33. Police standard commissions should be established in every state and be empowered to set mandatory requirements and to give financial aid to governmental units for the implementation of standards.

Source: Reprinted for President's Commission on Law Enforcement and Administration of Justice, *The Challenge of Crime in a Free Society*, pp. 91–123, 1967, Government Printing Office.

(National Advisory Commission on Intergovernmental Relations 1970, 7–10). Since the passage of the Law Enforcement Assistance Act, the federal government has influenced local policing through its funding process. Obviously, federal monies have played a major part in establishing standards, training, and innovations in police departments. Just as President Johnson wanted to improve policing in the 1960s, President Clinton has supported funding for those police departments initiating the community policing philosophy. In addition, the Clinton administration had created federal agencies to assist local police agencies that need training and professional consultants to establish community policing for their departments.

Police Response to a Decade of Turmoil, Violence, Chaos, and Change

As a result of the turmoil of the 1960s, police officers, responding to what they considered to be antipolice sentiment in the form of unwarranted attacks and unnecessary criticism, began to organize. Benevolent and fraternal organizations evolved into police unions to protect the rank-and-file officer. According to Samuel Walker (1992), the noted police scholar, police officers succeeded in organizing unions in the 1960s because of several factors:

1. Lagging salaries and benefits.
2. Poor police management.
3. Social and political alienation.
4. A new generation of officers.
5. The law and order model.
6. A new legal climate.

(Walker 1992, 371)

The police of the latter part of the twentieth century and early twenty-first century owe much to those police officers of the 1960s and 1970s for demanding respect and courtesy. The leaders of these decades helped reshape policing. Today, the police are not socially and politically alienated for their fellow Americans. In fact, community policing wants to bring the police closer to their fellow citizens.

National Advisory Commission on Standards and Goals

In 1971, the head of the Law Enforcement Assistance Administration (LEAA) established a National Advisory Commission on Criminal Justice Standards and Goals to formulate national criminal justice standards and develop goals for crime prevention at the local and state levels. The commission published six reports. *The Report on Police*, published in 1973, made several hundred recommendations to improve policing, including recommendations for recruiting minorities and women and for having all police agencies require a baccalaureate degree as a minimum condition of employment by 1982. Some of these recommendations have been incorporated into policing and some have not. For example, police departments generally do not require a baccalaureate degree as a condition for employment.

The Report on Police developed several standards that police administrators and supporters of community policing should review and incorporate into community-policing programs. These standards encourage that a police–community teamwork to control crime. Specific standards deal with:

- Local definition of police function
- Accountability to the public
- Communication with the public
- Public understanding of the police role
- Developing community resources
- Community crime prevention
- Police-public workshops and seminars
- Responding to personnel complaints

(National Advisory Commission 1973, 5)

Police Professionalism

1. *A lack of systematic knowledge available for appropriation by the occupation.* The vacuum is apparent and is reflected in the limited evolution of police strategies and formations of experts. The absence of sufficient systematic knowledge for occupational expertise is a serious shortcoming in professionalization. A prime characteristic of all professions is the presence of a coherent body of theory or practice that the occupation can

claim as its own and that can be transmitted through a lengthy training process.

2. *The bureaucratic structure of the police.* Centralization was a principal organizing force for police departments in England and subsequently was adopted in the United States as well. Today, an elaborate bureaucratic model has been built around the centralized structure. Among the many bureaucratic models that have been built around the police department are rules, specialization of functions, communications patterns, universalism, an elaborate control system of rewards and punishment, and the civil service structure. The development of a centralized command and a strict hierarchy of control was no accident. The Metropolitan Police of London, the historical model of American police, was formed to respond to civil chaos. Military discipline was imposed upon a civilian militia-type organization as a strategy for obtaining perform-ance. It was the judgment of early police leaders in both England and America that without strict supervision there was no guarantee that the patrolman would perform his duties. No presumption existed that highly motivated men of great dedication had been recruited.

3. *The internal leadership of the occupation.* Positions taken by police leaders, those who most often speak for the occupation, have created obstacles to the police's becoming professional. The generally conservative leadership directs more attention to efforts to protect its own position and keep external criticism to a minimum than to promote substantive change.

(National Advisory Commission 1973, 8–10)

The issue of professionalism is still with us today. Although the police claim to be professional, they have not yet achieved professional status. Most police departments do not require a baccalaureate degree to enter the field. Further, police officers, for the most part, do not believe in lifelong learning and do not feel that they have a responsibility to keep abreast of the knowledge in their field. Many officers stop learning anything new once they leave the police academy. They believe that the police department has the sole responsibility to train officers, and, if they are not paid for attending training classes, they refuse to attend training. In police departments that have unions, the officers are backed by their unions, which hold that they should be paid for training. Unlike members of the traditional professions of medicine, law, and the ministry, many police officers want to be paid for everything they do: not only training but court time and working overtime. Yet traditional professionals do not expect to be paid extra for putting extra time into their chosen profession, and they are expected to keep abreast of knowledge in their fields. Police who are not committed to their craft are more like mercenaries, who do their job only for money, than professionals. Police professionalism is highly controversial. According to James Q. Wilson (1978), the noted police scholar:

> Occupations whose members exercise, as the police do, wide discretion alone and with respect to matters of great importance are typically "professions"—the medical profession, for example. The right to handle emergency situations, to be privy to "guilty information," and to make decisions involving questions of life and death or honor and dishonor is usually, as with a doctor or priest, conferred by an organized profession. The profession certifies that the number has acquired by education certain information and by apprenticeship, certain arts and skills that render him competent to perform these functions and that he is willing to subject himself to the code of ethics and sense of duty of his colleagues . . . Failure to perform his duties properly, if detected, will be dealt with by professional sanctions—primarily, loss of respect. Members of professions tend to govern themselves through collegial bodies, to restrict the authority of their nominal superiors, to take seriously their reputation among fellow professionals, and to encourage some of their kind to devote themselves to adding systematically to the knowledge of the professions through writing and research. The police are not in any sense professionals.
>
> They acquire most of their knowledge and skill on the job, not in separate academies; they are emphatically subject to the

authority of their superiors; they have no serious professional society, only a union-like bargaining agent; and they do not produce, in systematic written form, new knowledge about their craft.

(29–30)

Eras of Policing

This history of policing has been subdivided by police scholars into "eras" of policing. These are not exact time frames, and the number of eras propounded varies depending upon who is presenting the information. The most well-known scheme is that of Kelling and Moore (1988), who described a political era, a reform era, and a community problem-solving era.*

Political Era

Kelling and Moore (1988) denoted the political era of policing as the period from 1840 to the early 1900s. During this period, there was a close relationship between the police and politicians. Cities and towns were growing, and modern policing was in its infancy. Policing came under the control of local governments. In urban centers, politicians oversaw police operations. The police and the politicians worked together to control the neighborhood, often referred to as a *ward*. It was the ward politician who controlled the police in his neighborhood: because job security was not available to ward police officers, they were obligated to the ward politician for their positions. Police tasks included not only crime prevention and order maintenance but also a broad range of social service activities.

Although police departments had a centralized, semi-military, hierarchical organizational structure, they generally did not function along these lines. Rather, they functioned as decentralized units, with the ward politician running the police department in his ward. Police officers reflected the ethnic makeup of the ward in which they lived and worked. Policing in the ward was conducted primarily by foot patrol. Communication between police officers and a centralized police headquarters was

---

* I deviate from several of Kelling and Moore's premises and include concepts contrary to their work in the following paragraphs.

almost nonexistent. When call boxes came into existence, they were used by the patrol officer to maintain contact with supervisors. Some police departments had detectives, but they were not well trained or held in great esteem. Detectives were often used by politicians to obtain information for political purposes. Their caseloads were usually based upon persons and not criminal offenses. The strengths of the political era of policing were:

First, police were integrated into neighborhoods and enjoyed the support of citizens—at least the support of the dominant economic and political interest of an area. Second, and probably as a result of the first, the strategy provided useful services to communities. There is evidence that it helped contain riots. Many citizens believed that police prevented crimes or solved crimes when they occurred. And the police assisted immigrants in establishing themselves in communities and finding jobs.

The political strategy also had weaknesses. First, intimacy with community, closeness to political leaders, and a decentralized organizational structure, with its inability to provide supervision of officers, gave rise to political corruption. Officers were often required to enforce unpopular law foisted on immigrant ethnic neighborhoods by crusading reformers who objected to ethnic values.

Because of their intimacy with the community, the officers were vulnerable to being bribed in return for nonenforcement or lax enforcement of laws. Moreover, policing closeness to politicians created such forms of political corruption as patronage and police interference in elections. Second, close identification of police with neighborhoods and neighborhood norms often resulted in discrimination against strangers and others who violated those norms, especially minority ethnic and racial groups. Often ruling their beats with the "end of their nightsticks," police regularly targeted outsiders and strangers for rousting and "curbstone justice." Finally, the lack of organizational control over officers resulting from decentralization and the political nature of many appointments to police positions caused inefficiencies and disorganization. The image of the Keystone Cops—police as

clumsy bunglers—was widespread and often descriptive of realism
in American policing.

(Kelling and Moore 1998, 4)

Hubert Williams and Patrick Murphy (1990) have critiqued Kelling
and Moore's description of the political era as pertaining primarily to
Northeast urban centers and as omitting mention of social and racial
conflicts related to police work, such as the work of "slave patrols" up to
the time of the Civil War to apprehend runaway slaves, racial oppression
by the police, the enforcing of racially biased laws, and the scarcity of
black police officers. During this period, blacks had limited legal rights
and were discriminated against in the North and eventually in the South
after Reconstruction, when slavery was outlawed.

In still another perspective on the political era of policing, Victor
Strecher (1991) questioned "whether policing was defiantly political or
simply part of an era which was inherently political" (2). During this
period, government services were developing not only for policing but
also for such areas as education, social service, and sanitation, name
"political era" on this period could lead to the erroneous interpretation
that politics no longer influences policing.

Reform Era

The reform era, according to Kelling and Moore, began in the early 1900s
and lasted into the 1970s. It was characterized by a movement to reform
policing by freeing it from the control of politicians. The implementation
of civil service for police departments decreased and in some cases
eliminated political patronage in the hiring and firing of police officers.
Political influence was considered as deviant and as indicating poor police
administrative leadership. The police emphasized their law enforcement
function over their previous social service role during the political era.

Administrators followed a management philosophy of control, unity
of command, and a division of labor. Attempts were made to routinize
and standardize police patrol. Communications within the police organization flowed downward but not upward. Police administrators showed
little interest, if any, in what lower ranking police officers had to
recommend. Unlike the political era, which had supported a close citizen-
police relationship, the reform ear deemphasized this relationship.

The goal of police administration was to distance the police from citizens, because during the political era police–citizen closeness had led to corruption and favoritism among neighborhood groups. Some communities decreased foot patrols while increasing automobile patrols. Police in cars definitely put a distance between police officers and citizens. In this era, police took the stance that they were the professionals who would handle crime control and that the general public had no business to be involved because they lacked the expertise and knowledge.

In the 1960s and 1970s, the reform era strategy ran into several obstacles:

First, regardless of how police effectiveness in dealing with crime was measured, police failed to substantially improve their record. During the 1960s crime began to rise. Despite large increases in the size of police departments and in expenditures for new forms of equipment, police had failed to meet their own or public expectations about their capacity to control crime or prevent its increase. More research conducted during the 1970s on prevention patrol and rapid response to calls for service suggested that neither preventive patrol and rapid response to calls for service was an effective crime control or apprehension tactic.

Second, fear rose rapidly during this era. The consequences of this fear were dramatic for cities. Citizens abandoned parks, public transportation, neighborhood shopping centers, churches, as well as entire neighborhoods . . .

Third, despite attempts by police departments to create equitable police allocations systems and to provide impartial policing to all citizens, many minority citizens, especially blacks during the 1960s and 1970s, did not perceive their treatment as equitable or adequate. They protested about not only police mistreatment, but lack of treatment—inadequate or insufficient services . . .

Fourth, the civil rights and anti-war movements challenged police. This challenge took several forms. The legitimacy of police was questioned: Students resisted police, minorities rioted against them, and the public, observing police via live television for the first time, questioned their tactics . . .

Fifth, some of the myths that undergirded reform strategy—police officers use little or no discretion and the primary activity of police is law enforcement—simply proved to be too far from reality to be sustained . . .

Sixth, although the reform ideology could rally police chiefs and executives, it failed to rally line police officers. During the reform era, police executives had moved to professionalize their ranks. Line officers, however, were managed in ways that were antithetical to professionalization . . .

Seventh, police lost a significant portion of their financial support, which had been increasing or at least constant over the years, as cities found themselves in fiscal difficulties . . .

Finally, urban police departments began to acquire competition: private security and the community crime control movement.

(Kelling and Moore 1988, 8–9)

Strecher (1991) did not completely agree with Kelling and Moore's reform era model. First, he took issue with the years initiating and ending the reform era and claimed that the reform era began in the 1880s with the establishment of the civil service. Second, he argued that a variety of research findings were not included in the reform era paradigm.

My own objection to Kelling and Moore's scheme is that it makes no mention of the crime prevention model, which came into vogue in the 1910s and lasted to the 1940s. As discussed earlier in this chapter, this model emphasized crime prevention and social work as the most important functions of policing and was a boon for women entering policing, many of whom were trained and experienced social workers.

In the 1930s, the crime prevention model began to lose ground to the crime control model discussed earlier in this chapter, which fits in better with Kelling and Moore's description of the reform era in that it discarded social service and preventative roles for policing began to decrease. The new model emphasized making arrests, and at this time men were considered better suited than women to this task.

The crime control model of the reform era has not completely fallen by the wayside. The reform era ideology has been ingrained into many police organizations, and it is difficult for police agencies to change.

Community Problem-Solving Era

Problem-Oriented Policing

In 1979, Herman Goldstein published an influential article that sought to initiate a new mode of problem solving in police departments. Goldstein maintained that in traditional police practice, a citizen calls the police about a specific problem and the police respond, handle the incident, and return to their patrol duties. Goldstein argued that this approach, which he called *reactive*, was standard operating procedure even though the beat officer might be called to the same incident over and over again without correcting the situation. He recommended that the police instead work proactively and direct their efforts toward solving the persistent problems that generate the calls. Eck and Spelman (1987) described this approach as "a departmentwide strategy aimed at solving persistent community problems. Police identify, analyze and respond to underlying circumstances that create incidents" (xv).

Although many police departments claim that they are doing community policing, they are often doing only problem-oriented policing. Chapter 5 will provide more detailed information about problem-oriented policing.

Community-Oriented Policing

In community-oriented policing, as in problem-oriented policing, police take a proactive role in problem solving, but they do so in partnership with the communities they serve. Community-oriented policing has been defined as "a philosophy of full service personalized policing where the same officer patrols and works in the same area on a permanent basis, from a decentralized place, working in a proactive partnership with citizens to identify and solve problems" (Trojanowicz and Bucqueroux 1994, 3). Community-oriented policing will be reviewed in much greater detail in later chapters of this book.

Community Problem Solving

Kelling and Moore described the era from the late 1970s or early 1980s to the present as the community problem-solving era, in that it combines problem-oriented policing with a community orientation. Community problem solving involves a variety of policing strategies that will be outlined in this book.

The wave of the future appears to be community-oriented policing. For several years community-oriented policing has had the support of the federal government. The federal government has provided funding for additional police officers to police departments for implementing community-oriented policing. In addition, grants have been made available to police agencies incorporating the community-oriented policing strategy.

As Strecher (1991) has noted, community-oriented policing is a slippery concept that academics have defined differently for different purposes, and it has stirred up many controversies (96). The purpose of this book is to address some of the questions that Strecher raised. Only by reviewing contemporary police innovations can we ascertain the strategies that make up problem-oriented and community-oriented policing and assess their value.

September 11, 2001

On September 11, 2001 or 9/11, an attack on American soil occurred that rivals the Japanese attack on Pearl Harbor on December 7, 1941. More Americans were killed on 9/11 than were killed in Pearl Harbor. More than 2,800 people were killed from 115 nations on 9/11 compared to 2,117 killed in Pearl Harbor. Of course, this is not including the one hundred who were wounded.

The terrorist acts of 9/11 in addition to others occurring before this date and after have now provided the police with a great responsibility in not only preventing crime but also in preventing potential terrorist acts.

There exist numerous definitions of terrorism but not one that has been universally accepted. The United States Code defines domestic terrorism and international terrorism. The U.S. Code states that the term

> domestic terrorism means activities that involve acts dangerous to human life that are a violation of the criminal laws of the United States or of any state; appear to be intended to intimidate or coerce a civilian population; to influence the policy of a government by intimidation or coercion; or to affect the conduct of a government by mass destruction, assassination, or kidnapping; and occur primarily within the territorial jurisdiction of the United States.
> (U.S. Code, Title 18, Part 1, Chapter 113B, $2332 (5))

The U.S. Code defines the term

> international terrorism to mean activities that involve acts
> dangerous to human life that are a violation of the criminal laws
> of the United States or of any state, or that would be a criminal
> violation if committed within the jurisdiction of the United States
> or of any State; appear to be intended to intimidate or coerce a
> civilian population; to influence the policy of a government by
> intimidation or coercion; or to affect the conduct of a government
> by mass destruction, assassination, or kidnapping.
>
> (U.S. Code, Title 18, Part 1,
> Chapter 113B, $2331 (1))

In the last several decades, there have been serious incidents of successful and unsuccessful acts of terrorism. In additional to the September 11,
2001 terrorism acts there was the 1993 domestic terrorist act carried
out successfully by an American. In 1993, terrorists placed a bomb in a
rental truck in an underground parking garage of the World Trade Center
in New York City. This act of terrorism caused the death of six people
and injuries to over 1,000. Eventually four Muslim men were arrested in
1994 for the World Trade bombing. In 1995, the Murrah Federal Building was a successful act of terrorism in downtown Oklahoma City. The
terrorist parked a rental truck with a bomb inside the truck adjacent to
the Federal Building, which exploded destroying the Federal Building
and killing 168 people and injuring hundreds.

International acts of terrorism have occurred against the United States
outside its borders. On August 7, 1998, the American embassies in
Tanzania and Kenya were badly damaged by two car bombs. These
bombings caused the deaths of 224 people and injured 5,000. Another
incident of international terrorism was the attack on October 12, 2000
on the U.S.S. *Cole* in Aden Habor, Yemen. When the U.S.S. *Cole* was
refueling offshore, a small water craft containing two men approached
the ship and exploded. The explosion left a 40-foot hole on the side of
the ship. This terrorist attack left 17 dead sailors and 39 injured. The
terrorist attackers were considered to be radical Muslims.

There have been unsuccessful terrorist attacks on American airlines.
On December 21, 2001 on a flight from Paris, France to Miami, Florida

Richard Reid, a British citizen, attempted to light a fuse to his shoe, which contained an explosive. He was subdued by the flight crew and passengers. Reid had converted to Islam and had contact with Muslim radicals. A similar incident to the Reid incident occurred on December 25, 2009, eight years after the shoe bomber incident: Umar Farouk Abdulmutallab on a Northwest flight from Amsterdam to Detroit. Abdulmutallab attempted to blow up the plane over American soil with an underpants bomb. The Christmas bomber was stopped by passengers and crew members.

The FBI in 2002 established the Office of Law Enforcement Coordination (OLEC) to strengthen relationships between the FBI and state and municipal police agencies. In 2003, the Terrorist Screening Center (TSC) was established to consolidate information from watch lists of terrorists and to provide around-the-clock operational support for policing agencies.

In the early decades of the twenty-first century, state and municipal police agencies have been on a new mission—the prevention of terrorism. Police officers are being trained as first responders to terrorist scenes, to gather intelligence on terrorists, to work closely with the federal terrorist investigators. It is anticipated that the police will work for the next several decades to prevent terrorism.

Summary

Community policing has been advanced as the new policing system for the twenty-first century. How can police administrators, political leaders, or students of policing support or even understand the value of and need for community policing in our contemporary world if they have no knowledge of where the police have been? How can effective decisions and policies be implemented if politicians and administrators making decisions lack knowledge or understanding of police history? Politicians, police administrators, community policing supporters, and students of policing should understand the history of policing, including its various strategies and methods, if they hope to have an impact on the field.

In ancient times, individuals were expected to follow the rules of the majority, and policing was conducted informally. The tribe, clan, and family had the responsibility to control individuals' behavior and to enforce the informal rules or customs established by the tribe or clan. Eventually, rules became law, and rule breaking was formalized as an act committed against the state.

With the development of formalized governments and states, laws became a prerequisite. The Roman Empire formalized laws when it formalized its government structure and gave the responsibility of enforcing the laws to its legions. When the Romans conquered the British Isles, they brought their legal system with them. But with the collapse of the Roman Empire, Germanic tribes invaded England, bringing with them their tribal customs and unwritten laws. These unwritten laws became integrated into the English legal system. During this period, the concept of king's peace evolved, whereby the king assured the people a state of security and peace in return for their allegiance to him. This peacekeeping system revolved around land ownership in that the landowner was responsible for all those on his land who violated the king's peace.

During the seventeenth century in London, night watches were paid a small fee to keep the peace. They were recruited from the poor, the old, and the weak and were ineffective in performing their task. During the eighteenth century, the term *police* began to be used. The idea of police involvement in crime prevention emerged during the early eighteenth century, along with that of citizens reporting crimes to the police. In the early nineteenth century, Sir Robert Peel, the Home Secretary, recommended to Parliament that a paid police force be appointed from the civilian population to maintain order in London. Parliament approved Peel's proposal, and the London Metropolitan Police was formed.

America traces its legal and police system to England. Americans used the London model to form American police departments. In 1845, New York City had the first "unified" police department in the United States: that is, a department combining the night and day watches in one police agency. Generally, American police, unlike the London police, did not function as professionals. Although municipal police departments were theoretically centralized, they tended to function as decentralized neighborhood units. Early police departments were often responsible to perform activities that had little to do with maintaining public order. For example, the police cleaned streets in New York City, distributed supplies to the poor in Baltimore, assisted the homeless in Philadelphia, and inspected vegetables in St. Louis.

In the latter part of the nineteenth century the police came under criticism for being under the influence of politicians, corruption, and inefficiency. Police critics advocated police training: eliminating corruption, police brutality, and inefficiency, and removing politics from police affairs. The goal of police critics was to professionalize the police. The police were given a new image: they were to become crime fighters. The expectation was that this would be the avenue to professionalized police.

The 1960s was a decade which began with hope, promise, and enthusiasm but ended in a state of disorder, disruption, and chaos. This decade saw the assassination of political and civil rights leaders, rioting in the streets, demonstrations against the Vietnam war, and anti-government disdain by certain segments of the American population. The police represented the government and the status quo; therefore, they received the abuse directed toward the government. Government commissions recommended that police officers receive training and eventually obtain a college degree.

This chapter also reviewed the eras of policing, which are not exact time frames. Police scholars have conceived of at least three eras, and not all scholars agree. George Kelling and Mark Moore outline three eras of policing. They are: political era, reform era, and community problem-solving. Hubert Williams and Patrick Murphy criticize Kelling and Moore because they completely eliminate minorities from their review of the eras of policing. Victor Strecher finds fault with a variety of premises advocated by Kelling and Moore: for example, he suggests that the police were not unique in their political involvement but a part of an inherently political involvement that included all government agencies.

In the last several decades America has been the target of terrorists. Municipal and state police agencies now work with federal terrorist investigators to prevent terrorism. It is anticipated that terrorists will be a problem for the next several decades.

KEY TERMS

- August Vollmer
- crime fighter
- crime prevention
- James Q. Wilson
- John Fielding
- National Advisory Commission on Criminal Justice Standards and Goals
- new police
- President's Crime Commission

REVIEW QUESTIONS

1. What value does an understanding of police history have for a student of policing?
2. Describe changes in American policing in the latter part of the nineteenth century.
3. What are the major differences between the crime control model and the crime prevention model?
4. Why is the 1960s considered a decade of violence?
5. Describe the various eras of policing.

2

UNDERSTANDING POLICE CULTURE

CHAPTER OBJECTIVES

1. Understand the importance of police culture to community policing.
2. Understand the meaning of culture.
3. Understand the various aspects of the police culture.
4. Be familiar with what makes police culture unique.
5. Be familiar with the various myths about policing.

Introduction

This chapter will concentrate on the value system reflected in the police culture. An examination of the police culture will provide a better understanding of why community policing is necessary. If the goal of community policing is to change the way the police do business, then an understanding of how police culture works and what its values are is a crucial prerequisite. How can any changes be made if the police culture is not taken into consideration? The culture of policing must be scrutinized to determine what effect community policing or any new policing philosophy or strategy will have on the police. Before a concept can be put in place, innovators need to be aware of the occupational culture they hope to influence or change. The philosophy of community policing, if completely adopted and integrated into policing, will change the culture of policing. The big question that remains is, can the police culture change to fit the philosophy of community policing?

Police Culture

The police culture cannot be overlooked if policing hopes to change its philosophy. Nevertheless, no student can be expected to understand the meaning of police culture without first having a general understanding of culture. What does the term culture mean? What is the culture of American society? What is meant by the culture of an occupational field?

Culture is the foundation upon which a social group functions. It consists of knowledge, beliefs, morals, laws, customs, and practices acquired by the group. Culture can be defined as "the total way of life shared by members of a society. It includes not only language, values, and symbolic meanings but also technology and material objects" (Brinkerhoff et al. 1997, 59). The concept of culture also encompasses our thinking, feelings, attitudes, and communications with each other. We learn culture from the people around us. This includes speaking, facial expressions, body language, and beliefs. Cultures are constantly being altered; people are exposed to new ideas, and new forms of technology are developed. For example, feminism and the computer have been added to our culture. Because police officers are members of American society, they operate within that culture's norms, customs, morals, and value system. In America, our culture includes the American dream, competitiveness, equal opportunity for everyone to succeed, and an attitude of independence ("No one can tell me what to do"). Culture not only changes constantly, at least in America, but also endures while humans die. Our American culture has been passed down from generation to generation through parents, relatives, and acquaintances. In contemporary society, culture is also being passed down through books, movies, music, museums, television, and entertainment parks.

Culture can be divided into material culture and nonmaterial culture. Material culture includes tools, streets, television, VCRs, forks, spoons, knives, houses, and automobiles, to name only a few items. Nonmaterial culture includes beliefs, attitudes, education, language, values, rules, norms, mores, folkways, laws, knowledge, and ways of dealing with similar problems and experiences, such as birth, death, raising children, and marriage.

A common language often reflects a common culture. The American version of English binds us culturally together as a people. Our English language symbolizes unity and gives us an identity as Americans. Values, after language, are central to culture. They guide our feelings about events in our lives and govern our sense of right and wrong. Different cultures have different values, and some social scientists have attempted to promote "dominant value profiles" for specific cultures. The American society has been characterized as a driven society, "one oriented towards achievement, competition, mobility, and an ever-higher standard of living" (McNall and McNall 1992, 60). McNall and McNall described the major American value system as follows:

1. Achievement/success. This is often measured by quantity and is dominated by the belief that only one's own effort will obtain success.

2. Activity/work. In colonial America and on the frontier, work had survival value. Idleness was dangerous not only from a practical point of view, but from a religious point of view as well. To be busy, useful, and active had intrinsic value besides the tangible results these qualities yielded.

3. Morality. The Pilgrims, the frontiersmen, and the prairie settlers were all strangers who migrated to a hostile land and struggled to master it. They also sought to recreate the civilization they had left behind . . . A strong link was forged between morality and civilization, since morality in America was associated with Protestant Christianity.

4. Efficiency/practicality. Americans value useful activity. Our emphasis on practicality and efficiency makes us tend to accept rational activity and science without question. Efficiency is the standard against which we judge nearly all activities. . . .

5. Progress. No idea has more greatly dominated or characterized the American approach to life than progress. The belief in progress is a conviction that the present is better than the past, and that the future will be better still. . . .

6. Humanitarianism. Americans believe in helping others, but this value, coupled with morality, has sometimes led to the belief that we must save other people from their shortcomings.

7. Materialism. Eighteenth and nineteenth century Americans certainly hoped for a good life. They strove to obtain the material goods that would fulfill such basic needs as food, shelter, and clothing, and some wanted, and got, luxuries like pianos, books, and large houses.
8. Democracy. Americans believe in freedom and equality.

(61–63)

Do American police officers share these values? Are these values brought with them when they enter the police field? We as Americans reflect the value system of our nation, neighborhoods, family, relatives, and acquaintances that we copied and adopted as our own. It has traditionally been accepted that police officers should be recruited from the community and should reflect the value system of the community. This unit will discuss in more detail the value system of police officers as it relates to their occupational culture. Other elements pertaining to culture that should briefly be reviewed include norms, folkways, mores, and laws.

Norms are rules of conduct. They designate what people should or should not do, think, or feel. The importance of norms can vary substantially in importance to individuals and society. For example, some people place no importance on their apparel, whereas other people consider it to be of extreme importance. There are two types of informal norms: folkways and mores. *Folkways* are customary, normal, and habitual ways of doing things. An example of a folkway could be setting off fireworks on July 4. Folkways have no right or wrong assigned to them. However, a person could be considered weird if he or she had green hair. *Mores* reflect a strong awareness of right or wrong. A violation of mores could be abusing a child. Someone who abuses a child, either physically or sexually, has violated not only mores but also a third type of norm known as a law. *Laws*, simply, are rules that are enforced by governmental authorities (Brinkerhoff et al. 1997, 67).

Folkways, mores, and laws are forms of social control. All cultures have checks on individual, group, and crowd behavior. The control of individual or group behavior may be either informal or formal. Individuals who do not follow the norms or mores of the culture will find themselves ostracized. However, if they break the rules, or more specifically the laws, of government, a more severe penalty can be imposed, such as a fine, confinement to a specific geographical location, or imprisonment. Governmental agencies involved in controlling behavior are criminal justice personnel: judges, prosecuting and defense attorneys, corrections personnel, and police officers. The vanguards in maintaining internal social control in American society are the police. The police are given the legal responsibility to assert social control and the option to use various means to achieve this goal; including arrests and the use of physical force— necessary, deadly force, or force with the potential of causing death. This book discusses the various philosophies, strategies, and methods of social control used by the police. Community policing is the latest social control philosophy to be adopted by the police.

Occupational Culture

Various groups of workers develop a culture unique to their specific occupation. Policing, like other occupations, has developed a unique culture. Before we examine the police culture in detail, an understanding of occupational culture will be helpful. To understand occupational culture, we need to understand how it fits into an organization and to answer several questions: How does occupational culture serve the organization and its members? How does occupational culture evolve? Where does an organizational culture come from? For starters, we know that the external social environment of an organization exerts an influence. Our American culture influences occupational culture—managers and workers bring the dominant culture to the workplace. The personality of the head of a specific organization may influence the culture of that organization. So may the management style of an organization, whether authoritarian or democratic.

Researchers of organizational cultures study organizational stories; language, including jargon and slang; jokes; rituals; ceremonies; myths; heroes; values; organizational structure; social roles; and standard operating procedures. They also study the intentions of organizational members, what members of the organization think is necessary to move ahead within the organization (Ford 1988, 346) and "the degree of trust, communications, and supportiveness that exists in the organization" (Hellriegel et al. 1983, 590).

It should be understandable that when people work together for any length of time, they will generate particular patterns of thinking, behaving, and feeling. The development of a unique understanding of the world and shared values, symbols, distinctive language, and behavioral norms separates occupational members from nonmembers and legitimately characterizes subcultures. Occupational cultures reflect a cooperative transformation to social and physical working conditions. People who perform similar tasks are exposed to similar experiences and are confronted with similar problems. They also interact with similar people and may receive comparable rewards. Workers who share experiences and interact create a feeling of cohesion. They develop knowledge unique to their occupations, a common language, and informal rules for dealing with problems. In addition, work clothing may become a symbol of membership in the group (Rothman 1987, 40–41).

Subcultural Occupations

Subcultural occupations tend to isolate individuals from outsiders and from the society. Occupations exist, such as the police, where segregation extends beyond the workplace to include leisure and social activities. Workers of specific occupations can form closed communities, associating only with people from their same occupation to the exclusion of individuals from other fields. The people they work with are the people they drink with, golf with, and entertain at home. Attitudes and behaviors that are distinctive and shared by a specific occupational group are instrumental in accomplishing the technical and social goals of the job. Shared work patterns, found in many occupations, ensure predictability and reliability. Occupational standards allow workers to anticipate how other workers will react in a specific situation. Career fields, through their subculture, provide protection from a social or physical environment that appears to be threatening. Symbols of subcultures integrate members into a feeling of solidarity. Uniforms, traditions, and ceremonials help create a cohesive group. Self-image, social status, and social placement are also achieved through an occupational subculture (Rothman 1987, 42–43).

What sort of young person enters the police field? Studies indicate that young people entering policing generally are recruited from lower-middle-class backgrounds. John Van Maanen (1978) gave several reasons why young people enter policing:

1. The literature notes that police work seems to attract local, family-oriented, working-class whites interested primarily in the security and salary aspects of the occupation. . . .
2. The out-of-doors and presumably adventurous qualities of police work (as reflected in the popular culture) were perceived by the recruits as among the influential factors attracting them to the job.
3. The screening factor associated with police selection is a dominating aspect of the socialization process.
4. As in most organizations, the police department is depicted to individuals who have yet to take an oath of office in this most favorable light. A potential recruit is made to feel as if he were important and valued by the organization.

(295–296)

In surveys of graduates from the New York City Police Academy, it was found that 80 percent of the fathers of police officers were employed either as service workers or as laborers. Most police recruits have not had high-status employment positions. Many of them have drifted from job to job. This is especially true when police agencies are in a hiring mode. It appears that police departments are not as selective about whom they employ when they are hiring a large number of recruits. The various scandals of police corruption during the last several decades have been reflected in this. Miami, Houston, New York City, and Washington, DC, all had police scandals due to poor recruiting. The general requirement for most police agencies is either a GED or a high school diploma. There are police departments that require a baccalaureate degree, but this is more the exception than the rule. The New York Police Department, the nation's largest municipal police agency, adopted in 1997 a policy requiring all police recruits to have two years of college or to substitute two years of military service for the college. Although more police officers are now entering police work with college degrees, many of them having a major in criminal justice, they are still a minority. Some police departments will give extra points on promotional examinations to police officers who have college degrees. Other police departments, such as the Wichita (Kansas) Police Department, require a college degree for promotion.

Since the late 1960s and early 1970s, police departments have concentrated on increasing the numbers of African Americans, Hispanics, Asians, and women in policing. The goal of police agencies is to have a department reflect the racial, ethnic, and gender makeup of the community. The numbers of minorities and women have increased substantially since the 1970s but are still small when compared against the composition of many communities.

Identification of Symbolic Assailants

Jerome Skolnick (1994) considered a continually watchful stance toward what he termed symbolic assailants to be an integral part of the police culture (51–63). Because of the danger associated with police work, according to Skolnick, the police develop intuitive techniques to identify undesirables or potential law violators. These indicators could include a person's appearance, such as clothing or hairstyle or, more recently, tattoos and body piercing. For example, gangs are known to use tattoos as symbols that other gang members would recognize. Characteristics of the symbolic assailant as described by Skolnick also include language, gestures, attitude, and body language. Police are trained to be suspicious (though suspicion should be controlled and not too obvious) and to look for the unusual: persons who do not "belong" where they are observed, automobiles that do not "look right," and businesses opened at odd hours, or not according to routine or custom.

The training that recruits receive while attending the police academy contributes to the identification of symbolic assailants. The police are trained to be suspicious. In fact, police officers believe that a suspicious nature is a key ingredient of being a good police officer. Police officers know the environment they patrol and often can detect the unusual. I myself know police officers who are familiar with the residents who live in their patrol areas and who know which automobiles go with which houses. Some officers are so good that they know what garage doors should be opened or closed and whether a car visor should be down or up. Good patrol officers who know how to work their beat are familiar with the small details of their patrol area. Police officers who develop the attitude of suspicion in their work are working hard to make arrests and to control crime.

Police officers who start working the street quickly learn to direct the "policeman's stare" toward the symbolic assailant. In our American culture, staring at an individual is considered rude or abnormal, but police officers consider staring as a means to control a situation. They are encouraged when patrolling in vehicles to do so with their windows open in order to pick up sounds or unique smells. They should use all their senses to determine if anything out of the ordinary, such as the smell of a gas main break, is occurring on their beat, and the law recognizes that they can use the evidence of their senses—seeing, hearing, smelling, touch, and/or taste—to make an investigation without a warrant.

Secrecy

"The concept of ethos encompasses the distinguishing character, sentiments, and guiding beliefs of a person or institution" (Kappeler et al. 1998, 99). A major ethos of policing is secrecy. As early as 1930, August Vollmer was critiquing the "blue code of secrecy" that he considered characteristic of many police departments.

Kappeler et al. (1998) listed the specific injunctions of the code of secrecy as follows:

- Don't give up another cop.
- Watch out for your partner first and then the rest of the guys working that tour.
- If you get caught off base, don't implicate anybody else.
- Hold up your end of the work; don't leave work for the next tour. Fails to follow this edict, other officers are expected to "cover" for him or her and to deflect attention from the group.
- Don't look for favors just for yourself.

(103–105)

Although the "code of secrecy" is not always as rigid as it is made out to be, secrecy does exist in all police organizations to some extent. Several factors contribute to the development of a code of secrecy in policing. First, policing is fraught with the potential for mistakes, and officers often observe the code of secrecy to protect their fellow officers from being accused of making inappropriate decisions, as they would wish to be protected themselves. They feel that they are often called upon to make split-second decisions that can be unfairly second-guessed by people not directly involved in policing. To some extent, this is true, even though the "split-second syndrome" is sometimes used by the police as a rationalization "to provide after-the-fact justification for unnecessary police violence" (Fyfe 1997, 540). John Crank (1998) has argued along these lines, observing that the veil of secrecy emerges from the practice of police work, from the way in which everyday events conspire against officers. The veil has no remedy. It may be desirable to penetrate the veil, but it is not reasonable. To look at secrecy in terms of good or bad, right or wrong, is to miss the point. It is a cultural product, formed by the environmental context that holds in high regard issues of democratic process and police lawfulness, and that seeks to punish its cops for errors they make. Secrecy is a set of working tenets that loosely couple the police to accountability, that allow them to do the work they do without interfering oversight. As long as police conduct law enforcement under a mantle of due process and accountability in the United States, police culture will be characterized by secrecy (226).

The trust that must exist between police officers who work together also provides a basis for secrecy. Police culture recognizes that officers can only function successfully when they work with colleagues whom they trust. Officers know the most about their fellow officers' performance, but if they revealed this information to superiors, they would jeopardize the trust on which they must rely.

The traditional or professional model of policing has reinforced an ethos of secrecy. Under this model, as discussed in Chapter 1, police are the experts in fighting crime, and the public has no business to know much about their work or to intervene. All nonpolice are outsiders whose knowledge of police activities could only harm the department or its personnel:

> Policemen are under explicit orders not to talk about police work with anyone outside the department. There is much in the nature of a secret society about the police; and past experience has indicated that to talk is to invite trouble from the press, the public, the administration, and their colleagues.
>
> (Wesley 1951, 30)

To maintain the integrity and reputation of a police department, the professional model of policing underscores the importance of policies, rules, and procedures that police officers must follow. Violating policies and rules can be a cause for suspension or even dismissal. Many departments use large loose-leaf notebooks to hold the departmental policies, procedures, and rules and expect all police officers to know them all. This is an impossible task for most people, but lack of knowledge about a departmental policy, rule, or procedure cannot be used as an excuse for violating it. Under such a system, officers feel so vulnerable to discipline for rule breaking that they are especially motivated to cover up their own and others' violations.

Further, many police officers have traditionally believed that they have the right, at times, to step out of legal and ethical bounds and to violate department policies and procedures while performing their duties, particularly in the interests of their own survival or job tenure. Because of the nature of police work, secrecy will always be a component of police work, and some aspects of policing, such as details of ongoing investigations and police personnel decisions that are required by law to be kept confidential, will always need to be kept secret and known only to a few individuals. Nevertheless, the code of secrecy is losing its dominance as police departments transfer from the professional model to the community-policing model. The philosophy of community policing requires that the police be more open with the information they have and gives them new roles as cooperative problem solvers and decision makers in the communities they serve. Unnecessary secrecy is an impediment to the police–community partnership, a major premise of the community policing philosophy.

Isolation

A by-product of police secrecy is social isolation. "Isolation is an emotional and physical condition that makes it difficult for members of one social group to have relationships and interact with members of another group" (Kappeler et al. 1995, 252). The police subculture isolates police from the rest of society. Often the police place restrictions on themselves that lead to limited interactions with the neighborhoods and people they serve. The "stay-out-of-trouble" mentality that some officers have contributes to the social isolation associated with the police field. Jerome Skolnick (1994) has cited James Baldwin's (1962) description, from the early 1960s, of the isolation of police officers from the people in black ghettoes of the 1950s and 1960s. Baldwin claimed that the only way the police could control the ghetto was through oppressive tactics, the police could not understand the people, and their very presence was an insult. The police represented the white world and were there to control black people—in other words, to keep them in their place. Even when a police officer had done nothing to be hated, he was serving as an occupying soldier of the group oppressing them, so people in the ghetto would wish to see him dead. Because police officers worked in a hostile environment, they had to patrol their walking beats in twos and threes (65–67). Baldwin's description may be more accurate for the 1960s and 1970s for policing under the professional model than it is today, when police agencies throughout America are making the transition to community policing and trying to develop cooperative relationships between communities and the police.

A number of forces contribute to the isolation of the police. First, individuals who have been subject to restrictive actions by the police resent the invasion of their privacy. Second, problems that have recurred throughout policing history, such as police incompetence, brutality, corruption, and pursuit of private interests, have created feelings of mistrust, fear, and disdain between the police and the public. Third, police operations are set apart from society because of their nature. Police work involves dealing with the seamy side of human behavior.

In addition, however, various governmental studies have claimed that since the police have been placed in patrol cars, they have lost contact with the community. They maintain that this chasm has been wider between the police and the public in some locales than others but that it exists everywhere. One of the reasons for adopting the community policing philosophy has been to bridge the gap existing between the police and the community. Police officers who are working the street (beat patrol officers) develop a set of beliefs that regulates the pace, style, and direction of their "on-the-street" behavior. These beliefs are produced by patrol officers' unique social role and their "outsider" position in the community, as well as the nature of police responsibilities and the requirements of personal survival while performing police work. The professional model of policing discouraged interaction with the community. The patrol officer had to be available to answer radio service calls. Police officers were not encouraged to get out of their cars to interact with the public. In fact, communication with the public was not encouraged. For example, as a young police officer, I worked for a midsized city police department that assigned officers a different patrol sector each day or night an officer worked. The purpose of this was to prevent police officers from becoming too familiar with the people on their beat. Police administrators who used this model were attempting to maintain the integrity of the police officers and the department by preventing overfamiliarity between police officers and people on their beat because it was believed that such overfamiliarity could lead to corruption. It should be kept in mind that the professional model of policing was instituted in reaction to the political model of policing which was associated with numerous police corruption scandals. However, community policing is taking the opposite approach from the professional model in that it encourages police officers to get to know the people on their beats so that they can solve problems of concern to the neighborhood. Today, police agencies that have adopted community policing have concentrated their efforts on ending the alienation that has existed for decades between the police and the community. Community members are being included in police policies that affect their communities and neighborhoods, and community-police cooperative efforts are breaking down the old barriers of hostility and mistrust. The more ingrained the community policing philosophy is in an organization, the less isolated the police will be.

Solidarity

Occupational groups have a sense of identification and inclusiveness. People working together, performing the same or similar tasks, and facing the same problems are most likely to bond and develop a sense of solidarity. Although all occupations have solidarity, this seems to be especially true of the police. The term solidarity implies consensus, integration, friendship, personal intimacy, emotional depth, moral commitment, and continuity in time (Durkheim 1966, 47–48). The sense of solidarity may change with a police officer's rank and age. According to Kappeler et al. (1998):

Police solidarity . . . may be said to be an effect of the socialization process inherent to the subculture and police work. New members are heavily socialized to increase their solidarity with the group, and those who move away from the subculture, either through age or promotion is gradually denied ties of solidarity. This cohesion is based in part on the "sameness" of roles, perceptions, and self-imagery of the members of the police subculture.

(102)

Three sources of solidarity are defensiveness, professionalization, and depersonalization. Defensiveness reflects in-group/out-group tensions and is an adaptation to an external social world perceived as hostile or critical. Police officers know that other officers will support them against outsiders, and this gives them the moral support to perform their duty. The sense of professionalism instilled in police recruit training further reinforces solidarity, the perception that outsiders can never know what policing is really like, and what it demands. Finally, solidarity is strengthened by the depersonalization of outsiders. Police officers who have this attitude often treat citizens inhumanely and may even abuse them. Possible contributors to depersonalization are the need for police efficiency, timed response to calls, and the requirement that the police are impartial (Harris 1973, 163–165).

The alienation from the public that is so often the flip side of police solidarity is partly based on the belief, held by some police officers, that the public does not support them, takes them for granted, does not respect them, and expects them to do a dangerous, low-paying job alone without any help from the community. Although the police have the responsibility to maintain order, they feel that the public should play a part. In addition, they may feel as depersonalized by ordinary citizens as citizens feel depersonalized by them.

The danger involved in policing alienates the police officer not only from the criminal offender but also from the law-abiding citizen (Skolnick 1994, 52–53). A similarity may exist between police and military solidarity; Janowitz (1964) has argued,

any profession which is continually preoccupied with the threat of danger requires a strong sense of solidarity if it is to operate effectively. Detailed regulation of the military style of life is expected to enhance group cohesion, professional loyalty, and maintain the martial spirit.

(175)

The professional policing model reinforces this kind of solidarity among police officers. But with the implementation of community policing and a restructuring of the police organization to allow community-policing strategies to be successful, there may be less need for solidarity among police officers because, as police officers increase their interaction with the community, there should be greater rapport and trust between the police and the community.

Cops' Rules

"Cops' rules" are an important component of police culture (Rubinstein 1973, 267–337). Police officers develop specific skills that help them perform their job successfully. Unlike many other career fields, policing is dangerous. Officers must be concerned not only about their own personal safety but about the safety of their fellow officers and citizens. When they confront citizens who want to harm themselves or a fellow citizen, they must be good manipulators who know when to cajole and when to threaten an individual or group to defuse a violent situation and keep the peace. The police officer on the street would say you have to be a good "bullshitter" to be a good police officer. Experienced police officers usually do not want to confront a disturbed, violent person or suspect; they want the person to voluntarily follow their directions. They do not want the reputation of being a "hothead" and do not want their fellow officers to think that every time they confront a citizen, no matter how trivial the matter, they must make an arrest or get into a scuffle.

Due to the nature of their work, officers develop an intimate knowledge of the street they patrol and become more familiar with the area than most of its residents. Police officers' knowledge about the territory they work during a tour of duty is extremely important to their safety and the safety of others. All police officers assigned to a beat or sectors are expected to know the houses, businesses, automobiles, adults, and children. They should know all the names of the streets, and the alleyways, one-way streets, parks, and playgrounds. Most police officers become familiar with what times businesses close, what lights are left on in the evening hours, and what days stores close. All this is expected of beat patrol officers in the police culture. At some point in their careers, police officers learn to read people and dangerous situations. To survive on the street, or at least not to be considered incompetent by their peers, they must be able to read threats and the possibility of resistance or flight. They must be familiar with all the tools available to them, including verbal and physical skills and weapons.

Cops' rules often change very little, if at all, under the community policing philosophy. Even under community policing, police officers are expected to be law enforcement officers. That means they investigate crimes, make arrests, interrogate suspects, and place themselves in dangerous situations. Community policing does not mean that police officers discontinue traditional policing. They are still expected to respond to radio service calls, stop traffic violators late at night, chase criminals down dark alleys, and go into darkened buildings searching for burglary suspects, so they need the skills and tools to protect themselves and other innocent people from harm. It would be unrealistic to assume that under community policing police officers would never be in a situation where they had to use force.

Technology

The most deadly tool at police officers' disposal is their service revolver. In many police departments, police officers in patrol vehicles have shotguns in a gun rack available to them. Today, police departments have a variety of sophisticated firearms at their disposal, but, for practical purposes, officers depend primarily on their service revolver for safety. Because firearms are deadly weapons, officers are trained to use them only as a last resort. They are also taught that the service revolver should not be used to threaten, but should only be pulled from the holster if one is willing to use it. It is a weapon of last resort to be used only to save the life of the police officer or another individual in imminent danger.

Another weapon of importance to the police officer is the nightstick or baton. Although the baton can be a deadly weapon, it should be used only as a defensive tool. It generally is used to get a suspect or violent person under control. The baton can do physical damage, but it usually does not cause serious physical injuries. Blows or raps to the shins, knees, elbows, or ankles can take the fight out of many people. The baton helps the police officer gain control of a potentially dangerous situation without causing excessive physical damage to the officer or to the offender.

A deadly weapon that some police officers carry is the slapjack or blackjack. The slapjack, a flat weapon, has a hard surface and thick edges and can cause serious cuts. The blackjack, a round weapon with a spring handle, has a whipping action that increases the force of a blow when used with a rapid motion. Both the slapjack and blackjack are lead pieces encased in leather. Because of the serious damage they can cause, many police departments have banned them.

For the last several decades the police have been searching for weapons that are not lethal but could be used to disable and subdue a violent individual for a short period without doing long-term physical harm. Less than lethal weapons can only be valuable to the police if the weapon incapacitates, debilitates, or disrupts the thought process of the individual for a period sufficient to allow the police to subdue the suspect (Downs 2007).

Less than lethal weapons include mace and pepper maces used by police officers to stop a suspect. Mace has been used since the 1960s, but pepper mace became more commonly used in the 1990s because it is generally more effective. Both mace and pepper mace are chemical irritants that act on the central nervous system and induce pain by activating receptor cells within the brain. Pepper mace causes a swelling of the eyes and breathing passage. An intense burning occurs in the eyes, throat, and the skin area sprayed. When pepper spray has been inhaled, breathing will be restricted, and the respiratory tract will be inflamed. The physical effects can include choking, shaking, involuntary closing of the eyes, nausea, lack of coordination, and loss of upper body strength. Disorientation and fear can also occur (Onnen 1993, 1–2).

Other weapons available to the police are the taser and the stun gun. The taser is a low-powered (5-watt) gadget that operates on a 7.2-volt battery and shoots barbs attached to 15 feet of wire. The taser causes "charley horse" spasms that cause subjects to lose control of their bodily movements. The stun gun generates an electrical current when it is placed against a suspect's body for several seconds. The taser and stun gun are both intended to keep police officers from using deadly force, which usually occurs with a firearm. Additional less than lethal weapons include beanbags, rubber bullets, and impact projectiles. Impact projectiles are used as an alternative to standard firearm rounds when trying to disperse a crowd from a distance or subdue dangerous combative people using lethal force (Vilke and Chan 2007).

It is expected within police culture that cops control the space around them. The control of space enables officers to control a situation and make the decisions that will keep them safe. Police officers do not like to go through buildings looking for a suspect or prowler because they do not have complete control of the situation: the suspect or the prowler may be able to see them without their seeing the suspect or prowler.

Controlling people goes along with controlling space. Police officers need to be in charge. In a potentially dangerous situation, whether it is a domestic disturbance, a shooting, or a traffic accident, they cannot allow a suspect, citizen, or criminal to seize the control; if they do, then for all practical purposes they cease to be police officers. Police officers control people by giving them commands, searching them, or arresting them. Police officers are not afraid to use their authority to control people.

An important tool possessed by police officers to control people is force. Although most police officers would prefer not to use force, they are almost required to use it against a rowdy or violent individual to gain control of the situation and to ensure their own safety and the safety of others. Rubinstein (1973) has described cops' attitudes about using force:

> Very few policemen use physical force gratuitously. A man will cajole, joke, advise, threaten, and counsel rather than hit, but once his right to act is questioned, once his autonomy is threatened, he is prepared to respond with whatever force is necessary. And once his power is contested, he can do no wrong. The legitimacy of this authority allows him to do whatever he must to preserve it. An attack on him is treated as an attack on the state. A man resisting a policeman is suddenly an alleged criminal, and although he has not been convicted, the policeman knows he can treat him in a manner in which he cannot treat others.
>
> (327)

Psychology Fitness for Policing

The psychological characteristics of police officers are probably contributing factors to the police culture. Psychologically, the police are generally considered to be more conservative. This view holds that traditional religious attitudes and gender roles are stressed and that people from different backgrounds who associate with each other should be voluntary. Police officers are often described as living in a "male-value" or hyper masculinity culture that emphasizes physical effectiveness and vitality. Although the number of female police officers has increased over the past decade it appears that the traditional masculine values have been accepted by female officers (Rostow and Davis 2004, 31–32). This is an example of the minority culture being dominated by the dominant culture.

Police officers often see their mission to be the guardians of morality who have the duty to protect society from the deviants and criminals. Philosophically, police officers are practical and generally have a distain for theory or abstraction. They resist change and innovation. Police officers have often developed some prejudicial attitudes toward minorities. These prejudicial attitudes have at times been adopted from senior police officers and supervisors. A good police officer is one who is suspicious. This is a quality admired by police officers of their colleagues. Skepticism has become an acceptable attitude of police officers. Police officers are often expected to use force without fear of being ostracized by their fellow officers. Generally, officers consider police work to be unpredictable. Often police officers may use deception, such as lying, to protect themselves from administrators or the courts. Policies, rules, and regulations put into place to control police behavior are generally considered to be "bullshit" by the line officer (Rostow and Davis 2004, 32–40).

Police officers should be psychologically fit before they are given the authority to function as police officers. Individuals applying for police positions must be psychologically screened prior to being employed as police officers. The screening of potential police officers has as its goals not only the screening out of inappropriate individuals but also attempts to identify and measure personal qualities that are associated with successful police careers. There are several psychological factors that are important for policing. These qualities (Fischler 2005) are:

- Intelligence: Police officers need problem-solving skills and to possess at least general intelligence.

- Judgment: Police officers need to act appropriately and decisively in stressful situations. The ability to have good judgment in a wide range of situations is critical to being a successful officer.
- Lack of Impulsivity: Police officers need to consider alternatives or consequences of their actions.
- Honesty and Integrity: These qualities are essential qualities for police work.
- Conflict Resolutions Skills: Police need the ability to relate in a positive compassionate way to citizens in crisis situations.
- Absence of Bias: Police officers must enforce the law fairly, regardless of ethnicity or gender of a victim, suspect, or citizen.
- Attitudes Toward Supervision: Police officers must be able to accept constructive criticism.
- Team Orientation: Police offices usually work in teams, and should be able to depend upon others for backup and be willing to develop a positive relationship with fellow police officers.
- Appropriate Motivations: Motivations such as service and not a desire for power should be the correct motivation for entering police work.
- Ability to Deal with Tedious or Boring Tasks: A great deal of police work can be tedious and boring and those entering policing will have to deal effectively with these tasks.
- Dependability: Generally, police officers score higher on tests of responsibility than the general public. Individuals who have shown irresponsible behavior in their driving records, arrest record, or school or work history would in all probability have difficulties as a police officer.
- Reasonable Courage: Individuals who show risk-averse behavior or reveal passivity may have difficulties as a police officer.
- Controlled Substance Abuse: Individuals with a pattern of heavy drinking, use of drugs, or a history of driving while intoxicated are negative signs to be qualified as a police officer.
- Absence of Serious Psychological Problems: Specific psychological disturbances are not compatible for police work. Recurring depression with suicidal tendencies or any type of recurrent psychotic disorder are examples of such disturbances. Other problems that render individuals unsuitable for police work include panic attacks, certain phobias, and personality disorders.

- Stress Tolerance: Individuals who react negatively to stress may exercise poor judgment in critical situations. The tolerance level of an individual may be inferred from an individual's history, test results, or observing the behavior of the individual.
- Absence of Sexual Disturbance: Individuals with deviant sexual attitudes or behavioral histories, which could pose a possible threat to public safety, should not be employed as police officers. Individuals with a gay or lesbian orientation should not be rejected solely because of their sexual orientation.

Myths About Policing

There are a large number of myths pertaining to policing. Some have been encouraged by police, administrators, officers, and unions. The entertainment and news media have also contributed to myths about policing by portraying police as superheroes. In real life, the police cannot realistically perform the acts or achieve the success that they do on television or in the movies. The news media frequently create a "crime wave" by leading the nightly news with the murder of the day. The media policy of "if it bleeds, it leads" often creates fear in the public that may be far more serious than the actual crime situation. The public can have unrealistic expectations of the police. The police are not all powerful, all knowing, or omnipresent. Students of policing know that police success in solving crime depends on individuals or groups coming forward to assist the police by providing information. Peter Manning (1997) defines the police myth as:

> Uncertainty, a basic informational matter, structures police work and is the basis from which the defining myth that grounds the work grows. The dramaturgical nature of policing is not an accident but is a function of information levels possessed by the police when considered in the context of their claimed place in a political-moral system.

He further states that:

> if we consider mythological formulations to be products of historical periods, then a change in social structure can produce

a change in beliefs, and previous beliefs and myths can become problematic.

(281)

David Bayley, in his book *Police for the Future* (1994), argued that the idea that the police prevent crime is the biggest police myth of all (3–12). The inability of the police to prevent crime has been a well-kept secret of modern times. Bayley asserted that the police have created an image of themselves as the public's best defense against crime and have managed to sell this myth to politicians and the general public, who have responded by giving them more resources, especially additional police officers. Yet, as Bayley pointed out, repeated analysis has consistently failed to find any connection between the number of police officers and crime rates, and the primary strategies adopted by modern police have been shown to have little or no effect on crime (3).

Bayley described three strategies of modern policing for which there is no evidence of effectiveness in preventing crime: patrolling of city streets by uniformed patrol officers, rapid response to emergency calls, and investigation of crime by detectives. Although the police maintain that these strategies are important for public safety, there is no support for their claims. Foot patrol makes people feel safer but does not prevent crime. A quick police response to a call has no bearing on preventing crime and has value only when the offender is still at the scene and can be apprehended when the crime is in progress. A predictable response time to a call appears to be more valuable than a rapid response. Criminal investigations by detectives have no major effect on public safety.

Bayley concluded that "police actions cannot be shown to reduce the amount of crime" (9) and that the police should "put up or shut up" (10). If the findings on police strategies are accurate, the police should change their tactics. According to Bayley, three fundamental issues need to be addressed if we really want the police to prevent crime more effectively:

1. Why haven't the police been effective in preventing crime?
2. What might the police do to become effective crime deterrents?
3. Considering the requirements, do we want the police to be effective?

(11–12)

Realistically speaking, the police cannot prevent or solve all crime. The police are recognizing that their success in preventing crime depends upon the average citizen. Only by giving the citizen a role to play in preventing crime can we expect a long-term decrease in the crime rate.

Police officers in my classes who read Bayley's theory strongly disagreed with him, claiming that the police do prevent crime. Police officers, former police officers, and those who feel the police can do no wrong may be angry about Bayley's thesis. But what is needed here is not anger but open-mindedness. A person can make a comment that the police do not like but still not be antipolice. Police philosophies and strategies should be open to evaluation, and, if they are not working or can be changed to work, then appropriate action should be taken. Although I myself do not completely agree with Bayley, I feel that he raises an important issue: whether the police should have the sole responsibility in crime prevention and what role, if any, the community, the neighborhood, and the individual have in crime prevention. In the community policing philosophy, the community, the neighborhood, and the individual must assume the primary role in crime prevention if they want to keep crime under control, and the police should provide them with training and assistance. A closer police–community partnership and a crime prevention orientation are emphasized.

Another myth sold to the public by the police is the "crime fighter" image. Studies indicate that police spend 80–90 percent of their time performing service activities. Further, if police are supported to be crime fighters, they are failures, because their performance record for solving crime is not impressive. For example, over the last several years, the police nationally solved approximately 65 percent of the homicides committed, about 52 percent of the forcible rape crimes, and 24 percent of the robbery crimes. It may not be the fault of the police that they have not solved more crimes. However, they should stop selling the myth that they are "crime fighters" if they cannot deliver on their promise. The "crime-fighting" image of the professional model of policing should be considered as one of this model's weaknesses. If police agencies keep what works from the professional model of policing and incorporate the strategies of community policing as well, they should be more successful in solving crime. The police should not have the sole responsibility to solve crime. The community has a responsibility not only for preventing crime but also for solving crimes. Community policing attempts to provide citizens with a sense of security by making them partners with the police in solving crime.

In all police departments, there are officers who joined up because they wanted to do the "real" police work of crime fighting. John P. Crank (1998) had the following to say about "real police work":

> Real police work engages the vital self, invokes the warrior's dream to make a difference in the battle against crime. Officers have the opportunity to use the special skills that derive from the unique experience and enforcement training—the powerful themes of danger, officer safety, weapon training, and protecting other officers come into play with real police work. Real police work is the "symbolic rites of search chase and capture." Such work gives the police a sense of self-worth absent in the give-and-take of normal everyday routines.
>
> (117–118)

Many police officers consider "real police work" to be catching bad guys: making arrests, conducting high-speed chases, catching burglars, stopping bar fights, and making the big bust. For them, real police work does not include such mundane tasks as doing paperwork and providing services. But in reality, except in a few busy patrol areas, paperwork and service activities, such as rescuing an elderly gentleman who has fallen on the floor and putting him back into bed usually make up 80–90 percent of a patrol officer's day. Some patrol officers feel that they are primarily report takers: they make a call, write up a report, and go back on patrol to take another call and make another report. They are expected to be in service to respond to citizens' calls, no matter how trivial these may be. They are not expected to solve a crime; if they do, it's a big event. If a crime has been committed, it normally will be turned over to the detectives to investigate. Such patrol operations do not necessarily make for happy patrol officers. Since most patrol officers would prefer performing "real police work," it is understandable that they are not necessarily big supporters of community policing, which they often consider "touchy feely."

Police work, with its image of action, offers individuals who want to work outdoors, have some autonomy, and put bad people away an opportunity that few professions offer. But community policing just expands the concept of real police work. Community policing can eliminate the dead time that officers complain about when not responding to radio calls for service.

Summary

The police culture cannot be overlooked if policing hopes to change its philosophy. The foundation upon which social groups function is referred to as culture. Culture consists of knowledge, beliefs, morals, customs, and practices acquired by a group. It also encompasses our thinking, feelings, attitudes, and communications with each other. We learn culture from the people around us. Because police officers are members of American society, they reflect American customs, morals, and values.

Elements pertaining to culture include norms, folkways, mores, and laws. Norms are rules of conduct. They designate what people should or should not do, think, or feel. Folkways are customary, normal, and habitual ways of doing things. Mores reflect a strong awareness of right or wrong. Laws are rules that are enforced by governmental authorities. All of these are forms of social control.

All cultures have checks on individual, group, and crowd behavior. Governmental agencies involved in controlling behavior are criminal justice personnel. The police are given the legal responsibility to assert social control and the option to use various means to achieve this goal, including arrests and the use of physical force—if necessary, deadly force, or force with the potential of causing death.

Various groups of workers develop a subculture unique to their specific occupation. Occupational subcultures tend to isolate individuals from outsiders and from the society at large. Workers of specific occupations can become closed communities, associating only with people from their same occupation to the exclusion of individuals from other fields. Policing is one such occupation.

Because of the dangers associated with police work, officers develop intuitive techniques to identify undesirable or potential law violators by their appearance, language, body language, gestures, and attitudes. They develop an alert and watchful stance toward what Skolnick (1994) has called the "symbolic assailant."

Another major feature of police culture is the ethos of secrecy. Police officers quickly learn that to survive in policing they must keep much of what they and their fellow officers do secret from their superiors and the public at large. The traditional police bureaucracy and the professional model of policing have supported the culture of secrecy in that police administrators wish to keep from outsiders any information that would reveal the inefficiencies and failures of the police department. Also, the perception of all nonpolice personnel as outsiders who should not be involved in police business has encouraged secrecy.

The term solidarity means consensus, integration, friendship, personal intimacy, emotional depth, moral commitment, and continuity in time. People working together and performing similar tasks are most likely to bond and develop a sense of solidarity. Policing is characterized by a high degree of solidarity, not only because of the dangers of the work but because of defensiveness toward what is believed to be a critical and nonsupportive public, shared professionalism, and depersonalization of outsiders.

"Cops' rules" are another important component of the police subculture. These are specific skills that help police officers to perform their job successfully. Police officers must be concerned about their own safety and the safety of fellow officers and citizens. They must be good communicators and be able to defuse volatile situations. An important tool possessed by the police officer to control people is force, including weapons. Although most police officers would prefer not to use force, they are almost required to use it against a rowdy or violent individual to gain control of the situation.

Many myths about policing have become a part of the police culture. These myths have been encouraged by police leaders, administrators, officers, and union officials. Some of them are the crime-fighting role of the police and the ability of the police to prevent crime.

KEY TERMS

- anomie
- cops' rules
- cynicism
- folkways
- isolation
- management cop
- material culture
- mores
- myths
- nonmaterial culture
- norms
- occupational culture
- out-groups
- "real police work"
- secrecy
- solidarity
- street cop
- symbolic assailant

REVIEW QUESTIONS

1. Define culture.
2. Define occupational culture.
3. Explain how the identification of symbolic assailants relates to the police culture.
4. Explain how secrecy relates to the police culture.
5. Discuss isolation and how it relates to the police culture.
6. Discuss solidarity and how it relates to the police culture.
7. Discuss cops' rules and how they relate to the police culture.
8. Discuss the division between street cop culture and management cop culture.

3

POLICE DISCRETION, POLICE MISCONDUCT, AND MECHANISMS TO CONTROL POLICE MISCONDUCT

CHAPTER OBJECTIVES

1. Have an understanding of police discretion.

2. Have an understanding of what constitutes police misconduct.

3. Have an understanding of the various mechanisms to control police misconduct.

4. Have an understanding of the value of community policing in controlling police discretion and police misconduct.

Introduction

Police discretion—the power to take action or not to take action or to arrest or not to arrest—is an important component of police powers and makes the police officer in our society an extremely powerful official. How officers use the discretion allowed them usually determines whether justice is done and whether the law has been applied fairly. Before the mid-1950s, our politicians and police administrators constantly told us that they enforced all laws and investigated all crimes equally. Today, we recognize that it would be impossible for the police to do this.

The major issues concerning the use of police discretion are the abuses that can occur with unchecked police discretion. Police abuses, often referred to as police misconduct, have been a major problem with many police departments in the 1990s and 2000s.

All vocations and professions have their outlaws, and policing is no exception. The police field has its share of officers who violate not only departmental policies and procedures but also the very laws they are to enforce. When a police officer is involved in misconduct, a scandal is created that tarnishes not only the reputation of the police officer but the reputation of the department that employs him or her and, even worse, the image of all police officers.

Since some police officers are involved in misconduct, mechanisms must be put in place to check police misconduct. These mechanisms investigate accusations of police misconduct and attempt to eliminate any police improbity when it is found. They are important not only for police personnel but for the community as well. Police officers following the rules of their department and doing their jobs strongly support mechanisms that punish and, if needed, remove police officers from the force. The community wants to have confidence in its police officers. Community policing cannot be successful without this trust.

Police Discretion

America is a nation of laws. Our laws are passed by the legislative branch of government and enforced by the executive branch. Cox and McCamey write that:

> The law explicitly grants some discretionary powers to police officers and creates a framework within which other discretionary judgments may legitimately be made. It is one measure of the importance of discretion in police work that these are among the first items that become incorporated into the officer's working knowledge of the law.
>
> (2008, 36–37)

Laws are passed to keep the peace and maintain order. Political scientists often claim that the purpose of laws is to "keep the underclass under control" for the benefit of the middle and upper classes. These groups could not remain affluent if chaos and disorder became rampant. Therefore, laws are passed and are enforced, not only for public safety purposes, but also to keep our society functioning well economically.

Individuals in our society, including those responsible for enforcing the law, do not always specifically follow the letter of the law. In addition, legal norms are constantly changing (Aaronson et al. 1984, 4). For example, a few years ago, it was acceptable to discriminate against homosexuals, but today this discrimination would be a violation of the law. Also, several decades ago it could be appropriate behavior to smack a youngster who talked back to a police officer and send him home to his parents, where he could expect to be smacked again. Today, this would be considered misconduct on the police officer's part.

Police discretion is the authority of police to decide how much effort they will apply to enforcing specific laws and which laws they will or will not enforce. According to Reiss (1984), the concept implies several things:

> One is quite simply that an officer who has discretion has the power to choose among alternatives. A second and closely related aspect is that a choice made by an officer in the exercise of his discretion must be permitted by law. A third is that an officer who has discretion exercises individual judgment in making a choice.
>
> (89–90)

Although the police are sworn to enforce all the laws all the time, they enforce only the laws they choose to enforce, and even when they choose to enforce specific laws, they often will enforce these laws only some of the time. In many situations, they will warn, reprimand, or release an individual rather than make an arrest. Often they decide not to arrest for crimes they do not consider to be violent or a serious threat, such as traffic violations, petty gambling offenses, and simple assaults between acquaintances. When the police decide not to arrest someone who qualifies to be arrested, it can be said that they are using discretion.

Joseph Goldstein (1960) argued that full enforcement would be difficult, if not impossible, to achieve. Police officers take an oath on the day they officially are sworn in as police officers that they will uphold and defend the U.S. Constitution, their state constitution, and federal and state laws. They are expected to respect individual rights of all people as outlined with the Bill of Rights of the U.S. Constitution, including the rights of those suspected of committing a criminal offense; to know and follow all the various court decisions establishing legal police procedures; and to protect the due process rights, as guaranteed by the Fifth and Fourteenth Amendments, of everyone that they arrest, search, or interrogate. Given the ambiguities in criminal law and due process boundaries, the conflicts between requirements, the time constraints, and the limitations of personnel and investigative techniques, full enforcement is simply not feasible. Therefore, actual enforcement of the law is inevitably selective enforcement (554–561).

Selective enforcement emphasizes the "spirit of the law" rather than the letter of the law. The unwritten selective enforcement policy of police departments enables police to enforce only the most serious laws and the laws the community wants enforced. Although legislation is written as if full enforcement is expected, lawmakers do not really expect it, and police agencies do not really expect it either. Kenneth Culp Davis (1971) argued that the police should not be expected to enforce all laws when prosecutors do not prosecute all cases. Prosecutors pick and choose what to prosecute, and police officers who observe them soon know what it takes for a prosecutor to take a case to trial. Further, insufficient funds allocated to police departments allow only for selective enforcement. Finally, lawmakers frequently pass laws that are difficult to obtain evidence to enforce (79–97).

The recognition of police discretion can be traced back to the early twentieth century, when the Supreme Court of Michigan, in Gowan v. Smith, 122 N.W. 286 (1909), asserted that

> the police commissioner is bound to use the discretion with which he is clothed. . . . To enable him to perform the duties imposed upon him by law, he is supplied with certain limited means. It is entirely obvious that he must exercise a sound discretion as to how those means shall be applied for the good of the community.

Although police discretion has been recognized by the courts since the early 1900s, it was not until the late 1950s that the police began to officially claim that officers possess discretion in performing their policing duties. The legitimating of police discretion was aided by an American Bar Association survey on the administration of justice in the mid-1950s. The survey found that criminal laws were frequently used for a variety of purposes other than their specified purposes—for example, to deal with numerous social problems, such as family problems, mental illness, and alcohol abuse. Thus, it was acceptable practice for police officers to use their own judgment about when to arrest and for what purpose (Walker 1993, 10). The 1987 U.S. Supreme Court ruling in McClesky v. Kemp, 411 crL 4107, further upheld the use of police discretion. Although police administrations under the professional model of policing have held onto the claim that the police fully enforce all the laws, progressive police administrators and personnel know that selective enforcement is the norm.

Discretion in when and whether to arrest or to use force against an individual places police officers in an extremely significant position in our society. Michael Brown (1988) went so far as to claim that "police discretion—the day to day decisions of policemen—is tantamount to political decision making, for the role of the police is based upon the legitimate use of coercion" (3–4). Brown further argued that

> the police have crucial policymaking powers by virtue of their power to decide which laws will be enforced and when. At issue is not simply the legality of these decisions, but the routine use of the legitimate means of coercion in society. The day-to-day choices of policemen affecting the meaning of law, order, and justice within American society.
>
> (5–6)

Fairness issues necessarily arise when race or class biases influence who is arrested or apprehended and who is not. Kenneth Culp Davis (1971) provides a realistic example:

> A statute, an ordinance, and a police manual all provide that a policeman "shall" arrest all known violators of the law. A policeman lectures a boy from a middle-class neighborhood, but he arrests a boy from the slums, although he knows that both are

equally guilty of violating the same statute. Because the evidence against both boys is clear, the policeman's decision is the only one that counts, for the release of the first boy is permanent and the conviction of the second follows almost automatically.

(218)

Further, police discretion can be abused. One common form of abuse is the dispensing of street justice. Street justice occurs when the police believe that someone should be punished for what he or she did or is about to do. The police usually have no qualms about using street justice on an individual who defies their authority or insults them. They feel that if they are to function effectively, they must be in control, and that if they are insulted and allow an individual to get away with it, then they have lost control of the situation. The Rodney King beating by the Los Angeles police officers could be considered an example of street justice. Rodney King gave the police a high-speed chase. He refused to stop when the police were in pursuit. According to police culture, when the police want you to do something, you do it. If you refuse to follow police orders, you may have to pay the price. Rodney King was beaten to teach him a lesson—and also to teach a lesson to the passengers in the vehicle King was driving.

Some police officers see nothing wrong with street justice. They consider it to be a part of their right and duty to teach an individual a lesson. However, when police officers dispense street justice, the individual has been denied due process and judicial review. By using street justice, a police officer has violated the law. Assaulting an individual is a crime, and police officers should not be immune from criminal charges if they have violated the criminal law or denied someone his or her constitutional rights.

The nature of the role assigned to the police by the community may be a factor contributing to the use of street justice:

> Studies of police discretion largely reinforce the view that street decisions to intervene, arrest, use force or issue traffic citations are primarily a function of situational and organizational factors that reflect interpretations of community needs and expectations by

police. "Street justice" in this sense is a response to a community mandate that something be done about situations where formal institutions cannot or will not respond for a variety of reasons.

(Sykes 1986, 498)

Sykes argued that the liberal reformers fear police repression and overlook the functional role of "street justice" in creating a sense of community. They choose to emphasize justice defined as due process over the community-based idea of justice as righting a wrong and protecting the physically weak from the powerful. Police accountability remains a problem, and order maintenance continues to create the potential for abuse of power. However, the answer provided by the professional model, which emphasizes the enforcement role, leaves many citizens without the means to civilize their community. The trade-off must be recognized and provides an ongoing moral dilemma in liberal society (507).

The dilemma here is that street justice is used by police officers to enforce the moral code of the community they police but that the use of street justice pushes justice aside.

According to Carl Klockars (1986), the police, for practical reasons, do not use street justice all that frequently. If an individual given street justice has been beaten severely, the police officer has to transport the individual to the emergency room and file a report explaining how the individual received his injuries. Because of the threat of departmental charges and the reactions of the community, which may not know the context of the officer's use of force, street justice is kept to a minimum (515–516)—although this may be hard to believe at a time when publicity has surrounded the Rodney King fiasco and the case of Brooklyn police officers accused of shoving a broom handle up a suspect's rectum. The next section will discuss the various forms of police misconduct in detail.

As Joseph Goldstein (1960) pointed out, police, unlike the other actors within the criminal justice process, generally operate without being seen, so their actions are not reviewed. If police officers assigned to investigate a disturbing event report the complaint as unfounded, in most cases their report will be accepted and not visible to the public. Even the records maintained by the police are usually too incomplete to be used to evaluate nonenforcement decisions (543–553). Because of concerns over fairness issues in police discretion, police abuses of discretionary powers, and the public invisibility of much police practice, many commissions and agencies have recommended that police departments establish rules to guide police discretion. In 1967, the President's Commission on Law Enforcement and Administration of Justice recommended such guidelines, stating that

> in view of the importance, complexity, and delicacy of police work, it is curious that police administrators have seldom attempted to develop and articulate clear policies aimed at guiding or governing the way policemen exercise their discretion on the street.
>
> (103)

In 1973, the National Advisory Commission on Criminal Justice Standards and Goals reiterated this theme. It recommended that

> every police agency should acknowledge the existence of the broad range of administrative and operational discretion that is exercised by all police agencies and individual officers. That acknowledgment should take the form of comprehensive policy statements that publicly establish the limits of discretion, that provide guidelines for its exercise within those limits, and that eliminate discriminatory enforcement of the law.
>
> 1. Every police chief executive should have the authority to establish his agency's fundamental objectives and priorities and to implement them through discretionary allocation and control of agency resources. . . .
> 2. Every police chief executive should establish policy that guides the exercise of discretion by police personnel in using arrest alternatives. . . .
> 3. Every police chief executive should establish policy that limits the exercise of discretion by police personnel in conducting investigations, and that provides guidelines for the exercise of discretion within those limits. . . .
> 4. Every police chief executive should establish policy that governs the exercise of discretion by police personnel in providing routine peacekeeping and other police services that,

because of their frequent recurrence, lend themselves to the development of a uniform agency response.

5. Every police chief executive should formalize procedures for developing and implementing the foregoing written agency policy.

6. Every police chief executive immediately should adopt inspection and control procedures to insure that officers exercise their discretion in a manner consistent with agency policy.

(21–22)

In 1974, the American Bar Association argued that

police discretion can best be structured and controlled through the process of administrative rule making by police agencies. Police administrators should, therefore, give the highest priority to the formulation of administrative rules governing the exercise of selective enforcement, investigative techniques, and enforcement methods.

(8)

Internal rule making gives police agencies a means of limiting the control of external agencies that can regulate police decision making. The courts, state legislatures, city councils, and county commissioners can all influence police policies and discretion. The numerous United States Supreme Court decisions have dictated police policies and have limited police discretion in many situations. State legislatures and city councils have directed the police to arrest the abuser during a domestic violence call. When the police observe or believe that a person has been assaulted by a spouse or live-in companion, they are legally required to make an arrest. This requirement to arrest during a domestic dispute is an example of how the legislative branch has taken away the power of the police to exercise discretionary decision making in certain situations. Rule making exists to increase predictability, fairness, and efficiency in daily policing activities. It should also contribute to more effective and responsive policing by minimizing procedural errors, improving police–community relations, establishing uniform policy, and centralizing accountability for decision making (Aaronson et al. 1984).

Although rule making has been advocated as a means of controlling police discretion and police behavior, most police departments have not followed the recommendations to implement rule making for the police officers. For the most part, departments initiate rules for their officers as a reaction to predicaments or in response to lawsuits, political pressure, or some other crisis. Rule making by police departments reflects a reactive approach rather than a proactive approach (Walker 1986, 362–363). But when police departments have failed to implement rules to control police discretion, the judicial branch has taken over this function. For example, the United States Supreme Court in Delaware v. Prouse has taken a strong stand against random traffic stops by the police. The Supreme Court in 1979 ruled that police officers could not randomly stop motorists without probable cause to suspect crime or illegal activity, to check the driver's license and auto registration (24CrL 3089). In 2000 the United States Supreme Court ruled in Indianapolis v. Edmond that police check points aimed at discovering drugs and other illegal activity are illegal and in violation of the Fourth Amendment rights of citizens (N99–1030).

Enlightened police leaders have realized that when police activities have intruded on the liberty of citizens, policies and procedures are required to give police officers guidance on:

1. The use of physical and deadly force.
2. Arrest and alternatives to arrest.
3. Stopping, questioning, and frisking citizens.
4. The handling of disorders and/or minor nuisances short of arrest.
5. The use of all intrusive investigative techniques including informants, infiltrators, and electronic surveillance.

(Walker 1986, 388–389)

How does police discretion fit into community policing? The community policing philosophy emphasizes a closer police–community working relationship. Traditional, or professional-model, policing requires that police respond to citizen complaints that are telephoned in to a dispatcher. When patrol officers have free time and are not responding to citizen calls or investigating a traffic accident, they are expected to look for crime on their beat—for example, by patrolling areas that are known to have a high rate of burglaries or a high rate of automobile accidents. Under the community policing philosophy, all police officers are community-policing officers. If this concept becomes operationally successful, the use of discretion by patrol officers may be more carefully thought out. As the beat patrol officer and the neighborhood develop a closer working relationship, breaking down barriers and sharing a stake in crime prevention and control, police discretion may become more attuned to community needs, and police misconduct may decrease.

Police Misconduct

According to organizational scholars, most occupations provide their members with the opportunities for behavioral misconduct, and police departments are no exception. Three elements of occupational misconduct are: "(1) opportunity structure and its accompanying techniques of rule violations, (2) socialization through occupational experiences, and (3) reinforcement and encouragement from the occupational peer group, i.e. group support for certain rule violations" (Barker 1977, 356).

The quality of work performance varies considerably from one police department to another. Most police departments employ police officers who generally function in a fair and impartial manner. However, some police officers become involved in police misconduct. Despite the publicity that police misconduct receives, police departments or even state or federal agencies keep few records of misconduct. It is not uncommon for departments to allow officers involved in police misconduct to resign their position rather than to be fired or prosecuted so that both the officers and the department can avoid publicity. In some states, policy agencies that do this may be violating state training standards that certify police officers. By these standards, an officer involved in police misconduct can lose his certification so that he is no longer employable as a police officer. But when a department allows a police officer to resign, this individual can obtain employment in another police department.

When the police are involved in misconduct, or even when the community believes that the police have committed acts of misconduct, the community loses confidence in the police. To obtain and maintain the community's backing, the police must refrain from wrongdoing. The community expects its police officers to be beyond reproach. When the police lose the community's respect and trust, the department cannot be an effective tool in criminal apprehension and in controlling crime. Without the community's support, victims and witnesses will not come forward. This is crucial because victims and witnesses willing to participate in the legal process contribute to the arrest and prosecution of offenders.

Forms of Police Misconduct

Since the formal organization of policing in the United States, police misconduct has inundated police departments. The police in the early decades of the twenty-first century are no closer to removing the misconduct problem than they were in the twentieth century. The police are in a position of authority and power. Their authority can lead to confrontation with citizens who challenge that authority. Often, police–citizen confrontations create the appearance that the police overstep their boundaries. It is important to recognize that the police have the duty to protect the constitutional rights of all citizens. It is not unusual for police officers to be accused of not fulfilling this role (Palmiotto 2001, 32).

Police misconduct may be either a criminal violation or a violation of departmental rules. It may be unethical or amoral without being criminal, and it does not have to result in personal gain, such as monetary rewards. It may be a reflection of the community, the police department, or an individual police officer. Misconduct of police officers include not only lying, protection of illegal activities, accepting of bribes, and theft occurring during investigations (Hyatt 2001, 75) but also the following misconduct actions:

> Sleeping on Duty—Sleeping on duty usually occurs on the midnight shift during slow periods when there are few calls for service. Although this violates police policies, there are officers who attempt to take catnaps during working hours. Some police officers have second jobs and work during the day and need to rest during their midnight tour of duty.

> Use of Illegal Drugs—In the modern era of policing, the use of drugs by police officers can be added to the police misconduct list. Police officers who were exposed to drugs growing up and who in all probability experimented with drugs do not necessarily

see anything wrong in using drugs. With drugs easily available in our society, it can be expected that some police officers will use illegal drugs.

Police Brutality

Police brutality is an ambiguous term that has had different meanings depending upon who uses it. Does police brutality include verbal abuse? To some people, it does. A number of police actions, including profane and abusive speech, commands to move or go home, field stops and searches, threats, prodding with a nightstick or approaching with a pistol, and the use of "physical force," may be called police brutality (Barker 1986, 71).

Citizens should recognize that police have the right to direct citizens' behavior. For example, if a person is double parked and blocking traffic on a city street, the police officer has the responsibility to require that person to move his or her vehicle. Also, if a group of teenagers are blocking access into a store and intimidating adults from entering the store, the police officer has the right to tell the teenagers to move. In these situations, the police officer should be civil and courteous but should expect the citizen or teenagers to comply with his or her request.

Many citizens are unaware that when police are patrolling their beat they are expected to conduct field stops and searches. The stops are to determine if the person or group stopped has legitimate business in the area. Generally, stops will take place during the evening hours. Citizens not versed in the law may not know that police officers have the legal right to conduct searches to protect themselves or others from potential harm. Whether police misconduct occurs during a field stop or search depends upon the specific situation and the police officer's behavior.

The use of physical force by police officers is not illegal or a violation of a departmental policy if it is justifiable. Every situation where physical force has been used must be judged on its own merit. Generally, acts of police brutality are known only to the police officer and a few witnesses, normally fellow police officers, who observe excessive force being used. Segments of the American population, especially minority members, who have the largest number of brutality complaints against the police, consider police brutality to be more of a serious problem than politicians or police administrators care to admit. Police brutality is usually discovered when the victim of police brutality reports it to police authorities or to other governmental agencies. Most states provide for a state investigative agency to investigate police brutality by local police officers. On the federal level, the Federal Bureau of Investigation has the authority to investigate police misconduct that can be in violation of federal laws.

Today, with the prevalence of video cameras, cases of police brutality can be videotaped and shown later. The videotaping of acts of police brutality is evidence that a specific officer or officers were involved in the use of excessive force. One case in which an act of police brutality was brought to the world by a citizen's videotaping was the beating of Rodney King on March 3, 1991, by Los Angeles police officers. George Holliday, the citizen who videotaped the Rodney King beating, brought the tape to the Los Angeles Police Department, who refused it. Upon the department's refusal, Holliday brought the tape to a local Los Angeles television station, which aired it. Eventually, CNN received a copy of the videotaped beating of Rodney King and gave it national and international coverage.

Another well-publicized case of police brutality took place on August 9, 1997, when a Haitian immigrant, Abner Louima, was taken into custody by police while sitting in a Brooklyn music club. The police took him to the 70th Precinct station house, where they strip-searched him and beat him. A New York City police officer allegedly shoved a toilet plunger into his rectum and then forced the toilet plunger into his mouth, breaking his front tooth. Louima asserted that while this was occurring, the officers taunted him, saying, "That's your shit, nigger," "We're going to teach niggers to respect police officers," and "This is Giuliani time, not Dinkins time" (Farley 1997, 38). Later, Louima recanted these comments. Eventually, Louima was hospitalized after a one and one-half hour ordeal in the station house. His injuries included a ripped bladder and a punctured lower intestine. The New York City police Commissioner Howard Safir called the incident a "horrific crime" and stated "We're going to make sure the perpetrators . . . go to jail." He also pointed out that a police officer who had been present had come forward to implicate his colleagues (Farley 1997, 38). One police officer was arrested and charged with sexual assault and sexual abuse, and 12 police officers were transferred, suspended, or demoted to desk duty.

When the public becomes aware of acts of police brutality in incidents such as the Rodney King or Abner Louima cases, they cannot have much confidence that the police will refrain from using excessive force. As acts of police brutality keep coming to the attention of the public before they can forget the last act of brutality brought to their attention, the police forfeit the community's trust more and more. The gap between police and minority communities grows wider or at least cannot be lessened while such inhumane acts are being committed.

Police brutality cannot be condoned. For community policing to be successful, police brutality must be eliminated. Why would citizens want to cooperate with the police when police are abusing community residents? The negative publicity from the Rodney King beating and the Abner Louima abuses will take decades for the police to overcome.

Throughout the 1990s, there have been numerous documented incidents of police brutality in American police departments of all sizes and in all parts of the country, rural and urban. But very little statistical information is available to document the overall extent of police brutality. Obtaining reliable data on police brutality is extremely difficult. To correct this deficiency, the U.S. Congress passed the Violent Crime Control and Law Enforcement Act in 1994, requiring the Attorney General to collect data on the use of excessive force by the police and to publish an annual report of the findings. The President's Commission on Law Enforcement and Administration of Justice (1967) reported in its task force report that physical abuse by police officers was not a serious problem but did exist. Commission researchers observed patrol officers in a number of cities and did observe instances where excessive force was used when none was necessary. Those abused were poor, drunks, sexual deviates, or youngsters considered hoodlums. The key ingredient discovered by the task force members was that those abused had verbally challenged the police officer's authority (181–182). If police officers are willing to use excessive use of force in the presence of the president's task force, what can the community expect when officers are not in the presence of witnesses?

In order to deal with the "use of force" misconduct issue the Community-Oriented Policing Service (COPS) national office with the New England Regional Community Policing Institute developed a curriculum on how to deal with the "use of force" in the community-policing environment. The training program was designed for police chiefs and senior managers with the authority and responsibility for overseeing, reviewing, and revising the department's use of force approaches. This training program makes the assumption that the administrators attending the "use of force" training will have experience in implementing policies, familiarity with internal affairs, and a commitment to community policing. The goal of the attendees for this "use of force" training is to identify and implement "the use of force" model for their department (Sweeney, n.d.).

Specific "use of force" training curriculums that are designed specifically for senior police administrators should go a long way in curtailing police brutality and excessive use of force by police officers.

Corruption

Police corruption is the abuse of police authority to obtain personal gain. This gain may be either monetary or nonmonetary. In committing acts of corruption, police officers gain financially by failing to perform services they are required to perform or by giving services that they should not be giving. Thirty years ago Barker and Wells characterized acts of corruption, which are still valid today, in three ways: "(1) They are forbidden, by some norm, regulation or law, (2) they involve the misuse of the officer's position, and (3) they involve a material gain, no matter how insignificant" (1981, 4).

Police corruption, according to veteran police officers, is always around and comes to life whenever the police department's vigilance subsides. For example, New York City police officers have been charged with selling protection to drug dealers and sometimes trafficking in drugs themselves. A report by the Mollen Commission investigating corruption in the New York City Police Department asserted that the department's internal affairs unit routinely buried corruption cases. The report also stated that police officers routinely made false arrests, tampered with evidence, and perjured themselves in court ("Policing the Police," 1994, 16).

Stoddard (1995) found that the police culture has an informal code that protects police misconduct and tolerates corruption. Recruits are indoctrinated into the police culture and soon come to the realization that they need the support of their fellow police officers, because their personal safety may depend upon a fellow officer being there when they need assistance. Further, recruits quickly learn that they themselves are bound to make mistakes, which may result in violations of departmental policy or criminal law, so that it may be best "not to see anything" if they observe misconduct by other officers.

Corruption has been found in many police departments—among them Atlanta, Miami, Houston, New Orleans, Philadelphia, Savannah (Georgia), and Los Angeles. Further, suburban and rural areas are not free from corruption. For example, a number of rural sheriffs from Georgia have been sent to prison for protecting drug dealers. Scandals involving police officers in corruption cannot benefit the police–community relationship. Police departments must check corruption if they hope to develop a successful community policing program.

Commission of Criminal Acts

A police officer lying in a court of law to obtain a conviction of a suspect has committed a crime. Lying in court has been termed perjury and is considered a criminal offense. Other violations of criminal law by police officers include murder, bank robbery, burglary, domestic violence, child abuse, and rape. In New Orleans, an off-duty police officer committing a robbery killed her partner, who was moonlighting as a security guard. Four Detroit police officers were charged with the murder of a black motorist who was beaten to death. In Galesburg, Illinois, a police officer was charged with bank robbery, and in Chatham County, Georgia, a police officer was caught robbing a convenience store on his own beat. In Wichita, Kansas, a police officer was charged with child molestation. In Savannah, Georgia, a police officer placed his own child in scalding hot water.

Although few police officers commit criminal acts, the few that do create a negative image for all police officers. Police departments must recruit people of integrity and investigate all complaints of improbity. Also, they must be proactive in their investigations and emphasize eliminating not only police crime but all police misconduct.

Mechanisms to Control Police Misconduct

For police misconduct to be controlled, mechanisms must be in place to control police behavior. These mechanisms can be either internal or external to the police agency. There are strong arguments for both approaches. Groups and individuals that distrust the police claim that the police cannot clean their own house, so that outside mechanisms are necessary to control police misconduct. On the other hand, police personnel find it offensive that "outsider" civilians who do not understand police work will be reviewing their behavior. This controversy is a hot topic in policing. If community policing is to be accepted by both the community and the police, this dispute will eventually have to be settled to the satisfaction of both.

Internal Affairs Units

Since the 1950s, midsized and large police departments have established internal affairs units to investigate citizen complaints of police misconduct. The size of an internal affairs unit can range from one officer to several hundred officers. The norm for staffing internal affairs is to have a ranking officer, captain or lieutenant, involved in investigating the conduct of police officers.

The ideal would be for every complaint against a police officer to be investigated impartially. When the internal affairs unit conducts an investigation, it interviews all witnesses and examines all pertinent evidence. The internal affairs unit commander reports directly to the chief of police. A report is made of the unit's findings to the chief, who then makes a decision for the appropriate action to be taken.

Civilian Review Board

The notion of a civilian review board can be traced to the 1930s. A civilian review board is "an independent tribunal of carefully selected outstanding citizens from the community at large" (Bopp and Schultz 1972, 146). Today, civilian review boards are often referred to as civilian oversight of the police. Although there may have been a name change, the two terms have similar meaning.

Every time there is a situation where the police are suspected of police misconduct, we hear the call for implementing a civilian review board if one does not already exist. Many of the same arguments made for a civilian review board in the late 1990s are similar to those made by supporters for civilian review boards in the 1960s and 1970s.

Civilian review boards review citizens' grievances against the police and are made up of only civilians, without any police representative. In 1967, the President's Commission on Law Enforcement and Administration of Justice recommended the adoption of such an external grievance system, stating that

the primary need is for the development of methods of external control which will serve as an inducement for police to articulate important law enforcement policies and to be willing to have them known, discussed and changed if change is needed.

(32)

Police acceptance of such an external grievance mechanism is a way of showing that their operations are open for inspection. The police can only create doubt and suspicion by rejecting an external grievance mechanism. In keeping with the community policing philosophy, with its emphasis on community-police interaction, it is a friendly gesture on the part of the police to accept civilian review boards, or civilian oversight bodies, as they are referred to today. Civilian oversight bodies have several characteristics in common. First, civilian oversight has been legally approved, either as an amendment to the city charter or by city ordinance. Second, civilian oversight bodies function independently of the police agency (Terrill 1990, 80).

Many of America's largest cities have some type of civilian oversight of police actions. In addition, many of America's midsized cities have adopted civilian oversight boards (Snow 1992, 51). The implementation of civilian oversight bodies does not necessarily mean that the police officer will always be found guilty. In all probability, the police officer will be exonerated. Civilian oversight boards are not in conflict with the community policing philosophy. In fact, civilian oversight boards indicate to the community the seriousness of police intentions to develop alliances and a cooperative spirit. The City of Wichita, Kansas, Police Department, which has a civilian oversight board, rarely has a recommendation of its internal affairs unit overturned by the civilian oversight board.

Civil Liabilities

For the past four decades, the United States Supreme Court has utilized Title 42, Section 1983 of the U.S. Code to control police misconduct. Section 1983 prohibits government employees from using any state law, ordinance, regulation, or custom as a technique to deprive citizens of their constitutional rights. The Court's purpose in establishing Section 1983 has been described as follows:

As a result of the new structure of law that emerged in the post-Civil War era—and especially of the Fourteenth Amendment, which was its centerpiece—the role of the federal government as a guarantor of basic federal rights against state power was clearly established. Section 1983 opened the federal courts to private citizens, offering a uniquely federal remedy against incursions under the claimed authority of state law upon rights secured by the Constitution and the laws of the nation. . . .

The very purpose of Section 1983 was to impose the federal courts between the states and the people, as guardians of the people's federal rights—to protect from unconstitutional action under color of state law, "whether that action be executive, legislative, or judicial" (Nahmond 1986, 4).

Section 1983 of Title 42 of the U.S. Code pertains to procedural remedies rather than substantial remedies. It provides an avenue of redress for violating the federal constitutional rights addressed in the Bill of Rights. In the 1960s, Section 1983 was expanded by the United States Supreme Court to afford the petitioner the right to take action against any person who—under color of law (state law, custom, or usage)—subjects another person to the deprivation of any rights, privileges, or immunities guaranteed by the U.S. Constitution. This means that the Fourth Amendment guarantees against unreasonable searches and seizures are equally applicable to the states via their judicial incorporation into the due process clause of the Fourteenth Amendment.

The Supreme Court of the United States has the authority to enforce the Fourteenth Amendment's provisions against state agents. This includes police officers who in some way fail to act according to their authority or who abuse their authority. The abused citizen, under Section 1983, can file a suit of equality, or other proceedings for redress, for being denied his or her constitutional rights, privileges, and immunities by an official's abuse of his or her position.

The United States Supreme Court concluded that local government officials under Section 1983 could be sued in their official positions for damages and retrospective declaratory and injunctive relief, even though local government may pay. A local government body can be held liable for traditions and customs that are unwritten and practiced by governmental departments or their employees.

When community members become stakeholders in the mission of police officers and have a major interest in crime prevention and control of disorder, a closer relationship between the police and the community can develop. With a police–community partnership, trust and confidence can grow, and fewer complaints will be made concerning police actions.

Summary

Police administrators used to claim that the police fully enforced all laws and investigated all crimes equally. But this has never been true. Full enforcement of the law would be impossible. In reality, selective enforcement is the norm. Police officers assigned to investigate a disturbing event can report the event as unfounded, and, in most cases, their report will be accepted and not visible to the public. Even the records maintained by the police are usually so incomplete that they cannot be used to evaluate nonenforcement decisions.

Although the police are sworn to enforce all the laws all the time, they enforce only the laws they choose to enforce and enforce even these laws only some of the time. In many instances, they warn, reprimand, or release an individual rather than make an arrest. Often, they decide not to arrest for crimes that they do not consider to be violent or a serious threat, such as traffic violations, petty gambling offenses, and simple assaults between acquaintances. In making such decisions, police are using discretion. Police discretion is the authority of police to decide how much effort they will apply to enforcing specific laws and which laws they will or will not enforce. It would be ridiculous to eliminate police discretion. Discretion is crucial to policing. But because it can be abused or applied unfairly, many commissions and agencies have recommended that police departments institute rules and procedures to guide and control the use of police discretion.

The quality of police work performance varies considerably from department to department. Most police departments employ police officers who generally function in a fair and impartial manner, but some police officers become involved in misconduct. Police misconduct is wrongdoing committed by a police officer. It can be either a criminal violation or a violation of departmental rules. It may be unethical or amoral without being criminal. Incidents of police misconduct include commission of criminal acts, corruption, excessive use of force, racism, and denying someone his or her civil rights. Police misconduct has taken place throughout history and still takes place today.

For police misconduct to be controlled, mechanisms must be put in place to control police behavior. These mechanisms can be either internal or external to the police agency. There are strong arguments for both approaches. Groups and individuals that distrust the police claim that the police cannot clean their own house and advocate outside mechanisms to control police misconduct. But some police personnel find it offensive that "outsiders"—civilians who do not understand police work—will be reviewing their behavior. Since the 1950s, midsized and large urban police departments have established internal affairs units to investigate citizen complaints of police misconduct. The size of an internal affairs unit can range from one officer to several hundred officers. The norm for staffing internal affairs is to have a ranking officer, such as a captain or lieutenant, involved in investigating the conduct of police officers.

One external mechanism for controlling police misconduct is civilian review boards. A civilian review board is an independent tribunal of carefully selected outstanding citizens from the community at large who review citizens' grievances against the police. Supporters of civilian review boards recommend that boards be composed of only civilians without any police representative. An additional remedy to check police misconduct is Title 42, Section 1983 of the U.S. Code. Section 1983 prohibits government employees from using any state law, ordinance, regulation, or custom to deprive citizens of their constitutional rights. The United States Supreme Court concluded that local government officials under Section 1983 could be sued in their official positions for damages and retrospective declaratory and injunctive relief, even though local government may pay. A local government can be held liable for traditions and customs that are unwritten and practiced by government departments or their employees.

KEY TERMS

- Abner Louima
- actual enforcement
- civil liability
- civilian review board
- corruption
- full enforcement
- Gowan v. Smith

- internal affairs units
- police brutality
- police misconduct
- Rodney King
- rule making
- selective enforcement
- street justice

REVIEW QUESTIONS

1. Explain police discretion.
2. What did the American Bar Association study discover about police discretion?
3. Provide an example of police discretion.
4. What do the terms full and selective enforcement mean?
5. Describe rule making as it pertains to police discretion.
6. Describe the meaning of street justice.
7. What does the term police misconduct mean?
8. Describe the purpose of an internal affairs unit.
9. What are the functions of a civilian review board?

4

CONCEPTS, STRATEGIES, EXPERIMENTS, AND RESEARCH FINDINGS THAT HAVE INFLUENCED COMMUNITY POLICING

CHAPTER OBJECTIVES

1. Be familiar with the police–community relations concept.

2. Be familiar with the team policing concept.

3. Be familiar with the Kansas City Preventive Patrol Experiment.

4. Be familiar with the directed patrol concept.

5. Be familiar with the response time concept.

6. Be familiar with the ministation concept.

7. Be familiar with the value of research to the evolution of community policing.

Introduction

This chapter discusses various concepts, strategies, experiments, and research findings that have influenced community policing. Community policing should not be considered a completely new philosophy. Many of its concepts and strategies are based on those that have been used by police departments in the past. For instance, community policing has adopted ideas about police–community relations that have been propounded since the 1960s. The team policing concept that developed in the 1980s could also be considered a forerunner of the philosophy of community policing. The strategy of directed patrol, or patrolling guided by analysis of crime patterns and directed toward the solution of specific neighborhood problems, was developed in the 1970s and is still used in community policing today. Ministations, or police substations that cover a small geographical area, have been in use for decades as a means of putting police officers in closer contact with the people they serve. Experiments in bringing back foot patrols as an alternative to motorized patrolling were first conducted in the 1970s and early 1980s. They have helped decrease the "fear of crime" and to develop rapport between patrol officers and their neighborhoods and have been recognized as an important aspect of community policing. The "broken windows theory," first advanced in 1982, has been extremely important in exploring how disorder creates a fear of crime and may even lead to a neighborhood's decay and an increase in crime. The theory of broken windows has played an important part in developing strategies for community policing. Finally, research on policing over the last several decades has corrected many misconceptions about policing and has provided a great deal of support for the community policing concept. Further research will be required to determine which aspects of community policing work.

Police–Community Relations

Police–community relations are an important focus of policing today, especially under the community policing model. The International City Managers' Association (1967) defined it as a police-department initiated program designed to offer an opportunity for police and other public agencies and individuals in the community to discover their common problems, ambitions, and responsibilities and to work together toward the solution of community problems and the formulation of positive community programs. It is not merely a problem-solving device. It is a problem-avoidance methodology which, when correctly recognized, can create healthy community attitudes (3).

Raymond Momboisse, in his book *Community Relations and Riot Prevention* (1967), defined police–community relations as meaning exactly what the term implies—the relationship between members of the police force and the community as a whole. This includes human, race, public, and press relations. The relationship can be bad, indifferent, or good, depending upon the attitude, action, and demeanor of every member of the force both individually and collectively (97).

The concept of police–community relations developed during the 1960s, a period of turmoil in America's cities. There were demonstrations against the war in Vietnam, civil rights demonstrations, and numerous riots, and the police often came into direct confrontation with the people they were to serve. Because of the chaos in American cities and alienation that existed between the police and the community, President Lyndon Johnson appointed a Commission on Law Enforcement and Administration of Justice in 1965. In 1967, the commission published a report stating that police indifference, police mistreatment of citizens, and citizen hostility toward the police were disruptive influences on the community (President's Commission 1967a). According to the report, police officers who work in a community that is hostile toward them will have difficulty providing police protection to that community, because citizens who are hostile toward the police will not report crimes to the police or provide them with the information necessary to solve crimes. When a community has negative feelings toward the police, tension rises, and aggressive actions against the police begin to occur, which in turn can trigger irrational behavior on the part of police officers (100).

Conversely, as the commission's report pointed out, poor police–community relations weaken the police ability to solve crime and make arrests because community residents who have hostile feelings toward the police will not report crimes or come forward as witnesses when they observe a crime taking place. It also influences police officers' attitudes and behavior in the field. Officers who feel unappreciated by the citizens they serve tend to be more abrasive and even more abusive.

This last point deserves special emphasis. Police–community relations should be a consideration in all aspects of police work, including departmental policy, supervision, personnel procedures, records and communications, acceptance of complaints against departmental members, and planning and research. Ideally, it is an attitude, a way of perceiving police responsibilities that permeates the entire police organization (Niederhoffer and Smith 1974, 3).

Community policing fosters good community relations in that it emphasizes listening to people rather than telling them what to do. It stresses that the police need to take seriously the concerns and the input of citizens who live and work in the community. In addition, the police are listening, because they now recognize that:

1. Citizens may legitimately have ideas about what they want and need from the police that may be different from what police believe they need.
2. Citizens have information about the problems and people in their areas that police need in order to operate effectively.
3. Police and citizens each hold stereotypes about the other that, unless broken down by nonthreatening contacts, prevent either group from making effective use of the other.

(Wycoff 1988, 105–106)

The police can also improve their relations with the community by establishing citizen police academies and community advisory councils. Citizen police academies are schools operated by police departments that offer courses to citizens on police subjects once a week for 15 weeks. Citizens walk away with a better understanding of police problems. Graduates of citizen police academies also constitute a source of police volunteers who can perform a number of services that leave officers free to perform police tasks.

Community advisory councils meet with police operations personnel to work on decreasing the crime rate, eliminating disorder, and reducing the fear of crime. A partnership between a community advisory council and the police can be linked to improving the quality of life for community citizens. The community advisory council can identify and prioritize problems within the community that a majority of residents want rectified. Once the problems are identified, strategies can be developed to solve the problems.

Finally, police departments need to be more open if they hope to gain the confidence of the people they serve. They must recognize that not all police information need be kept confidential, even though criminal investigations and other confidential information should obviously not be discussed with citizens or even with officers who have no need to know. The police must agree that they should be accountable not only for misconduct but also for any policies, procedures, or activities that are questionable. As communities and police develop a partnership, we may expect fewer complaints against the police and a greater success rate in solving crime.

Collaboration

The concept of police–community relations has as its goal communications with the community the police serve. Police–community relations offer an excellent jumping-off point for taking the relationship between the police and community a step further. The next step should be the development of a partnership between the police and community. This police–community partnership is a collaboration to jointly solve public safety issues and problems.

Various terms and concepts have been used to improve interaction and the relationship between the police and citizens. Since the inception of formalized police, there have been conflicts and confrontations between the police and the citizens to whom they provide public safety. In recent years the terms partnership, collaborative, and coalition have all been used to bring organizations and citizens together to solve community and neighborhood problems.

Some individuals consider the term "partnership" is straightforward and understandable. Others consider it to be legalistic and formal. The term "coalition" has several meanings: a narrow focus with a common goal or the bringing together of two or more entities. The term "collaborative" means working together (Blank, Rollins, and Ingacio 1999, 3). Blank, Rollins, and Ingacio define collaborative as: "A collaborative is a group of community leaders who use an inclusive strategy to establish shared goals and agree to use their personal and institutional power to achieve them" (3).

Currently, several available sources can assist in community-police collaboration. Many of these may not be specifically for police–community collaboration but they can be used as a model. One such toolkit was developed by Blank, Rollins, and Ingacio for the Institute for Educational Leadership. The toolkit provides a frame of reference on how to develop a partnership for collaborative problem solving. The toolkit provides a step-by-step outline on how to develop collaboration between the community and the police. The authors also provide an evaluation that can be utilized to assess and improve the quality of the collaboration. In addition to this toolkit, there are numerous resources available on collaboration. Many of these are available on the World Wide Web.

Team Policing*

Early Systems of Team Policing in Great Britain

Team policing began in Aberdeen, Scotland, following World War II. The Aberdeen experiment was an effort to counter low morale and boredom among police officers patrolling their beats. This project provided for 5–10-member teams of foot patrol and car officers assigned to different areas of the city. The number of officers assigned to an area was determined by the volume of service calls and the crime rate. The team policing method eliminated loneliness and boredom for the foot beat officer.

A further development in team policing was unit beat policing (UBP), introduced in Lancashire, England, during the summer of 1966 and later spreading to other areas of England. It was introduced as a means of improving police–community understanding, increasing clearance rates by encouraging information and intelligence flows within the department, creating a more challenging and attractive beat for the beat officer, utilizing manpower more efficiently by combining resources, and minimizing response time (Gregory and Turner 1968, 42).

In creating the UBP, the English hoped to design a patrol system that would reduce response time while maintaining a level of police–community relations. The English had a high regard for community cooperation and communication so they devised a system with a quick response time. Until the implementation of UBP, the primary method of patrol was the foot patrol. The use of patrol car beats increased substantially under UBP, and foot beat constables were all provided with two-way radios to communicate with dispatchers. Beat car constables were encouraged to leave their vehicles periodically to make a closer examination of conditions on their beat. The UBP strategy, although adding a beat car to an area to respond to emergency calls, still assigned a beat constable to the area to maintain community relations, gather

---

* Source: Data from E.J. Albright and L. Siegel, Team Policing: Recommended Approaches, pp. 8–17, 1979, Government Printing Office.

intelligence information, and provide general police work. The patrol beat constable was given the option to work flexible hours and to wear either a uniform or plainclothes. He was also responsible for performing initial investigations for major investigations, homicide and those covering a large geographical area, handled by the central investigative division of the police department (Gay et al. 1977b, 45–46).

Under this scheme, a UBP team was assigned to a geographical area and was responsible for the beat on a 24-hour-a-day basis. The team was decentralized, and the personnel assigned to the team were assigned specialized tasks. Each beat had a sergeant as a supervisor who would plan the team's activities. The foot constable had considerable discretion to perform a variety of functions. Three constables were assigned to the car beat to work 24-hour coverage. In some cities, the beat had an investigator. In contrast to the American policing system, the English emphasize foot patrol over motorized patrol. The English believe that crimes are prevented and can be detected and cleared when a constable knows his community and the people of the community. The UBP system recognizes that problems exist with specialization. Investigations are assigned to the beat to improve clearance rates and to enlarge the constables' role. The English recognized that police–community isolation usually exists when patrol officers are all motorized and are expected to react to 911 calls. UBP recognized that a mobile patrol force is needed along with strong police–community relations. Therefore, both motorized and foot patrol are a part of the UBP (Gay et al. 1977b, 45–47).

The National Advisory Commission on Criminal Justice Standards and Goals

The 1973 Commission on Criminal Justice Standards and Goals (National Advisory Commission 1973) recommended that both large and small police departments adopt a team policing strategy, which they defined as "essentially . . . assigning police responsibility for a certain area to a team of police officers. The more responsibility this team has, the greater the degree of team policing" (154). For example, team policing units that have investigative duties are more complete than those lacking these duties. Ideally, teams develop strategies specifically geared to the neighborhood they serve. The goal of team policing was to overcome the isolation of the police from the community under the traditional model of policing in order to facilitate crime control (154–156). Team policing would combine the line operations of patrol, traffic, and investigations for a specific geographical area into one unit under one supervisor. Teams would include generalists and specialists who would be permanently assigned to the area and would have responsibility for all police services for the area.

The Police Foundation study found that those departments that were successful in implementing the operational elements had strong organization support in the following areas: unity of supervision, lower-level flexibility in policy making, unified delivery of services, and combined investigative and patrol functions (Sherman et al. 1973, 5–6). The unity of supervision principle (patrol officer reports to one supervisor) led to effective team performance. When a police officer has more than one supervisor, he or she is often caught in the middle, with the two supervisors giving conflicting orders. Lower-level flexibility in policy making (the ability of low-ranking officers to make their own decisions) was of extreme importance for teams' productivity. Several police departments pushed decision making down to the teams because teams had the most accurate information about their neighborhood; this increased the authority of the lower levels of the hierarchy and responsibility and accountability of the team officers. Some police departments put in place a unified delivery of services, in which the team had complete control over the delivery of all police services in the team neighborhood. The unified delivery of services included the authority to decide when specialized police units could be assigned to the neighborhood. The idea was to recognize the knowledge of the team officers about their neighborhood and to give police generalists more authority as decision makers for their neighborhood.

The ingredient of combined investigative and patrol functions (investigators and patrol officers working as a unit) increased information sharing among team members, thereby increasing officers' familiarity with the neighborhood and making investigations more effective.

The simplest form of team policing employs basic patrol teams. This program decentralizes the patrol function by reorganizing patrols into teams responsible for preventive patrol, radio, and traffic duties. Teams are instituted to improve manpower allocation, reduce response time, and increase clearance of service calls. This program hearkens back to the traditional police precinct organization, for example, in New York City.

Programs using patrol-investigative teams connect the basic features of the basic patrol team with the assignment of follow-up investigative responsibilities to the team. The Rochester, New York, Police Department is an example of the patrol-investigative approach. The entire police department—patrol officers, supervisors, and administrators—contributes to the investigative process. The City of Rochester, New York, developed this approach in response to a rising crime rate, a poor clearance rate for crime cases, and the apathy and ineffectiveness of the police department's investigative division.

Team policing has been an elaborate experiment in American law enforcement. During the 1970s, approximately 60 police departments established team policing programs. Many of these programs were evaluated, and most of these evaluations are available for review. This chapter could not possibly cover all the evaluations of team policing programs.

Preventive Patrol

Traditional Preventive Patrol

Generally, police departments assign 60–70 percent of their police officers to patrol. The patrol unit has been called the "backbone" of the police department. Uniformed officers are assigned either on foot or in vehicles to patrol a specific geographical area, often referred to as a beat. Although other units such as investigations may be accorded more prestige, the patrol division has the most influence on public perceptions of the police. During the 1970s, police departments began to review the goals and functions of patrol operations. Traditionally, patrol operations function to provide a multitude of services, both crime and noncrime related.

The police functions can be divided into four categories: calls for service, preventive patrol, officer-initiated activities, and administrative tasks. Calls for service are usually referred to as reactive policing. A citizen calls the police for service—for example, about a dog barking in the wee hours of the morning—and the police respond. In most cases, the patrol officer is expected to correct the situation and to satisfy the citizen's complaint. When a patrol officer is not reacting to a citizen's call, he or she should engage in preventive patrol—that is, walking or driving around the area and keeping a lookout for potential problems. The notion behind preventive patrol is the belief that patrol prevents and deters crime. While on patrol or perhaps even while eating lunch, a patrol officer could stumble upon or observe a crime occurring. The patrol officer has the responsibility to initiate corrective action on his or her beat regardless of whether it is a criminal or noncriminal matter. Finally, all patrol officers have administrative tasks that they must perform, including writing reports, running department errands, appearing in court, transporting prisoners, or having the police cruiser cleaned. Traditional preventive patrol has five goals: (1) deterrence of crime, (2) apprehension of criminals, (3) satisfaction of the public demands for services related to crime, (4) development of a sense of security and confidence in the law enforcement agency, and (5) recovery of stolen property (Szynkowski 1981, 169). Patrol officers have more opportunity to recover stolen automobiles on their beats than many other types of stolen property.

All patrol officers have been taught in the police academy that they are out on patrol to deter crime. However, they do not know if they are a deterrent. They realize that most individuals will not commit a crime in their presence. Most seasoned patrol officers realize that an individual will commit a crime when police leave the area if the desire is there. Arrests may require not only hard work but a great deal of luck.

Patrol officers are asked or given the responsibility to provide services that other governmental agencies are unwilling or unable to perform. Also, they may be left with performing a variety of services simply because they are available 24 hours a day.

Kansas City Preventive Patrol Experiment

The Kansas City, Missouri, Police Department, under a grant from the Police Foundation, initiated in 1972 an experiment to determine the effectiveness of routine preventive patrol. The experiment involved 15 preventive patrol beats within Kansas City, randomly divided into three groups of five beats. Group 1 beats were reactive: officers were instructed to respond only to calls for 911 services. Group 2 beats were controls: standard preventive patrol was maintained at its usual level of one car per beat. Group 3 beats were proactive: regular preventive patrol was intensified by two or three times the usual level by assignment of additional patrol cars and by the frequent presence of cars from reactive patrols (patrols looking for crime, such as drug buys) beats (Kelling et al. 1974, 3). The experiments were developed to test the following hypotheses:

1. Crime, as reflected by victimization surveys and reported crime data, would not vary by type of patrol.
2. Citizen perception of police service would not vary by type of patrol.
3. Citizen fear and behavior as a result of fear would not vary by type of patrol.
4. Police response time and citizen satisfaction with response time would vary by experimental area.
5. Traffic accidents would increase on the reactive beats.

(3)

Several of the findings directly challenge the assumptions of traditional preventive patrol. But this study should not be interpreted as meaning that patrol officers should be removed from their patrol beats or that police presence may not be of value in reducing crime. Nor should the study be used to justify reducing the levels of policing. Also, the fact that a majority of a police officer's time is typically spent on noncriminal matters does not mean that the officer's role in preventing crime is not important.

The findings of the Kansas City Preventive Patrol Experiment were not welcomed by all police administrators and police officers; indeed, they are still being debated today. But the study is important because it tested a long-held belief that preventive patrol deterred crime. Students of community policing should be aware of this research because it may affect decision making pertaining to community policing. Also, the Kansas City Patrol Experiment has been given credit for the initiation of directed patrol programs.

Directed Patrol

Directed patrol developed in the 1970s out of a sense that random preventive patrol was ineffective in addressing the growing crime problem and was an inefficient use of limited police budgets. The idea behind directed patrol was that patrol officers could function more effectively if they received formal guidance and detailed crime analysis. Directed patrol has three major components:

1. Identification, through rigorous crime analysis, of the places and times when crimes are occurring and are most likely to occur in the future.
2. Preparation of written directions describing in detail the way problem areas are to be patrolled.
3. Activation of these patrol directions at specific times determined by crime analysis.

(Gay et al. 1977a, 13)

Crime analysis may perhaps be the most critical component of directed patrol. The collection and analysis of crime information to detect crime patterns can assist in establishing patrol procedures to combat specific crimes. The crime analysis unit identifies order maintenance, traffic, and crime problems, and the information produced is used to guide police operations in solving criminal or order maintenance problems. Directed patrol units can target specific crime or traffic areas and can become more effective and efficient in solving problems on their beats. In Kansas City, for example, the police department established a Crime and Intelligence Unit that gave patrol officers information on the most active criminal and problem offenders (Directed Patrol Project 1979, 41–43). Directed patrol uses uncommitted patrol time for implementing its activities and strategies. Citizens' calls for service are prioritized so that patrol officers have more time to carry out directed patrol strategies. Citizens are encouraged to telephone in reports or walk in to the precinct station and make a report instead of calling 911. Calls that are not serious can be handled by a delayed response. In Charlotte, North Carolina, the police department created an "expeditor unit" to conserve the time of patrol officers who had the task of taking reports over the telephone. Directed patrol also involves scheduling and deploying patrol officers by computer geographically, in ways that are matched to workload conditions.

Response Time

One of the key objectives of the professional model of policing was a rapid response time. Police administrators believed that a rapid response time would increase arrests, produce more witnesses, and produce greater citizen satisfaction with the police, and they proclaimed this belief to the general public as a fact. Police chiefs have considered rapid response so important that they have tried to enable their patrol officers to respond to a call within three minutes of a dispatcher receiving the call. In a study of 1,100 emergency calls dealt with by 24 police departments, patrol officers arrived within three minutes 50 percent of the time, within five minutes 75 percent of the time, and within 11 minutes 95 percent of the time (Attunes and Scott 1981, 165–179). Police have accepted the premise of O. W. Wilson, a leader of the professional model of policing, that "the likelihood of arrest is far greater if a patrol officer arrives within three minutes of the time a serious crime takes place" (Wilson and McLaren 1977, 345).

Wilson's premise certainly holds for crimes in progress, when it might be possible for the patrol officer to make an arrest. I myself have been in situations where a rapid response time has led to an arrest. But will a rapid response be of any use when a homeowner who has been on vacation for a week comes home to find his or her home burglarized? What value does a rapid response time have in this situation?

One study on rapid response time in five cities found that fewer than 3 percent of rapid police responses resulted in an on-scene response-related arrest. This study also found that 75 percent of crimes committed are discovered after the fact and that in many cases citizens wait an average of 10–15 minutes before notifying the police (Spelman and Brown 1980, 48). Citizens delay reporting crime to the police for the following reasons:

1. Apathy
2. Being unsure about police assistance
3. Contacting security
4. Investigating the incident scene
5. Telephoning another person or receiving a call
6. Waiting or observing the situation
7. Injury
8. Not being informed or being misinformed about the incident

(Van Kirk 1977, 32–33)

Ministations

One of the goals of community policing is to get the police into closer contact with the public. To meet this goal, police departments in big cities like New York, Chicago, and Philadelphia have always divided the city into districts, each of which has its own substation. More recently, many midsized and small cities have established district stations as well. Some cities have gone further and established ministations, or substations, that cover a smaller geographical area than a district, such as a mall or other business area or a public housing complex.

Detroit

In the mid-1970s, the Detroit Police Department established ministations under a grant from the Law Enforcement Assistance Administration. The city installed 52 ministations, with each police precinct having a minimum of three. The ministations were considered to be neighborhood police stations and were staffed 24 hours a day. An officer was permanently assigned to a ministation and was not required to respond to 911 calls or to patrol an assigned beat. Neighborhood ministations encouraged walk-in calls for police service and the filing of crime reports and were charged with crime prevention duties (Skolnick and Bayley 1986, 53–57).

Public Housing Ministations

Savannah, Georgia, was one city among many that initiated ministations to restore order in public housing. In the late 1980s with the introduction of crack cocaine, Savannah experienced a dramatic increase in crimes committed by offenders using drugs—both crimes against persons and crimes involving drugs. The Savannah Police Department identified ten areas, by citizen complaints and arrests, as being heavily drug infested; five were public housing areas.

In these areas, drug use and sales were conducted openly. The crime rate was high, and residents were fearful for their safety. Public service utility crews could not openly walk in these neighborhoods without being harassed or approached to buy drugs. Drive-by shootings averaged one to two per week, and police usually confiscated weapons in encounters with suspicious persons.

In 1990, the City of Savannah received a Drug Control and Systems Grant from the federal and state governments, and the Housing Authority of Savannah received a grant from the Department of Housing and Urban Affairs. The city and the Housing Authority, working together, contributed funds to a program entitled "Project Shield," whose purpose was to implement police ministations to control crime and eliminate drugs in public housing and to enable tenants to become active in neighborhood revitalization. The initial public housing area selected for Project Shield was Garden Homes because it had one of the worst drug problems in the city. Six officers and one sergeant were assigned to Garden Homes full time. Officers were divided into two overlapping shifts of three officers each, from 4.00 p.m. to midnight and from 9.00 p.m. to 5.00 a.m. The sergeant overlapped the two shifts, working from 8.00 p.m. to 2.00 a.m.

Police officers assigned to the ministation at Garden Homes were instructed in problem-oriented policing, departmental resources, and community resources. The officers and sergeant assigned to the ministation were handpicked by the lieutenant responsible for Garden Homes in order to select officers who were able and willing to work in a public housing complex. The officers assigned to the ministation saturated the complex with walking patrols to eliminate drug dealers and nontenant drug customers. Residents involved in drug activity were informed by the Housing Authority's resident management that they were subject to the eviction process already in place.

Like other residents of public housing, Garden Homes residents were more vulnerable to being victims of crime than other segments of the population. They also were disturbed by the disorderly behavior of rowdy young people, addicts, and drug merchants and by the deterioration of their physical environment, as manifested by graffiti, broken windows, and poorly maintained apartments. With the implementation of the ministation in the Garden Homes public housing complex, the "fear of crime" substantially decreased, and the residents were able to take back their neighborhood. The children were able to play in the playground, which had become the domain of drug merchants. Drive-by shootings were all but eliminated, and residents' victimization by crime was greatly reduced. Outsiders who did not reside in Garden Homes and who caused most of the problems within Garden Homes were chased away by the police. Those individuals who wished to buy drugs within Garden Homes were unable to do so. Graffiti was removed, grass was planted, and vacant apartments were remodeled.

Project Shield provides a model for other police departments and communities. It shows cooperation of the police department with another city agency, the use of problem-oriented policing, the development of a partnership with community residents, and the value of the ministation in curbing crime and disorder in a small geographical area (Palmiotto 1998).

Foot Patrol

Patrol has often been called the backbone of the police department. Generally, other services provided by the police department evolve from the work of the patrol division. The patrol units are the primary line units that have as their mission the prevention and control of criminal conduct. If the aphorism "thin blue line" is to be considered accurate, then it has to be applied to the patrol force. The patrol force, more than other police operations units, provides the first line of defense against the street criminal and predatory crimes. The delivery of police service to the community by the patrol force has become expected by the community. Most police–citizen contacts occur at the patrol level.

The oldest procedural method, one that has received much attention and has continued to be proven valuable, is the foot patrol. Before the advent of the automobile, foot patrol was the primary means of patrolling the community. When the automobile became popular with the police department as a patrol technique, foot patrol lost favor. Foot patrols are useful for special events such as parades, dignitary visits, and public relations. They are also valuable for patrolling shopping malls, beaches, apartment complexes, schools, and areas where motorized vehicles cannot gain access.

Officers on foot patrol can observe more than officers in vehicles. By being on the street, an officer's sense of smell and sense of hearing are improved. Foot patrol is "an effective method of improving face-to-face communication between community residents and the police. The increased communications often culminates in the exchange of information needed to prevent and solve crime" (Trojanowicz 1984, 49). In addition, foot patrol officers, making personal contact with citizens on their beat, can function as community organizers, as dispute mediators, and as valuable links between social services agencies and the community (Trojanowicz 1984, 47).

Broken Windows

The broken windows theory was first set forth in a 1982 *Atlantic Monthly* article by James Q. Wilson and George Kelling. Based on the results of the New Jersey Safe and Clean Neighborhood Program and the findings of the Newark Foot Patrol Experiment, it argues that minor public disorder offenses such as vandalism, littering, rowdy behavior, public drunkenness, and prostitution can start a downward spiral of neighborhood deterioration and fear of crime that leads to more deterioration and more serious crime.

Social psychologists and police officers tend to agree that if a window in a building is broken and is left unrepaired, all the rest of the windows will be broken. This is as true in nice neighborhoods as in run-down ones. Window-breaking does not necessarily occur on a large scale because some areas are inhabited by determined window-breakers whereas others are populated by window-lovers; rather, one unrepaired broken window is a signal that no one cares, and so breaking more windows costs nothing (Wilson and Kelling 1982, 31).

When rowdy behavior is not checked, community controls break down: residents no longer take care of their homes, watch out for and correct one another's children, or scowl at unwanted intruders. When they abandon property, windows are broken and weeds and debris are allowed to grow, creating an environment of "not caring." When drunks, panhandlers, prostitutes, drug addicts, unruly teenagers, loiterers, and the mentally ill throng the streets, frightened residents no longer go out much, and their control over the public realm is lost. When gangs spray-paint street signs and the streets department takes three months to remove the graffiti, the impression is given that the gang has more power than the city, the police, or the residents. When teenagers are allowed to block city streets and be rowdy, the disorderly behavior will escalate to even more serious criminal behavior (Wilson and Kelling 1989, 47–48).

Conversely, police enforcement of public order can help to revitalize a neighborhood and ultimately reduce crime. As officers patrol their beats and enforce informal rules that are familiar to all the beat residents— for example, telling teenagers to keep the noise down or vagrants not to bother people at bus stops—they restore public order and provide a sense of security to residents, encouraging residents' higher presence and involvement in their neighborhoods.

Wilson and Kelling (1989) argued that we must return to our long-abandoned view that the police ought to protect communities as well as individuals. Our crime statistics and victimization surveys measure individual losses, but they do not measure communal losses. Just as physicians now recognize the importance of fostering health rather than simply treating illness, so the police—and the rest of us—ought to recognize the importance of maintaining, intact, communities without broken windows (38).

Neighborhood crime for the most part has been found to be committed by offenders who reside near their victims. This makes it primarily a local problem that must be locally solved.

Clearly, the concept of broken windows fits well into problem-solving approaches and into the overall philosophy of community policing. The theory of broken windows has been incorporated into the community policing philosophy of many police departments. In their 1996 book, *Fixing Broken Windows*, George Kelling and Catherine Coles compared the broken windows approach with the approach of traditional criminal justice processes in dealing with crime.

Value of Research

The importance of research to improving police strategies and tactics cannot be overemphasized. According to Brown and Curtis (1967):

> Many practitioners within criminal justice have met with repeated failure over the years because they relied upon only their common sense. Thus, millions of dollars have been spent on police patrol efforts that do not reduce crime, judicial practices that are widely perceived as unfair, rehabilitation programs that do not rehabilitate offenders and countless other failures.
>
> (3)

Police operations have often been based on untrue or outdated assumptions. The myth that the police are primarily crime fighters who deter crime has been deeply ingrained into our American culture. This myth has been reinforced for several decades not only by the police agencies promoting their interests but also by the news and entertainment media. Not only do the general public believe it, but the police have bought into it themselves. Young people are often drawn to police work because of the glamour of the crime-fighter image, and they are reinforced in this attitude by their recruit trainers. In general, the training curriculum emphasizes the law enforcement aspect of policing. In fact, many police administrators, middle managers, supervisors, and police officers consider community policing to be social work or "touchy-feely" activity and not "real" police work. A good number of police officers have told me that they did not enter policing to "hug" citizens but to make arrests, perform investigations, and deter crime. Even those police administrators who claim to support community policing may stress or at least claim they are crime fighters.

The myth of the police as crime fighters has shaped traditional patrol operations. For example, the automobile was initially used to increase the geographical patrol area and to enable officers to move swiftly from one area to another. Preventive patrol evolved from the notion that officers could be everywhere on their beat or at least create that impression. Such patrolling, along with fast response to calls, was sold as a useful means of controlling crime. But, in reality, this approach had little effect on controlling criminal activity, and an examination of crimes solved by the police indicates that the police are not very successful. Research has found that most police departments spend most of their time in service-related activities, such as dealing with noisy youngsters, settling domestic disputes, and handling derelicts.

A vast number of police studies have corrected misconceptions about policing. They have also provided support for the community policing approach in that they highlight the importance and effectiveness of strategies that improve police–community relations and develop a police–community partnership in solving and preventing crime and in maintaining public order and arresting community decline.

Summary

The concept of police–community relations developed during the 1960s, a period of turmoil in American cities. This decade saw the police in direct confrontation with the community they were to serve. In 1967, the President's Commission on Law Enforcement and Administration of Justice argued that when a community has negative feelings toward the police, tension rises, and aggressive actions against the police begin to occur, which can in turn trigger irrational behavior on the part of the police. Further, citizens will not report crimes to the police or give the police the information they need to solve crimes. Thus, it recommended that police–community relations be considered in all police operations, including departmental policy, supervision, personnel procedures, records and communications, the acceptance of complaints against departmental members, and planning and research. Ideally, police–community relations emphasizes listening to people rather than telling them what to do and taking seriously the concerns and input of community members.

The goal of team policing was to overcome the isolation that police had experienced under the traditional model of policing. Basically, team policing assigns responsibility for a certain geographical area to a permanent team of police officers. The more responsibility this team has, the greater the degree of team policing. In some cities, teams include generalists and specialists and provide all police services to an area, including patrol, traffic, and investigations, under one supervisor.

Team policing, like the community policing of the 1990s, requires the police to be responsive to the neighborhoods where they are assigned and to develop rapport and cooperate with the community. Many of the strategies of team policing have been incorporated into community policing. In addition, both concepts require organizational change and a shift away from the traditional authoritarian management style.

Another set of innovations concerns preventive patrol, or the regular patrolling of an area, either in cars or on foot, with the purpose of preventing crime and spotting and responding to problems. Generally, police departments assign 60–70 percent of their police officers to patrol; thus, the patrol unit has been called the "backbone" of the police department. When patrol officers are not responding to a call or performing an administrative task, they are expected to engage in preventive patrol.

The Kansas City Preventive Patrol Experiment was a study conducted in 1972 to determine if preventive patrol was effective. The study found that preventive patrol did not have any effect on crime rates, delivery of services, or citizens' feelings of security. These findings, and increasingly tight budgets, led police departments to institute changes in preventive patrolling to make it more efficient and effective. The new system was called directed patrol.

The idea behind directed patrol was to provide officers with guidance that was lacking in random preventive patrol. Patrol officers would be scheduled and deployed by computer in ways that matched workload conditions in an area. Crime analysis units would identify specific problems for police to target and would give patrol officers information— for example, on active offenders—that could guide patrol activities. Like team policing, directed patrol was abandoned in the late 1970s and early 1980s, but many of its strategies are being reintroduced into community policing.

A rapid response time to calls for service has long been considered a key objective of policing. Police chiefs have considered rapid response time so important that they have tried to ensure, or at least claim, that their patrol officers would respond to a call within three minutes of a dispatcher receiving the call. They have assumed that rapid response will increase arrests, produce more witnesses, and produce greater citizen satisfaction with the police. But a major study conducted during the 1970s found no support for any of these assumptions. It found that: (1) most Part I (serious) crimes are discovered after the crime has taken place, so that rapid response does not enable the officer to make an arrest at the scene of the crime or even, in most cases, to locate witnesses; (2) citizens typically delay calling the police for so long that a rapid police response becomes irrelevant; (3) reporting delays are due to citizens' attitudes and actions rather than to any uncontrollable problem they confront; and (4) if the citizen does not take an exorbitant amount of time to notify police, a prompt police response can have a significant impact on some property crimes but otherwise has a limited impact on crime outcome.

Another innovation of the 1970s was the ministation, or a police substation, that covers a smaller area than a district, such as a mall or other business area or a public housing complex. Ministations are used to bring the police into closer contact with the public. They can decrease crime and increase reporting of crime and citizen cooperation with police in the areas where they are opened.

Still another innovation of the 1970s and early 1980s was the replacement of some car patrols with foot patrols that provided full law enforcement services for a neighborhood, referred individuals to social services, and organized crime prevention activities cooperating with the community. Foot patrol officers who had a permanent beat were able to develop good rapport with citizens and increase citizens' feelings of security. Many of the suggestions of the foot patrol experiments have been incorporated into community policing. Whereas foot patrols under traditional policing were low-prestige assignments, the foot patrol experiments of the 1970s gave walking beats legitimacy.

A theory that has greatly contributed to community policing is the broken windows theory of Wilson and Kelling (1982). According to this theory, public order offenses such as vandalism and rowdy behavior, if not checked by the community, can create a downward spiral of neighborhood deterioration and fear of crime that leads to more deterioration and more serious crime. This is because graffiti, broken windows, abandoned properties, and public drug use, drunkenness, and prostitution give the impression that "nobody cares" about the community and that residents, police, and the city have lost control over it. Conversely, increased police presence and enforcement of informal rules of conduct as well as laws can make a neighborhood seem less chaotic and more safe, thereby encouraging heightened presence and involvement of residents in their community and lowering crime rates. The broken windows theory has been shown to work and has been incorporated into community policing.

This chapter has emphasized the value of research on policing in dispelling numerous misconceptions about policing that have guided police work and rendered it ineffective. Police research has led to the acceptance by progressive police administrators and students of policing of a need for police to develop a positive and cooperative relationship with the community in order to reduce crime. Most currently, this viewpoint has been expressed in the philosophy of community policing, which has incorporated many of the policing innovations of previous decades that this chapter has discussed.

KEY TERMS

- basic patrol teams
- broken windows theory
- citizen police academies
- community advisory councils
- COMSEC
- directed patrol
- English unit beat system
- full-service teams
- ministations
- patrol-community service teams
- patrol-investigative teams
- random preventive patrol
- response time
- team policing

REVIEW QUESTIONS

1. Outline the principles of good police–community relations.
2. How have principles of police–community relations been incorporated into community policing?
3. What is team policing and how does it work?
4. Discuss the four types of team policing.
5. Describe random preventive patrol.
6. Describe directed patrol.
7. Why does rapid response time have little effect on solving or preventing most crimes?
8. Explain the broken windows theory.

5

COMMUNITIES AND NEIGHBORHOODS

CHAPTER OBJECTIVES

1. Have an understanding of the term community.

2. Have an understanding of what produces and reinforces a sense of community and the role of community policing in strengthening community.

3. Have an understanding of the term neighborhood.

4. Have an understanding of how police can contribute to community empowerment.

5. Have an understanding of the term multiculturalism.

6. Have an understanding of how multiculturalism relates to community policing.

Introduction

The focus of this chapter is on communities and neighborhoods. The community policing officer works in a community, a neighborhood, and often a multicultural environment. According to the community policing philosophy, the police need to develop a partnership with the community. How can a partnership between the police and the community be developed if police have no understanding of the concepts of community, neighborhood, and multiculturalism?

For community policing to be successful, police officers must be open to new ideas and experiences and be willing to take risks. Unlike the traditional model of policing, in which the police rarely react to a crime or social problem, the community policing model requires police to be proactive, searching for crime and disorder problems to solve. Community policing officers serve their communities and neighborhoods not only by solving crime and social disorder problems but by preventing them before they occur. This requires understanding what communities and neighborhoods are and how they work.

In the last several decades, multiculturalism has received a great deal of attention. The police in general, and particularly community policing officers, must have an understanding and knowledge of multiculturalism in order to be respectful and appreciative of various cultures within the community and neighborhood where they work. For community policing to be successful, police departments and officers need to grasp what comprises a community and neighborhood. Once an understanding of these concepts has been established, then, and only then, can a successful partnership between the police and community take place. Many of the communities and neighborhoods in our country are multicultural, and, by attempting to understand multiculturalism, the police are showing the members of their communities and neighborhoods that they are reaching out to establish a partnership.

The Community

The term community has a variety of meanings. Generally, a community is conceived of as a group of people occupying the same geographical area by which they can identify themselves, and in which a degree of solidarity exists (McNall and McNall 1992, 179). Thus, it is about both territorial settlement and social relationships. The word is often used to identify local, small geographical units with communal relationships, such as villages, towns, or neighborhoods (Gusfield 1975, 32–33), but it can also be used to describe larger units, such as whole cities. According to the sociologist Robert MacIver (1936), it means "an area of common life, village or town, or district, or country, or even wider area" (22). MacIver further stipulated that, "to deserve the name community, the area must be somehow distinguished from further areas, [and] the common life may have some characteristics of its own such that the frontiers have some meaning" (23). The community has been considered a territorial group that embraces all aspects of social life—a local area over which people usually are using the same language, conforming to the same mores, feeling more or less the same sentiments, and acting upon the same attitudes. According to Robert Nisbet (1966):

> The word, as we find it in much nineteenth- and twentieth century thought, encompasses all forms of relationship, which are characterized by a high degree of personal intimacy, emotional depth, moral commitment, social cohesion, and continuity in time. Community is founded on man conceived in his wholeness rather than in one or another of the roles, taken separately, that he may hold in a social order.
>
> (47)

The term community can be used to describe people's associations around skills, professions, or interests independent of locality: for example, university professors belong to a "community of scholars." However, in community policing, the term usually has a geographical component, because the areas that police patrol are geographically based.

Communities are commonly classified as rural or urban. Rural and urban communities are usually distinguished by population size, but this distinction has been criticized as arbitrary and devoid of significance. Other distinguishing criteria used have been density of population and legal status of the locality as rural or urban.

A rural community consists of a group of families living on contiguous land who generally think of themselves as living in the same locality, to which they give a name, and who interact with each other through visiting, borrowing, and lending tools, exchanging services, or participating in social activities. Frequently, a community has a center of common activities that includes such institutions as a school or church. Community members know one another, and their relationships appear to be intimate.

The urban community usually consists of a large group of people living in a small geographical area who have their own local government and carry on various economic enterprises. Urban communities are often only loosely "communities" in the social sense. They are more likely than rural communities to be characterized by anonymity: an individual who travels two blocks from his or her home may not be known by anyone. Urban communities are also generally more heterogeneous. Urban people are likely to associate with each other chiefly based on interest rather than locality, and there is less general association among people than occurs in rural communities.

Until recent years, it was generally accepted that urban communities had a higher rate of crime, violence, narcotics, divorce, desertion, prostitution, and other forms of deviance. Nevertheless, today rural communities are seeing an increase in violence, crime, narcotics use, and other forms of deviant behavior that are normally associated with the urban community.

Sense of Community

For community policing to be a success, there must exist a "sense of community." Officers involved in community policing have to understand, and, more important, strive to create and reinforce, a sense of community.

Elements of a Sense of Community

A sense of community can be defined as "a feeling that members have of belonging, a feeling that members matter to one another and to the group, and a shared faith that members' needs will be met through their commitment to be together" (McMillan and Chavis 1986, 9). It consists of four elements:

1. Membership—the feeling of belonging.
2. Influence—a sense of mattering, of making a difference to a group and of the group mattering to its members.
3. Integration and fulfillment of needs—the feeling that members' needs will be met by the resources received through membership in the group.
4. Shared emotional connection—the commitment and belief that members have shared and will share history, common places, and time together, and similar experience.

                                        (McMillan and Chavis 1986, 9)

Membership. McMillan and Chavis (1986) have described five aspects of community membership—a sense of belonging, boundaries, emotional safety, personal investment, and a common symbol system. Community membership gives one a feeling of belonging. The sense of belonging and identification includes feelings, expectations, and beliefs that are consonant with those of other community members. The boundaries of a community allow some people to belong whereas others do not. The community gives its members a sense of structure and security. Members feel personally invested in the community. Finally, a common symbol system is important in creating and maintaining the sense of community (9–11).

Influence. In a community, the individual both influences and is influenced by the group members. McMillan and Chavis (1986) outlined the following postulates concerning influence:

1. Members are more attracted to a community in which they feel that they are influential.
2. There is a significant positive relationship between cohesiveness and a community's influence on its members to conform. Thus, both conformity and community influence on members indicate the strength of the bond.
3. The pressure for conformity and uniformity comes from the needs of the individual and the community for consensual validation. Thus, conformity serves as a force for closeness as well as an indicator of cohesiveness.
4. Influence of a member on the community and influence of the community on a member operate concurrently, and one might expect to see the force of both operating simultaneously in a tightly knit community.

(12)

Integration and Fulfillment of Needs. Integration and fulfillment of needs is reinforcement of the shared values of the community. For a sense of community to exist, reinforcement must be used to bind members of the community together. According to McMillan and Chavis (1986):

1. Reinforcement and need fulfillment is a primary function of a strong community.
2. Some of the rewards that are effective reinforcers of communities are status, membership, success of the community, and competencies or capabilities of other members.

3. There are many other undocumented needs that communities fill, but individual values are the source of these needs. The extent to which individual values are shared among community members will determine the ability of a community to organize and prioritize its need-fulfillment activities.

4. A strong community is able to fit people together so that people meet others' needs while they meet their own.

(13)

Emotional Connection. Emotional connection is the connection or identification of members of the community with the history of the community and with each other. McMillan and Chavis (1986) made the following assertions about emotional connection in communities:

1. Contact hypothesis: The more people interact, the more likely they are to become close.

2. Quality of interaction: The more positive the experience and the relationships, the greater the bond. Success facilitates cohesion.

3. Closure to events: If the interaction is ambiguous and the community's tasks are left unsolved, group cohesiveness will be inhibited.

4. Shared valiant event hypothesis: The more important the shared event is to those involved, the greater the community bond. For example, there appears to be a tremendous bonding among people who experience a crisis together.

5. Effect of honor and humiliation on community members: Reward or humiliation in the presence of community members has a significant impact on attractiveness (or adverseness) of the community to the person.

6. Spiritual bond: This is present to some degree in all communities.

(13–14)

Solid communities provide members with avenues to interact, events to share, and ways to recognize members. They also give members opportunities to invest in the community and to bond with other members (14).

Sense of Community and Community Policing

The concept of a sense of community has importance to the community-policing strategy. Community policing will be much more successful in a place that has a sense of community than in one that does not. For community policing to be a success, the police and the community must work together to maintain or improve the quality of life of the community members.

Generally, communities organize around needs, and members of communities join communities that meet their needs. Many successful communities have associations to represent their interests (McMillan and Chavis 1986, 15–16). Such interests might include dealing with crime in the community. Community-policing officers should be aware of the community associations and make contact with them to find out what they consider to be safety and crime issues. The community-policing officer who becomes aware of a community's concern about safety and crime issues may be able to implement crime prevention strategies or initiate problem-solving strategies before a crisis occurs.

In a study of the relationship between a sense of community and individual well-being, it was found that people who had a strong sense of community scored high on social well-being and happiness and that a sense of community contributed to people's happiness. In addition, people with a strong sense of community had a better grasp of how to use the resources of their community than people who had no sense of community (Davidson and Cotter 1991, 251). It is important that community-policing officers recognize the contribution of a sense of community to the success and happiness of members of a community and that they encourage developments that enable members of the community to help each other.

Empowerment

Empowerment is "the processes by which people organize, attain a collective objective, and learn about their own personal power" (Heskin 1991, 63). An empowered community is structured in a way that provides members with the opportunity to participate in community activities and to be responsible for the community, and its members are willing to use that structure (Heskin 1991, 64). Community empowerment begins with community organizations and groups that take an activist role with a common purpose. Such organizations have deep and strong roots in America. They draw on:

- the American traditions of self-help and the building of voluntary associations;
- the civil rights and self-determination movements among blacks, Hispanics, and other minority and ethnic groups;
- the churches' quest for greater social justice and a renewed sense of community;
- the neighborhood movement and people's determination to resist outside institutions that injure or neglect their neighborhoods and to build their own institutions;
- the desire, throughout America, for new vehicles to give people greater control over the political process and economic decision making;
- the desire for new, human-scale organizations and mediating structures in a society in which too much has been left to massive, unaccountable, alienating, and often ineffective institutions.

(Mott 1992, 12)

Community-policing officers should be aware that community organizations empower the community and that this movement has a long tradition. Community organizations can make the community-policing officer's job easier, and, in turn, the community-policing officer can be helpful to community organizations. Consequently, the intelligent community-policing officer will respect the organizations within the community; learn about their mission and goals, and work to develop a partnership with them. Police agencies that have adopted the community-policing philosophy should recognize that community groups have solved some very tough problems and have been successful in taking on street crime and criminal justice issues. Community organizations have demonstrated that they can play major roles with great effectiveness, including:

1. Organizing and mobilizing people to press for improvements.
2. Creating self-help programs to provide community services and develop housing and economic development projects.
3. Pursuing changes in public policy through voter registration, research, education, litigation, and legislative and political action.

(Mott 1992, 12)

Organizations typically go through stages of community building before they can become fully empowered. Jason (1997) described four stages. First, there is pseudo-community, in which people avoid disagreements and just pretend to be a community. During the next stage (chaos), healers attempt to heal and convert others; this is a time of considerable fighting and struggle. During the third stage (emptiness), people begin to remove barriers to communication, such as expectations, prejudice, and ideologies. During the final stage—aptly called community—a peaceful, soft sense of quietude descends. People feel safe to share their vulnerability, their sadness, and their joy (73–74).

One way that community organizations can become more empowered is by periodically reappraising their current activities to determine if they are still relevant and effective. Mott (1992) offered several basic rules to be followed in this process:

1. Learn, synthesize, and innovate. Groups should look at [the reappraisal as an opportunity for] learning and synthesis, knitting together the strongest elements of the approaches those different organizations have followed.
2. Let the leaders lead. Groups should deeply involve their leadership and membership, as well as their staffs, in the appraisal. This should be seen not only as a matter of principle for community-based organizations, but also as a matter of hard pragmatism. People from the community are far more likely to take a tough, dispassionate look at their needs and the advantages of alternative courses of action than are staff people who have records, budgets, and jobs to defend.
3. Go back to basics. The reexamination should start by going back to the long-range, fundamental goals that led to creation of the

organization. That vision undoubtedly is far larger than the sum of the organization's current activities. Is the organization on track, or should it make substantial changes to gain the power and capacity to achieve those goals over time?

4. Go beyond localism. The group should also raise its sights beyond the neighborhood. To gain the resources, allies, and institutional changes that the community will need if there is to be either development or social progress, the group must decide how it can have an impact that reaches beyond its borders and affects government and private institutional policies.

(14)

Generally, members of the community are the core of community organizations, but nonmembers may also play a role, including organizational helpers such as consultants, professionals, and volunteers; government officials, such as public housing officials; and, most recently, community-policing officers.

The role of community members in a given program as compared to that of outside professionals or officials will vary depending on the organization and its influence. Wandersman (1981) has described the following patterns:

- Creation of parameters and objects: [Community members have] the decision-making power and generate plans without preconceived parameters from professionals or others.
- Self-planning: [Community members] generate alternative plans within available parameters and [have] the responsibility and decision-making power for decisions. (The professional can play a consultant role.)
- Choice: [Community members] choose between alternative plans generated by professionals or government officials.
- Feedback: [Community members are] asked for [their] ideas and opinions about a plan. This information is evaluated by the professionals or government officials who [have] the responsibility and decision-making power.
- No participation: The decisions are made by the professional or government officials for the [community].

(45)

Generally, community-policing officers should encourage a high degree of participation and responsibility for programs among community members. Techniques of participation such as surveys, public hearings, or game simulation all allow members of the community to have input on issues that they consider to be important in their community. Participation in community organizations can affect the individual and the community in a variety of ways:

1. Individual Level

   - Evaluation of the community organization: degree of satisfaction or liking of the organization and evaluation of specific qualities of the organization
   - Evaluation of the community: degree of satisfaction or liking of the community and evaluation of specific qualities of the community
   - Attitudes toward participation: favorable or unfavorable views about participation in community organizations generally
   - Attitudes toward the authority figures: attitudes about the planners', leaders', and politicians' concern for the individual
   - Feelings about oneself and one's role in the community: feelings of creativity, alienation, responsibility, anonymity, helpfulness, or being "a good citizen"
   - Behavioral effects: interactions with the social and physical environment of the community, including use of community services and facilities, investment in home improvements, mobility, and contact among neighbors

2. Organizational Level

   - Organizational growth: increased membership, attendance at meetings and actions, resources (e.g., money, in-kind contributions), and new chapters or affiliates
   - Leadership development: advancement of group leaders to more powerful positions within the community and city, development of secondary leadership, and emergence of leadership skills

- Legitimacy: amount of publicity for the organization, representativeness of the organization, degree of credibility, and organizational image among nonmembers and elites
- Adaptiveness: flexibility in response to changing the environment, development of collective problem-solving techniques, and creation of new organizational capabilities, new issues, committees, structures, etc.
- Congruence between the goals and the activities of the organization: extent to which the organization is achieving its goals as well as any additional goals individual members may have

(Pearlman 1979, 43–63)

3. Community Level

- Environmental effects—changes, for example, in noise and density levels
- Ecological effects—changes such as number of settings or facilities available
- Social effects—changes in the social characteristics of the community, such as composition of the population, social networks, norms, and functioning (e.g., crime rates, quality of service delivery)

(Wandersman 1981, 48–49)

Community-policing officers should be aware of the various effects of participation between the various levels. The community-policing officers should know the nature and extent of the interrelationships between the various levels. It is important that community-policing officers become integrated into the community. The more the community-policing officers know and understand the nuances of community organizations, the better they will be able to understand community organizations and to achieve the goals of the community-policing philosophy.

The role of the police in community empowerment has perhaps been best summarized by Cheryl A. Steele, program coordinator for the community-oriented policing program in Spokane, Washington, and founder of Spokane's first volunteer substation. She tells the police that it is all right to make a commitment to do community policing as an agency—but don't think you are going to do it to your community. You must get community members to drive the initiative for themselves. In doing so, the stewardship of public safety is then totally owned by the entire community.

(personal communication, June 17, 1998)

Rather than trying to fix all the social ills of a community, police should concentrate on what they know the most about—law enforcement and crime prevention. The police need to call community meetings, release the information, and then participate in the changes for which they have the resources. Steele calls this the "EMOM" model—Educate, Mobilize, Organize, and Move out of the way!

The Neighborhood

The study of urban centers by sociologists has tended to focus on neighborhoods, or small geographical areas that are embedded in a larger area, such as a town or city, and that include residential dwellings. By one definition:

The most sensible way to locate the neighborhood is to ask people where it is, for people spend much time fixing its boundaries. Gangs mark its turf. Old people watch for its new faces. Children figure out safe routes between home and school. People walk their dogs through their neighborhood, but rarely beyond it. Above all, the neighborhood has a name: Hyde Park or Lake View in Chicago; Roxbury, Jamaica Plain, or Beacon Hill in Boston.

(Williams 1985, 33)

An individual might describe his or her neighborhood by referring to such landmarks and geographic features as rivers, lakes, expressways, parks, schools, and malls. The terms neighborhood and community are often used synonymously, but the term community can be used to describe larger areas as well, such as an entire town or city that contains many neighborhoods.

Bursik and Grasmick (1993) have stated that a neighborhood has some degree of

> collective life that emerges from the social networks that have arisen among the residents and the sets of institutional arrangements that overlap these networks. That is, the neighborhood is inhabited by people who perceive themselves to have a common interest in that area and to whom a common life is available.
>
> (6)

They also state that "the neighborhood has some tradition of identity and continuity over time" (6). But neighborhood residents do not necessarily share a culture, associate cooperatively, or form many kinds of ties with each other.

Wellman and Leighton (1988) have discussed several problems with the assumption that a neighborhood is, automatically, some kind of "container for communal ties." They argued that "even though space-time costs encourage some relationships to be local," it does not necessarily follow that the neighborhood has a well-developed social organization. Further, "even the presence of many local relationships does not necessarily create discrete neighborhoods," because "there may well be overlapping sets of local ties, the range of these ties being affected by the needs and physical mobility of the participants." And "there are important ties outside of the neighborhood even in the most 'institutionally complete community'"—especially work relationships (59).

In other words, a sense of community does not necessarily coincide with the divisions marks on maps. As Wellman and Leighton (1988) argued, "administrative officials have imposed their own definitions of neighborhood boundaries upon the maps in attempts to create bureaucratic units. Spatial areas, labeled and treated as coherent neighborhoods, have come to be regarded as natural phenomena" (58). Further, "territory has come to be seen as the inherently most important organizing factor in urban social relations rather than just one potentially important factor" (58).

A neighborhood can develop interpersonal ties, networks of sociability and support, sentiments of solidarity, and shared activities and, if residents focus their energies in this direction, it can become a political entity if residents perceive it as a base for building power. Community-policing officers are often assigned to specific neighborhoods. They need to be aware of the extent to which the neighborhood they serve is a cohesive social unit.

A neighborhood that offers many opportunities for sociability, from block parties to front-porch visiting, for the exercise of interpersonal influence through opinion sharing, for mutual aid among neighbors in time of need or emergencies, for the discussion of common concerns, for the development of local pride, and for the achievement of status among neighbors already has many resources and strengths that a community-policing officer can draw upon (Williams 1985, 37).

Neighborhood Crime

Neighborhood organizations are frequently established to combat the crime problem. The neighborhoods that are most likely to formally establish neighborhood anticrime organizations tend to have the following characteristics:

1. They are of moderate size in the urban environment, several square blocks to perhaps a square mile.
2. Their boundaries are fairly clear.
3. Their inhabitants are somewhat homogeneous in background, lifestyle, and income.
4. Residents perceive the neighborhood as a good place to live, at least more desirable than bordering neighborhoods. Their neighborhood in fact may be quite deteriorated, however.
5. Residents feel threats to their neighborhood's stability.
6. Residents are somewhat optimistic about the future of their neighborhood; this optimism is based on a sense that they control the neighborhood social order to an extent.
7. There are preexisting organized sub groupings, although they must interact very little with each other.

(Williams 1985, 43)

There are several theories about the causes of crime in neighborhoods. One is that crime could be caused by the unwillingness or inability of neighborhood residents to exert social control by informal means over the public behavior of residents or nonresidents in their neighborhood. Another is that economic deprivation could possibly be a cause of crime by operating as a justification for alienation and reducing an individual's future opportunities. On the basis of both theories, action taken to alter the neighborhood environment can reduce crime (Williams 1985, 176). And if the neighborhood environment plays a role in crime, then neighborhood organizations, aided by community-policing officers, have an important role to play. Neighborhood organizations can deter crime in several ways:

> First, they organize residents to watch out for each other (for children, the elderly, one another's homes, and so forth) on an informal basis. A variant of this is the Whistlestop Program, in which residents buy whistles for a dollar or so at a block meeting. One blows the whistle if one is attacked; the goal is to startle and repel the offender while at the same time summoning help.
>
> Second, some neighborhood organizations create more formal civilian patrols. These groups work closely with police, carry walkie-talkies, and do not attempt to apprehend suspects. This last point differentiates them from vigilante groups. They may walk or ride in cars; they may be tenants in a housing project or taxi drivers. They function as people taking some formal responsibility for attending to public behavior. When behavior improves, these patrols often cease.
>
> Third, the ordinary operations of the neighborhood organization in creating block clubs, disseminating information about the neighborhood to its residents, and involving them in its neighborhood-wide activities, all help to weave social fabric. . . . The sense of neighborhood identity—which one not only resides in an area, but that one belongs to and therefore cares about it is a less tangible but extremely important outcome of everything the neighborhood organization does.
>
> Fourth, neighborhood organizations squelch crime in cooperation with the police. This is perhaps what residents might think of first but for a variety of reasons is the most difficult

to accomplish. Police assistance is essential, of course, for those situations involving public behavior or outright criminal activity that cannot be handled by residents alone.

(Williams 1985, 177–178)

Traditionally, neighborhood cooperation with the police has been hard to achieve in the low-income neighborhoods that are likely to have the most crime because police and residents have had a relationship much like that between white colonizers and black African natives: police have been seen as "motorized bwanas cruising, hunting, and foraging among the natives in the urban jungle" (Williams 1985, 178). Under the traditional model of policing, police have distanced themselves from the neighborhood residents, locking themselves in police cruisers and developing a siege mentality of "us versus them." But the community-policing model, unlike the traditional policing model, which segregated the police from the neighborhood, gets the police involved in the neighborhood. Foot patrols are one means of accomplishing this. Also, police act as consultants in helping residents to solve crime and disorder problems. They recognize that residents have a stake in their own safety and can do a great deal to secure it through community action.

Fear of Crime

Not only crime itself but fear of crime is a major issue facing neighborhoods. Fear of crime, as stated earlier, often reflects actual rates of victimization by crimes against persons and crimes against property. But there also exists a third category of offenses that creates a fear of crime among neighborhood residents: the disorderly offenses, which include loud noises, loitering, defacing public property with graffiti, drunkenness, prostitution, drug trafficking, gambling, and rowdiness (Wilson and Kelling 1982, 30). Thus, the fear of crime may in reality be much greater than the actual statistics on crime. Fear of crime can be related to both neighborhood characteristics and individual characteristics such as socioeconomic status, gender, and age. At the neighborhood level, it is often related to the perception that the neighborhood is on the decline (Austin 1991, 81). As discussed in Chapter 4 in the section on the broken windows theory, "Fear of crime has been hypothesized as one factor, perhaps in a chain of other factors, that can lead to abandonment and deterioration of neighborhoods" (Brown and Wycoff 1987, 71).

The fear of crime can lead to a sense of anomie that has four components:

1. A sense of neighbors as strangers.
2. A sense of physical, social, and psychological distance from the police, who, especially in a rapidly changing environment, may have an even greater responsibility for being the visible symbol of social control.
3. A feeling of powerlessness caused by the sheer size of the city, with the subsequent physical distance from City Hall and the involvement of local government with a vast array of problems, many of which do not bear directly on the neighborhood where a given individual lives.
4. A lack of accurate information about the nature and extent of crime in neighborhoods.

(Brown and Wycoff 1987, 74)

Community-policing officers can break down this anomie by reducing their physical, social, and psychological distance from neighborhood residents, and they can reduce feelings of distance from neighbors and of neighborhood by encouraging neighborhoods to organize to protect themselves and develop more familiarity and solidarity among themselves. They can also provide accurate information on neighborhood crime.

Community-policing officers can dispel many of the inaccuracies of residents' perceptions of crime in their neighborhoods. But they can only learn about residents' perceptions by interacting with residents and listening to them talk about crime in their neighborhood. Neighborhood police officers should be able to obtain crime statistics from the crime analysis unit of their department for their neighborhood and for specific areas where a reported crime has occurred. They should freely share these statistics with neighborhood residents and organizations. If the neighborhood members or organizations consider the crime statistics to be inaccurate, the officer can inform the residents that the statistics reflect crimes reported by citizens to the police but, that if crimes occur and are not reported to the police, it cannot be expected that the police will have a record of the crime. Therefore, all residents need to report all crimes to the police, no matter how minor, so that the police can have an accurate record of crime for the neighborhood. The police can only concentrate on solving, preventing, and controlling crimes when residents report the crime.

Communities that want to successfully control crime and disorder must develop programs that strengthen neighborhoods by developing strong levels of social control either informally or formally through a network of associations among neighborhood residents and between residents and local governmental and private agencies. The police can assist in creating this network and in channeling outside resources to the neighborhood.

Intelligence-led Policing

Since the terrorists attacks of September 11, 2001 the importance of intelligence gathering and analysis has substantially increased. Intelligence operations can be directed not only toward criminal offenders but also toward terrorists. The community has become of greater importance in partnering with the police. Community infrastructures that are critical to preventing terrorist acts include food, agriculture, public health, tele-communications, energy transportation, and banking as potential terrorist targets. Community policing now includes these stakeholders who are not partners with the police in crime control and preventing terrorism. In the early decades of the twenty-first century community and problem-oriented policing have to be integrated into intelligence operations dealing with conventional crime issues. Community policing now involves the police collaborating and engaging with the community at all levels (Peterson 2003, vii).

Intelligence-led policing can be described as "a collaborative enterprise based on improved intelligence operations and community-oriented policing and problem solving, which the field has considered benefi-cial for many years" (Peterson 2003, vii). Some intelligence units use a problem-solving methodology as recommended for problem-oriented policing. Community policing is important in providing the context for the success or failure of the intelligence-led policing process (Ratcliffe 2003, 5).

The goal of intelligence-led policing is to obtain greater efficiency in policing. One potential problem with intelligence-led policing is that some police departments are performance oriented and want to measure everything possible. This may not be possible in all cases. Important aspects of intelligence-led policing suggest that the police should collaborate with outside agencies such as housing authorities and health and educational departments. The increased sharing of intelligence by the police may lead to a substantial crime reduction (Rattcliffe 2003, 6).

Compstat

Community policing was initiated by the New York City Police Department in July 1984 when it introduced the Community Patrol Officer Program (CPOP) as a pilot program. Each community-policing officer was to maintain order and to handle crime on his beat. The community patrol officer reported to a sergeant who reported directly to the commander of the precinct. By 1990 community policing involved the entire department (Silverman 1999, 55–56). Although community policing involves problem solving and working closely with the neighborhood this may be difficult if department support has been lacking. Two important issues are important here. First, crime statistics were never up to date, and second, precinct commanders did not consider crime reduction as a responsibility of theirs. In the mid-1990s, the New York City Police Department had a Police Commissioner who wanted up-to-date crime statistics and held the precinct commanders accountable for crime in their precincts. Compstat was implemented to change the police culture perception of crime. This new approach of commanders obtaining current crime information would be valuable in reducing crime and assisting community-policing officers in problem solving and working with their neighborhoods.

The term Compstat comes from Compare Stats, a computer file name. Compstat operated under the premise that all New York Police Department crime information would be available immediately so that top administrators and commanders could make key decisions in crime-fighting meetings. Police administrators were expected to share information and to interact with each other. Upper administrators and commanders met periodically to discuss crime strategies (Silverman 1999, 109). Compstat has not only been successful in the New York City Police Department but has been adopted by many other police departments as well.

Summary

A community is a cluster of people living within a continuous geographical area who share, to some extent, a way of life. A local territorial group is also a social group. A community can be a small aggregation, such as a neighborhood, village, or town, or a large one, such as a city. A neighborhood is a small geographical area that is embedded in a larger area, such as a town or a city, which includes residential dwellings. As is the case for communities in general, the extent to which it is a cohesive social unit will vary. For community policing to be successful, there must exist a "sense of community." Officers involved in community policing must have an understanding of what factors create a sense of community, how police can assist in creating a sense of community, and the extent to which the area they serve functions as a cohesive social unit.

Neighborhood organizations have an important role to play in deterring crime. They can organize residents to watch out for each other and form civilian patrols. They can work to clean up the neighborhood, thereby sending the message that residents care about their community and will not tolerate crime and disorder. Finally, by organizing neighborhood activities, they can increase neighborhood solidarity and residents' familiarity with and concern for each other.

The role of community-policing officers in these efforts is to encourage neighborhood organizing, provide information and guidance related to crime and crime prevention, and assist in channeling outside resources to the neighborhood and networking with outside agencies.

Two important concepts that have practical value for communities and neighborhoods are intelligence-led policing and Compstat. These concepts deal with reducing crime, making neighborhoods safer, and providing community-policing officers with information to assist them in problem solving.

KEY TERMS

- community empowerment
- community organizations
- neighborhood
- sense of community

REVIEW QUESTIONS

1. What is a community?
2. What is meant by sense of community?
3. What is meant by empowerment?
4. What does the term neighborhood mean?
5. Why are neighborhood organizations important?
6. How can police help to develop a sense of community in the areas they serve?
7. Why is multicultural awareness important in community policing?

6

MULTICULTURALISM AND ORGANIZATIONAL CHANGE

CHAPTER OBJECTIVES

1. Have an understanding of the term multiculturalism.

2. Have an understanding of how multiculturalism relates to community policing.

3. Understand the need for organizational change as the police profession makes the transition to community policing.

4. Understand the need to maintain support for communications for community policing.

5. Understand how work environment is important to community policing.

Introduction

As the United States enters the second decade of the twenty-first century it finds that America is having economic problems with an unemployment rate around 10 percent of the American workforce. Some economists consider that the unemployment rate may be higher when those unable to collect unemployment benefits are no longer counted in the unemployment rolls. To make matters worse the second decade of the twenty-first century may have an unemployment problem through most of it.

During the coming decade, from 2010 to 2020, the population of the United States will grow from about 312 million people to almost 350 million people. The white population in the second decade of this century will decrease substantially while the Hispanic, Afro-American, and Asian population will increase in proportion to the white population. International migration will have an impact on the growth of the American population. Most of the migration is expected to come from Hispanic and Asian countries. Even if international migration remains relatively low, the Hispanic population will increase substantially since they normally have more children than other segments of the population.

One group that will be adding to the population growth and to the diversity of the country is older Americans. Those who are 65 and older are referred to as senior citizens. By 2020, the population of older Americans will be approximately 54 million (Administration on Aging 2008, 3).

America in the coming decade will pay greater attention to multiculturalism and the American society will become more diverse. The goal of this chapter is to define multiculturalism and diversity and explain its value to community policing.

Multiculturalism Explained*

Multiculturalism is an approach to cultural diversity that emphasizes understanding, respecting, and adapting to other cultures and cultural differences. In today's world, cultures are coming into contact more often and more rapidly. The issues surrounding such contact have major implications for community policing. In addition, changing population distributions in the United States, with increases in percentages of minority populations and a concurrent decrease in the percentage of the majority population, have led to questions about the interaction of these populations in the workplace and in the larger society.

Some futurists have already predicted that by the year 2050, the current minority/majority distribution will be radically changed, with the minority population representing the majority of United States citizens (Henry 1990, 4). These predictions are based on two population phenomena. First, the traditional migration sources for the United States have shifted from the European continent to the Asian Pacific rim, to Central and South America, and to Africa and the Middle East. Changes in immigration law and the percentages of immigrants from these areas have changed the distribution of whites and people of color in the immigration streams. Second, whites and nonwhites have different birth rates. These changes have had a major

---

* Source: Copyright © 1999, Dr. Anna Chandler.

impact on the composition of the workforce, with a decrease in the number of white males predicted to enter the workforce and an increase in the number of females and nonwhites over the next several years.

These immigrants bring cultural beliefs and practices that may not be compatible with the mainstream American culture. What happens when people engage in various forms of cross-cultural contact, and how does this affect community policing?

What Is Culture?

As discussed in Chapter 2, culture includes artifacts, concepts, and behaviors. Humans must display four features in order to be considered as having a culture. There must be an identifiable group, whether identified by geography, language, and/or religion; the group must have a shared set of beliefs and experiences; the group must attach feelings of worth and value to those beliefs and experiences; and there must be a shared interest in a common historical background (Brislin 1981).

Culture is not innate, it is learned. Humans born into one culture but adopted into another will be products of the adopted culture. This is especially evident when children are adopted cross-racially. To be learned, culture must therefore be transmissible. Transmission occurs by words and by nonverbal actions. The libraries of a culture exist in the minds of the people. The best way to learn about a culture is through daily, long-term socially intimate contact. Because most humans do not have access to different cultures on this level, it is difficult to learn well all the facets of a different culture. Culture is dynamic, never static; it evolves. It changes through inventions, such as the wheel, the automobile, or the computer; infusion of elements, such as the adoption of words in a language, foods in the diet, or religious practices; and calamities such as war, plague, or natural disasters.

Each culture is selective. Of the myriad possible human behaviors, each culture selects those behaviors that will be acceptable and rewards its members who engage in those behaviors. Conversely, the culture punishes members who engage in behaviors unacceptable to the culture. Because not all behaviors can be acceptable, different cultures will select different combinations of behaviors as acceptable. Each culture selects the behaviors that are important to that culture. Differences in the acceptability of human behaviors define the boundaries between cultures. Facets of culture are interrelated.

To understand culture, one must recognize that the cultural behaviors exhibited by individuals are the product of two interrelated "histories": the history of the group or culture of which an individual is a member and the personal history of the individual, or the individual's exposure to concepts and his or her treatment by others. The individual has little control over these events. Napoleon Bonaparte defined history as "a set of lies agreed upon." History in the United States can be defined as an accident that occurred at an intersection with five corners: the five geopolitical groups of African Americans, Asian Americans, European Americans, Hispanic Americans, and Native Americans. The way in which the history is then reported and recorded is dependent on which corner an individual or group occupies. Thus, historical events such as the Civil War will have different labels, heroes, causes, and perceived outcomes depending on who reports and records them.

Culture also is the mechanism that gives the individual the processes and frameworks for organizing and negotiating the real world. Just as not all behaviors can be acceptable in a culture, not all physical phenomena can be processed by individuals in a culture. The culture determines which events in the world must be attended to and dealt with. Three major areas of culture determine how individuals view the world and how individuals treat people different from themselves. These are (1) the language that people are expected to learn, (2) the way in which people are reared and disciplined, and (3) education and the mass media.

Language

There is a relationship between language and interaction with others. Language gives people concepts, structures, and vocabulary that form the basis for reacting to others, especially to out-groups and to strangers. Limits are placed on interaction by language. People speaking different languages experience the world in very different ways. For example, the Eskimo have many words for snow, because their survival is dependent upon being able not only to accurately label the type of snow but also to engage in the type of behavior that will ensure their survival in that type of snow. Cultures in less wintry climates have no need to have such precise definitions. Therefore, language gives individuals and the culture the labels of various physical phenomena in the world, the descriptions of them, and the expected behavior when encountering them. Unless the phenomena can be labeled, described, and reacted to, then for all intents and purposes they do not exist.

Culture includes values, technology, and religious practices as well as a particular and peculiar cognitive structure. Language, then, extends beyond being able to recognize and reproduce sounds and words. It is more than mere vocal skills; it is the worldview of the group. Langston Hughes said, "The limits of my language are the limits of my world" (Brislin 1981, 34).

Some aspects of language that involve out-group members define the treatment of out-groups. In English, certain structural characteristics facilitate the development of concepts that have an effect on how outsiders are perceived and help define how they should be treated. First, words that are used to describe individuals can be used to describe groups. This allows ease in expressing generalizations from the observation of one individual to the group to which that individual belongs. It also makes it easy to form and to think in terms of stereotypes. Second, the use of collective nouns without qualifications contributes to stereotypes and generalizations and masks any variation of individuals within the group. Because any qualification would require explanation and complex grammatical construction, people find it easier to talk about groups in the same way that individuals are talked about. It is also easier to use categories that listeners are certain to understand.

Color words are also a source of reference for treatment of out-groups. Certain color words used to label skin color have negative connotations in English. Black is one such word. Children learn the connotation as part of the language and then transfer the connotation to people who have the skin color. Color symbolism in the Western tradition reveals a tendency to use black when connoting evil and white when connoting good. Concepts associated with black include woe, gloom, darkness, dread, death, terror, horror, curse, mourning, and mortification. It is no accident that mourners wear black to funerals, or that the day of the stock market crash was labeled Black Tuesday or that the series of virulent diseases that wiped out much of the population of Europe was labeled the Black Plague.

Other color words have positive connotations. White in the Western tradition has been associated with triumph, light, innocence, joy, divine power, purity, regeneration, happiness, gaiety, peace, chastity, truth, modesty, femininity, and delicacy (Gergen 1997, 397). It is no accident that brides wear white, or that souls are washed whiter than snow, or that the heroes wear white hats. In the 1950s, Chrysler Corporation had an advertising slogan, "All us good guys wear white hats!" When questioned, their reply was that they were following the Western movie tradition in which the hero rode in on a white horse wearing a white hat. They acknowledged that some heroes wore black hats but stated that the white hat made the heroes instantly recognizable. This use of color to connote good and evil extends even into the Saturday morning cartoons, where the villains are always in black and the heroes are always in white. One manifestation of this connotation is that among darker skinned people, those whose skin is somewhat less dark are more desirable marriage partners (Brislin 1981, 32).

Affective connotation exists in all languages and has three dimensions: evaluation, potency, and activity. People from different cultures rely on these same dimensions when explaining the meaning of concepts. "Out-group" is a concept, and members of the out-groups are reacted to as other concepts. When encountering a member of an out-group, people pose three questions based on the three dimensions: (1) Does this person seem good or bad? (2) Does this person seem weak or strong compared to me? And (3) Do the actions of this person require passivity or activity on my part? Depending on the perceived appearance of the person, contact or no contact will occur (Osgood and Osgood 1975, 102).

Because the decision for contact cannot be based on long-term socially intimate interaction, it must be based on the concept that this person matches. That concept has a label, a description, and a behavior already embedded in the culturally prescribed worldview of the group. It should come as no surprise that women will clutch their purses when confronted by young black males. The culturally prescribed worldview is that they are deviant, dangerous, and to be avoided and feared. This may or may not be true of individuals, but the decision to find out has already been made by the cultural definition of them. Conversely, contact may be attempted with a person from a group, such as bankers or lawyers, who are labeled as safe by the culturally prescribed worldview but who actually may be deviant, dangerous, and to be avoided at all costs.

Phrases that use the names of the different ethnic groups as referents contribute to the tendency to attribute specific characteristics to ethnic groups. Such phrases as "Jew him down" reinforce stereotypes that discourage interaction with out-group members. A study done by the National Conference of Christians and Jews (1994) supported the existence of this use of referents and pointed to its universality among the ethnic groups of the United States. All ethnic and religious groups were found to have stereotypical views of all other ethnic groups and/or religions and to base their decisions about the treatment of those groups and members of those groups on these stereotypes.

Child-Rearing Practices

There is a relationship between parents' child-rearing practices, especially discipline practices, and attitudes toward out-groups (Brislin 1981, 34). Adults acquire their initial attitudes about out-groups from their parents. Parents control access to out-groups. Given the housing and other population distribution patterns in the United States, children generally have little long-term socially intimate contact with out-groups. Children raised in cultures with traditional and conservative norms generally exhibit negative attitudes toward out-groups. These norms include such practices as shunning or declaring the child dead to the group if behavior deemed deviant, such as marriage to an out-group member, occurs. In cultures where there is little encouragement for children's self-development and where children are to follow the occupational and living patterns of the parents without question, there may be negative attitudes toward out-groups. A pattern of dominance by adults such that the child is in a subservient position and punishment is ensured if the child does not conform with the parents' wishes has also been associated with negative attitudes toward out-groups. Also, when adults ignore children, keep them from becoming an important part of the family, and disregard their needs, negative attitudes toward out-groups may develop. Children have not developed the sophistication or had the experience to allow them to compare their treatment with the treatment of others in the larger world. Adults who experience mistreatment as children acquire the point of view that such treatment is normal and treat out-group members accordingly (Brislin 1981, 35). Much has been written and debated about the legacy of child abuse. It is speculated that children who are abused often go on to become abusers. Because most of such abuse occurs within the confines of family, the attitudes developed by children in such situations have a major impact on how they will interact with other members of society, especially out-group members.

Education and the Mass Media

Two features of schools have a major impact on children's attitudes toward out-groups. One is the organization and operation of the schools themselves. The age-stratified organization of schools reflects nothing of real life. Also, schools with very punitive discipline policies and disparate application of those policies generally have been shown to produce students with negative attitudes toward out-groups (Stephan and Rosenfield 1978, 802). Some experts have gone so far as to suggest that the organization of schools and the treatment of children in schools are tantamount to the teaching of racism ("U.S. Schools Teach Racism" 1992, ID, 3D). However, the feature of schools that has the most far-reaching and long-lasting impact on children's attitudes is the school curriculum and the materials used to teach it. Beginning with the initial introduction to reading and mathematics, the materials, counting rhymes, and illustrations teach children that some ethnic groups are to be treated as objects. Also, the illustrations used in the material bear little resemblance to real life in America. They are based on nuclear families with the father employed and the mother as a full-time homemaker. Currently only about 30 percent of students in America's schools reflect this family organization.

Furthermore, life in the United States is portrayed as easy and comfortable. The people, who generally are white, blond-haired, and of northern European origin, are kind and generous. The underlying suggestions are that there may be other kinds of people in the world, but they live in faraway places and in faraway times, and they certainly have no place in the American scene (Klineberg 1964). When any attempt is made to include other ethnic groups, it is usually unrealistic, such as one black or Asian family in the all white neighborhood. Also, in the teaching of the development of the country, little or no mention is made of groups other than Europeans in the building of the United States beyond the mention of slavery, the Civil War, and Martin Luther King, Jr.

Finally, the following five myths of America are taught and inculcated into students' psyches every day:

1. America is great because of individualism or reliance on one's self. We hold up icons such as Horatio Alger as the hallmark of all that is good and proper in this country. Competition rather than cooperation is the guiding value. Contrary to this myth, cultures in this country know and understand that cooperation is the key to survival, and the idea of competition is antithetical to them. If these icons were truly examined by an unjaundiced eye, one would know and understand that they, too, built on cooperation.

2. We must distrust foreign alliances and be concerned only with internal affairs. From the isolationist views prior to World War I to the current debate of our role in conflicts in Europe, Africa, the Middle East, and the Far East, the sentiments expressed reflect this stance. Growing out of a sense of betrayal and a sense that foreign alliances would require participation in other peoples' wars that surfaced during the time of the Revolutionary War, this debate has guided the country's foreign policy and the conduct of that foreign policy to the present.

3. America is a "melting pot," and all cultures need to divest themselves of "foreignness" and become "Americans." In fact, it was once predicted that by the year 2000 all Americans would be a uniform color somewhat akin to weak tea. But this can scarcely happen if certain groups are not allowed into the mix. Further, because culture defines not only who we are but also how we view, organize, and behave in our world, the melting-pot ideal is unattainable.

4. It is acceptable to impose one's views on others. This myth is evident in the doctrine of "manifest destiny" that governed the settlement of the American West and in incidents that led to the Spanish-American war and the Monroe Doctrine. It also undergirded the entire institution of slavery, Indian removal, and the importation of Asian laborers into the West.

5. The status quo is perfectly acceptable in race and in gender relations. The question is often asked, "What do 'you people' want?" This rhetorical statement reflects the lack of knowledge and understanding of the questioners.

(Brislin 1981, 18–30)

The mass media reinforce the same stereotypes and display unrealistic attitudes about out-groups that are found in school materials. The depiction of minorities in the media is most often a caricature. A caricature may be defined as a pictorial representation in which the subject's distinctive features or peculiarities are intentionally distorted or exaggerated to generate a comic or grotesque effect (Webster's II 1984, 231). This caricature of minorities dehumanizes, but it is inspired and made acceptable by earlier dehumanizing influences, namely an absence of information on who minorities are and where they have been (Brislin 1981, 30).

In analyses of the depiction of minorities in print media in one mid-western city, it was found that Native Americans and Asian Americans were virtually invisible in the local paper, whereas Hispanic Americans were somewhat more visible and African Americans were highly visible. However, the areas in which African Americans had a major presence were crime, sports, and entertainment; their visibility in business and government was low. This was in a city with sizeable populations of the four above-mentioned minorities. Ironically, the city itself had been named for a Native American nation and was located in a state named for a Native American nation. This is hardly surprising when in 1993, just 5 percent of reporters in print media were minority and 45 percent of newspapers in the United States had no minority reporters on staff (Chideya 1995, xv).

But the most influential area of the media is television. As of 1990, 95 percent of all homes in the United States had at least one television set. Children spend more time watching television than they spend in any other activity except sleep (Brislin 1981, 37). It is estimated that by the age of 18, children in the United States will have spent more hours in television viewing than in classroom instruction. Television reinforces the same stereotypes and displays the same attitudes toward out-groups that are found in school materials and in the print media. Not only the content but the structure of television material has a major effect on how children view the world and especially out-groups. Issues are simplified to be covered in a small amount of time, and problems can be solved within a time slot. Happy endings are common, and complex problems are resolved to everyone's satisfaction. Characters are overdrawn, larger than life, and clearly labeled. The world of television bears little resemblance to real life (Brislin 1981, 37).

Multicultural Communities

In contemporary America, the term multiculturalism may have a different meaning depending on how you understand the concept. Multicultural-ism can be referred to as "a society that is made up of many different ethnic and racial groups and does not refer to a 'movement' or political force" (Shusta et al. 1995, 3). Traditionally, America has referred to itself as a "melting pot" but in the past several decades we hear more of America being a multicultural and diverse society. In the initial decades of the twenty-first century multiculturalism in America includes immigrants, refugees, and ethnic minorities. However, during various segments of America's history it always had to deal with new waves of immigrants who came from all four corners of the world. Like today, many Americans have difficulties accepting the recent arrivals and ethnic peoples into the mainstream of our society.

We need to recognize that all of us, except native-born Americans, all come from a multicultural society, which is very diverse. All cultures bring their values, attitudes, and beliefs and are often intolerant of people who are different from them. The police who reflect the value system of society generally are mainstream Americans who often do not understand people from different cultures who are different from them. This can often lead to prejudice against people from a different culture. "Prejudice is a judgment or opinion formed before facts are known and it usually involves negative or unfavorable thoughts about groups of people. Discrimination is action based on the prejudiced thought" (Shusta et al. 1995, 23).

Prejudices if conducted by police officers are illegal and frowned upon. Prejudice encourages narrow-minded thinking. It stereotypes racial groups such as Afro-Americans and Hispanics and religious groups such as Jews and Catholics with viewpoints not based on factual information. Prejudice and discrimination are connected but not the same. Discrimination puts prejudice into action, which is a belief or attitude. One form of putting prejudice into action is stereotyping. One form of stereotyping is racial profiling which can be defined as "any arbitrary police-initiated action based on race, ethnicity, or natural origin rather than a person's behavior" (Schaefer 2006, 45).

Although prejudice still exists in America it is not as great as it once was. Over the last several decades, America is becoming more tolerant. However, prejudice has been found to be as diverse as the nation's population. Not only does prejudice exist between dominate and subordinate groups but also between subordinate groups. Laws and court decisions have played a role in combating prejudice in society (Schaefer 2006). It also seems that since the 1960s prejudice and discrimination has declined.

Intergroup prejudice and hostility may be as diverse as the country's population. Conflict exists between minorities. Minority groups, similar to whites, have negative beliefs, attitudes, and stereotypical views against other ethnic and racial minorities. The National Conference on Christian and Jews (1994) found the following information about the views of various racial and ethnic groups about one another. Most blacks, Hispanics, and Asians consider whites to be bigoted, bossy, and unwilling to share power. Many Hispanics and blacks consider Asians to be unscrupulous, crafty, and devious. African Americans and Asians consider that Hispanics have larger families than they can afford. Asian Americans and Hispanics consider that African Americans want to be welfare recipients. It seems all racial and ethnic groups have stereotypes and negative views about one another.

Diversity can be found anywhere in America. It exists in America's cities, suburban areas, and rural communities. Rural police officers must be prepared to deal with residents who have diverse backgrounds. People from all races, ethnicities, religions, and cultures can be found anywhere in contemporary society. Police officers must learn lifestyle differences that they are unfamiliar with. Only by learning the cultural differences and respecting those differences can the police develop good police–community relations. The police need to recognize diversity and value it. A community that is culturally diverse offers opportunities and benefits that should not be overlooked. Police need to be fair and respectful and tolerant of diversity if police–community relations are to be held to a high level of integrity.

The community functions as a cultural influence of all citizens who reside in a specific neighborhood. The police need the trust from the community to function effectively. The police need to address the social and cultural needs of communities that are racially and ethnically diverse. Discrimination and prejudices that should be eliminated must start with the lowest level between the individual citizen and the beat officer. Just as a community has diversity so must the community's police department. A community that has a mixture of whites, Hispanics, blacks, and Asians should have community-police agencies that reflect the diversity of the community. Those agencies that do not recruit, hire, or promote officers who reflect the cultural, racial and ethnic groups of their city are doing an injustice to the citizens of their city (Green 2009). In order to establish an effective police–community relationship in a diverse community several principles suggested by the Department of Justice are as follows (Principles of Good Policing 2003): (1) The agency should strive to maintain a workforce consisting of officers from diverse ethnic backgrounds that appropriately represent the community. (2) The agency should attempt to hire employees with a wide variety of educational backgrounds. (3) The agency should strive to hire individuals who are emotionally capable to handle the difficulties and complexities of the job.

Police–community relations can become effective when the police and community develop a partnership that combines their efforts and skills. Effective policing in a multicultural community requires that a strong partnership exists between the police and community. There must be trust and honesty if cooperation and a partnership have any chance of working between the police and community.

Racial and Ethnic Groups

When examining multiculturalism and diversity there are several racial and ethnic groups that deserve attention. One group that seems to receive a great deal of attention since 9/11 is Arabs. Since 9/11, Arab Americans have seen discrimination and abuses against them increased. Arab Americans have been murdered, beaten, threatened, and had their mosques burned to the ground. They are subject to racial and ethnical profiling. Some police agencies are working with Arab Americans to learn their culture and some are recruiting Arab Americans for their police departments (Jackson 2006).

Asian Americans have been under attack and discriminated against since arriving in America. Although there are 32 Asian American groups, most Americans consider Asians to be either Chinese or Japanese. Similar to most minorities Asians have been the victims of prejudice and discrimination. Asians migrated to America for economic and educational opportunities, to escape political chaos, or as refugees. America has a long history of treating Asians poorly. The most shameful act the American government did against the Japanese Americans was to force them into relocation centers during World War II. The Japanese Americans were forced to stay in these relocation centers under military guard. When compared to other minority groups the Japanese Americans are lower status (Jackson 2006). Asian Americans often find themselves targets of hate crimes, for the following reasons:

1. The growth of the Asian American population.
2. Economic factors such as the trade deficit.
3. Increased numbers of corporations (e.g., automobile manufactures) closing means greater competition for jobs.

4. Conflict with African Americans.
5. The escalating conflicts in China and North Korea.
6. The success image: Asian Americans have established more businesses in African American communities.

(Jackson 2006, 140–141)

A major minority group that has a long history in America of being abused and being discriminated against are African Americans. Police–African American incidents that create conflict between the police and blacks include the 1991 Rodney King incident in which King was videotaped being beaten by Los Angeles police officers; and the 1999 killing of Amadou Diallo who received 41 bullets in him from New York City police officers. Incidents such as these and racial profiling have created a chasm between the police and African Americans in many communities. For decades, African Americans have complained of verbal abuse and excessive force. Blacks more than whites have a tendency to believe that it is not unusual for police officers to abuse citizens, treat whites better than blacks, and not be accountable for their cruel behavior (Weitzer and Tuch 2006).

Not only do the police stereotype minorities, minorities stereotype the police. People tend to communicate stereotypical information and to embrace a stereotype of other groups. African Americans stereotype the police and reinforce it with their folklore about black encounters with the police. The history of urban police–black encounters has been intergraded into the folklore of black neighborhoods. The attitudes of all citizens, including blacks, play a major role in how they perceive the police. If they have a negative view of the police then most likely they will consider their encounters with the police in a negative light (Holmes and Smith 2008). This may be an approach many African Americans have towards the police, whether based on an accurate account of an encounter with the police or by a misinterpretation of a police action.

In addition to the minorities mentioned there are other minorities that have been discriminated against. Almost no group that has come to America was welcomed by those currently there. Now the early immigrants who have been assimilated into the culture have bad feelings against newcomers and some minorities who have been in America for decades. Minorities who may not have been fully accepted into American society include Native Americans, Middle Eastern groups, new arrivals from

Central and South America along with new arrivals from Asia. A new group that has been added to the list of minorities who are not always treated with respect and courtesy are gays and lesbians. Homosexuals have not been accepted by all people. Many homosexuals have kept their identity a secret for fear of the abuse that could be used against them. Like other minorities it is unlawful to discriminate against them but like other minorities this will not protect those who dislike their sexual orientation (Jackson 2006).

How can policing be improved in a diverse community? The police in the twenty-first century will have to become more tolerant of minorities and that includes minorities' attitudes toward other minorities. The cultural, racial, ethnical, and religious makeup of America is changing and we as Americans will have to make adjustments to our changing world. This definitely includes the police. Shusta et al. (2008) in their book provide nine suggestions for the police and a diverse community to practice good police–community relations. These suggestions are:

1. Make positive contact with the community group members from diverse backgrounds. Do not let them see you only when something negative has happened.
2. Allow the public to see you as much as possible in a non-enforcement role.
3. Make a conscious effort in your mind, en route to every situation, to treat all segments of society objectively and fairly.
4. Remember that all groups have some bad, some average, and some good people within them.
5. Go out of your way to be personable and friendly with minority group members. Remember many do not expect it.
6. Do not appear uncomfortable with or avoid discussing racial and ethnic issues with other officers and citizens.
7. Take responsibility for patiently educating citizens and the public about the role of the officer and about standard operating procedures in law enforcement. Remember that citizens often do not understand "police culture."
8. Do not be afraid to be a change agent in your organization when it comes to improving cross-cultural relations within your department and between police and the community. It may not be a popular thing to do, but it is the right thing to do.

9. Remember the history of law enforcement with all groups and ask the question: Am I part of the past or part of the future?

Police agencies must face multicultural and diversity issues if they are to win the support of the community. In the twenty-first century, the police must be respectful to all cultures regardless of how diverse they may be from the cultures they assimilated in their childhood and adult development. Only by respecting all peoples can community policing develop a partnership with the police. Police departments may have to go through an organizational change for the police partnership to work.

Organizational Change*

The American workforce is changing in many ways. Workers' self-efficacy and attitudes about work are becoming increasingly important to organizations. Like other fields, policing needs to go through organizational transformation to remain competitive and to attract and retain quality employees. The adoption of a community-policing philosophy will also require this transformation.

To the casual observer, policing has made praise worth advances during the twentieth century. Police practitioners and academics alike have seen police agencies change quality employees. The adoption of a community-policing philosophy will also require this transformation.

Implementing change within police organizations as they are traditionally run is not an easy task. As Victor Strecher (1997) pointed out, "The status quo is easier—it is easier to defend (people know it; they're more comfortable with a predictable, known quantity) and it is less risky" (12). Nevertheless, organizational transformation, also referred to as organizational engineering, must be initiated and should be the first of many steps in the community-policing process. It is not uncommon for people to stereotype their interaction with others.

Change in policing, as in any field, has been driven by a wide range of factors:

1. Increase in crime in a particular area and/or the fear of crime.
2. Budgetary concerns—a need to do more with less.
3. Citizens' greater expectations of the police.

---

* This section was written by Michael Birzer.

4. An increase in specific types of crime (i.e., juvenile crime and domestic violence).
5. Technological changes to the nature of police work.

The trends require the police to critically rethink the way in which they provide police service. Traditionally the police have failed to keep up with societal complexities.

As discussed in previous chapters, community policing is a response to these complexities. It requires that the police become proactive problem solvers in the communities they serve. The police are expected to become resource catalysts and direct links to the many public and private agencies that may foster the problem-solving process. Community policing is also coactive in that the police and community work together to solve problems of the community. It requires the police to become street-level criminologists and to think more in terms of the root causes of the problem—for example "Why is this area of the community having a large amount of reported burglaries?" In this case, police would be expected to investigate a variety of potential causal factors that might include environmental characteristics, victim characteristics, and offender characteristics. They might link the burglaries to truancy rates at schools in the area. For example, the burglaries were occurring during the day. Then they might address the problem of truant juveniles (root cause) to solve the burglary problem (result).

Because community policing represents a fundamental change in the way that police do business, it requires organizational change. Effective organizational change will involve virtually all aspects of the police organization. These include training, promotions, leadership, and organizational structure.

Community

It is critical that the police agency involve the community early on in the community-policing implementation in order to begin building public support. The first of many steps involving the community is usually educating the community about what community policing is and what it means for their neighborhoods. One of the most effective methods of educating community members is to hold several small community meetings. These should be open to any member of the public and should be publicized extensively. The police executive should be present at each of the meetings, as well as precinct or sector commanders and as many lower-ranking personnel who wish to attend. The presence of the chief or sheriff reinforces the importance of these meetings and assures the public that they are not merely "show-and-tell" sessions (Watson et al. 1988, 76). During these meetings, police executives and community-police officers should provide the community with a general overview of community policing and the roles of the police and the community. At this time, leaders within specific neighborhoods will begin to emerge and be identified. Neighborhood leaders take on a crucial role later in the implementation process, assisting community-policing officers in organization groups and neighborhood teams and encouraging other citizens to become involved.

The location of meetings should be readily accessible to all community members. Schools, recreational centers, and neighborhood police stations work well for meetings. The site for the meeting should comfortably accommodate a large number of people.

The Chicago Police Department held regular beat meetings during the transition to community policing in an effort to gain the support of community residents. The officers who attended were those officers that patrolled the neighborhoods where citizens in attendance resided. The meetings accomplished a number of objectives. There were many opportunities for the police and citizens to exchange information. Participants learned about police procedures, including when to call 911 rather than a list of alternate nonemergency numbers, and police learned something about residents' priorities (Skogan and Harnett 1997, 113). Furthermore, the Chicago Police Department, by bringing residents and officers together, began to nurture community support for community policing and build relations of trust between the police and the community.

After neighborhood meetings are conducted, frequent meetings should be held for the purpose of identifying problems, cares, and concerns of the community. The police and affected community should be involved in tailoring solutions to identified problems. When citizens become engaged with the police in the problem-solving process, their support will become even stronger.

Communication

To maintain support for community policing, communication must be continual between management and rank-and-file police employees. Police employees must be kept appraised of the change process and what exactly is occurring within the department. In many organizations, this is difficult due to the many layers that separate the command staff from the line-level police officer.

Within police organizations, there are basically three types of formal communication channels: downward, upward, and lateral. In most police organizations, the upward and downward communication channels appear to be used the most.

Downward communication transmits information from the top of the organizations to the bottom. Most of the information is in the form of standard operating procedures, directives, special orders, and general orders. In essence, downward communication is the flow of information down the chain of command.

Upward communication transmits information from the bottom of the organization to the top. This is the communication channel used by subordinates in the organization. Upward communication usually focuses on making management aware of the problems, presenting ideas, suggesting improvements in performing certain tasks, and expressing feelings about certain aspects of the job. Upward communication can be somewhat frustrating for line-level police officers because of the chain of command that the information must flow up through. For example, a police officer who wants to communicate with a major must first go through his or her sergeant and then the lieutenant, the captain, and finally the major. This can be frustrating in and of itself, not to mention the problems that may be created in the process. In some cases, it may reach the top command after a delay of several weeks. Or it may reach the top and be ignored, so that the subordinate never receives a reply or an answer to a request or proposal. This can be debilitating for any true form of community policing. Yet another problem with upward communication is that often employees communicate only what the boss wants to hear.

The lateral communication channel is the channel used by peers. For example, a police officer working on the day watch may report an activity to a detective or an officer working the night watch. This type of activity is critical in policing for the coordination of activities and events. For example, day watch officers may be competing with night watch officers to get additional officers for that specific shift.

Nevertheless, lateral communication with the police organization is important so that functional units can be continually appraised of what the other is doing. To foster change to community policing, police management must correct obstacles to the organizational communication process. This may involve deviating from the traditional chain of command when upward or downward communication is desired. The traditional style of formal communication must be relaxed, and information from the top must be articulated directly to the subordinates at the bottom of the pyramid.

The traditional information system must be altered and perfected both inside and outside the organization to sustain effective change. In traditional policing, communication is organized around a need-to-know basis, and information is distributed according to position and rank. In contrast, community policing demands open communication with the community, and frequent exchange among units with other public and private agencies (Gray et al. 1997, 41–48).

The recent influx of technology within policing is altering many of the traditional communication channels. Computers, with their e-mail and information networking capacity, allow for a diagonal form of communication that jumps across the traditional chain of command. The new communication channel is increasing the responsiveness of today's organizations. The traditional chain of command often takes too long to negotiate (Buhler 1997).

Computer communication technology will correct some of the problems that past communication channels created. Further, e-mail will allow police employees to communicate with members of other agencies and community members with ease and may improve on the dissemination of information both in and outside the police organization. Management must support and implement new styles of communication systems and encourage subordinates to suggest ways of providing better services and not just say what the boss wants to hear. An empowered, engaged, and high-trust police organization has a free-flowing relaxed system of communication.

Work Environment

One final area in which management must be willing to support in the process of implementing community policies is that of the work environment. Police employees want to work in a meaningful environment where their ideas and suggestions are taken seriously. Police management must be committed to continually improving the working environment of the organization. Successful organizational improvement can only come about through a three-stage process:

1. Change yourself.
2. Improve the workplace (primarily by improving the organizational leadership style).
3. Ask your employees to treat customers the same way you are trying to treat them: i.e., improve service to citizens.

(Couper and Lobitz 1993, 18–19)

Changing oneself means examining issues and reflecting in a way that one has not engaged in previously. It means being receptive to all viewpoints and becoming more democratic in thought. Supporting a democratic work environment entails changing to a more democratic proactive style.

Improving the workplace involves thinking in terms of a system approach in terms of creating a learning organization where processes are continually examined and alternate methods explored. It involves being willing to listen to subordinates and encouraging innovation. Improving organizational leadership involves leading by example and living the core values and visions that have been articulated to the rank and file.

Managers who support a customer service environment where employees are asked to treat others as they would want to be treated are well on their way to creating a community-policing organization. Police officers must be treated with dignity and respect all who require and request police services and treat every citizen's concern as if it is the most important. Here is how a meaningful work environment may be fostered:

1. Share the company vision in detail with employees.
2. Show how individual jobs contribute to achieving the vision.
3. Include employees in decisions that affect their job.
4. Foster a spirit of collaboration.
5. Celebrate diversity.
6. Promote open and honest communication.
7. Don't punish employees for taking risks.
8. Empower employees to share equally in decisions that affect the shape and direction of the organization.
9. Provide ongoing growth and development opportunities.
10. Encourage regular feedback.

(Caudron 1997, 24–27)

Summary

Multiculturalism is an approach to cultural diversity that emphasizes understanding, respecting, and adapting to other cultures and cultural differences. It is important for all police personnel, especially those involved in community policing, to become aware of and sensitive to diversity issues and to develop cross-cultural skills.

Organizational change is a crucial prerequisite for the implementation of community policing. Traditionally, police organizations have been modeled after the principles of the classical organizational theory. Police executives must allow police operations to decentralize and move into the community. They must allow supervisors and commanders working in neighborhood stations to have more input into matters affecting police operations.

KEY TERMS

- community empowerment
- community organizations
- neighborhood
- sense of community

REVIEW QUESTIONS

1. What is a community?
2. What is meant by sense of community?
3. What is meant by empowerment?
4. What does the term neighborhood mean?
5. Why are neighborhood organizations important?
6. How can police help to develop a sense of community in the areas they serve?
7. Why is multicultural awareness important in community policing?

7

CRIME PREVENTION AND
COMMUNITY POLICING

CHAPTER OBJECTIVES

1. Understand what is meant by crime prevention.
2. Understand what the police role is in crime prevention.
3. Understand the relationship between crime prevention and community policing.
4. Be familiar with the various crime prevention strategies.
5. Be familiar with situational crime prevention.
6. Be familiar with community crime prevention.
7. Be familiar with crime prevention media campaigns.

Introduction

The police sell themselves as the best defense against crime and argue that with more resources they would do a better job in protecting the community from crime. But according to David Bayley (1994), the noted police scholar, "The plain fact is that police action cannot be shown to reduce the amount of crime" (9). Differences in crime rates cannot be attributed to variations in the number of police, and additional police officers do not slow, even temporarily, rates of increase in crime. Although there are probably critical thresholds beyond which changing the number of police would affect crime, no one knows what these thresholds are. There is no evidence that patrolling by uniformed officers, rapid response to emergency calls, and expert investigation of crime by detectives will prevent crime. Police foot patrols make people feel better, but they do not prevent crime; and research has consistently failed to show that the intensity of random motorized patrolling by uniformed officers has any effect on crime rates, victimization, or even public satisfaction. Finally, the success of police in criminal investigations has no appreciable effect on public security (4–7).

Other police researchers have also found that many police strategies are not effective in preventing crime (Bouza 1990; Kelling et al. 1974; Walker 1989). The reactive approach to crime has been especially criticized. The use of 911 by citizens to call the police after a crime has been committed does not prevent crime. In many cases, the police are working merely as report takers—taking a report after the fact. Although they need to respond to emergencies and crime-in-progress calls to arrest an offender or come to the aid of a citizen who requires assistance, they probably should not respond to every 911 call. Many nonemergency calls can be taken over the telephone, or the citizen can come to police headquarters to file a report. Some police departments even take some criminal reports over the telephone: for example, the Wichita Police Department does this with stolen car reports.

The alternative strategy to reactive policing is proactive policing, which involves taking an active part in going after criminals. Sting operations are one example: the police establish a fencing operation, getting the word out to the street criminals that they are purchasing stolen merchandise, then purchase stolen goods from the thieves and then arrest them.

The community-policing philosophy is a proactive approach to policing that emphasizes crime prevention through working with the community. If crime prevention is not incorporated into the community-policy philosophy, the strategy of community policing is substantially weakened, and in all probability community policing will not succeed. Certain police strategies, such as directed patrol and proactive arrests, which were discussed in Chapter 4 in greater detail, have shown tangible evidence of preventing crime. The police can prevent robbery, disorder, and domestic violence, but only by using specific methods under certain conditions.

When Sir Robert Peel first established the Metropolitan London Police in 1829, he listed crime prevention as a major goal of policing. Today the police need to return to this goal. All officers should be knowledgeable in crime prevention techniques and strategies. The purpose of this chapter is to provide police officers and potential police officers with a foundation of knowledge about crime prevention. In departments adopting the community-policing philosophy, an understanding of crime prevention is essential.

What Is Crime Prevention?

Several definitions of crime prevention are used, depending upon the program or research conducted. Lab (1997) stated, "crime prevention entails any action designed to reduce the actual level of crime and/or the perceived fear of crime" (10). Another definition, from the National Crime Prevention Institute (1986), described crime prevention as "any kind of effort aimed at controlling criminal behavior" (2). The institute classified crime prevention efforts into direct controls of crime—those that "reduce environmental opportunities for crime"—and indirect controls, which would "include all other measures, such as job training, remedial education, police surveillance, police apprehension, court action, imprisonment, probation and parole" (2). Crime prevention advocates believe in "preventing specific kinds of crimes; mobilizing residents for prevention efforts; and developing physical and social environments inhospitable to crime" ("Crime Prevention" 1996a, 4). They assume that people can take measures to avoid becoming victims of crime and that neighborhoods can reduce crime by becoming more vigilant with regard to checking both potential serious crimes and public nuisance offenses (vandalism, graffiti, public drunkenness) that lead to deterioration of a neighborhood's quality of life.

Responsibility for Crime Prevention

There are many views about who has the responsibility for crime prevention. One is that the individual bears the sole responsibility of avoiding becoming a victim of a crime. Another is that the neighborhood or community bears this responsibility. Still another is that the police bear sole responsibility. A fourth approach is consonant with the philosophy of community policing: obviously, the police have an obligation to concentrate on crime prevention, but they cannot do it alone; they need the cooperation of the neighborhood and of the citizens who live in the neighborhood. Crime prevention cannot be successful unless it involves the participation of all formal and informal structures, the cooperation of all neighborhood residents, and a heightened awareness, among individual residents, of the dangers of crime and how they may be avoided.

Role of the Police in Crime Prevention

As Sir Robert Peel stated when he first established the London police, the police have the responsibility of preventing and controlling crime. No other component of criminal justice has the vantage point that the police possess in working with the community. The police are the first to know if a crime has been committed. They have to investigate crimes, solve crimes, arrest criminal offenders, and recover stolen property. By the nature of their positions, they also know how offenders commit crime—knowledge that can be used to prevent crime from occurring.

In 1971, the National Advisory Commission on Criminal Justice Standards and Goals was appointed by the Law Enforcement Assistance Administration (LEAA). The purpose of the commission was to establish national criminal justice standards and goals for reducing and preventing crime at the municipal, county, and state levels. In 1973, the commission completed its task and published its standards for crime prevention in the report *Police*. The standards for crime prevention as it applies to the police are as follows:

> Every police agency should immediately establish programs that encourage members of the public to take an active role in preventing crime, that provide information leading to the arrest and conviction of criminal offenders, that facilitate the identification and recovery of stolen property, and that increase liaisons with private industry in security efforts.
>
> (66)

Police style should be considered as important as substance. Both the style and substance of police practices must be considered reasonable from the public's viewpoint. Scientific evidence supports the conclusion that the less respectful the police are toward suspects and citizens, the less people will comply with the law (Sherman et al. 1997, 1).

Traditionally, police departments have established crime prevention units or at a minimum have had an officer who does security checks for residents and businesses. But departments that have adopted the community-policing philosophy have gone further by incorporating crime prevention into community policing. They attempt to obtain the cooperation of neighborhood and business associations in implementing crime prevention strategies, and they provide education, training, and consulting services to the neighborhood through programs on preventing such crimes as rape, mugging, shoplifting, and juvenile delinquency.

Role of the Community in Crime Prevention

The term community has multiple definitions. It can mean an entire city, for example the community of Wichita, or merely a section of a city, such as the north side or the east side. Crime prevention strategies or plans function more efficiently when they are geared to a small, specific geographical area or neighborhood. According to Bursik and Grasmick's (1993) definition,

> first, and most basically, a neighborhood is a small physical area embedded within a larger area in which people inhabit dwellings. Thus, it is a geographical and social subset of a larger unit. Second, there is collective life that emerges from the social networks that have arisen among the residents and the sets of institutional arrangements that overlap their networks. That is, the neighborhood is inhabited by people who perceive themselves to have a common interest in that area and to whom a common life is available. Finally, the neighborhood has some tradition of identity and continuity over time.
>
> (6)

Different neighborhoods in a city will have different crime problems. The biggest crime problems of poorer neighborhoods may be drive-by shootings and drug dealings on street corners, whereas the upper-middle-class neighborhood's biggest crime problem may be burglaries.

Police departments are well aware of where violent crimes, and specific crimes such as robberies, burglaries, auto theft, and drug dealing, usually take place. To keep these crimes under control, police need the cooperation of citizens who live in the places where the crimes occur.

A study sponsored by the National Institute of Justice on Crime Prevention in the late 1990s concluded that

> communities are the central institution for crime prevention, the stage on which all other institutions perform. Families, schools,

labor markets, retail establishments, police, and corrections must all confront the consequences of community life. Much of the success or failure of these other institutions is affected by the community context in which they operate. Our nation's ability to prevent serious violent crime may depend heavily on our ability to help reshape community life, at least in our most troubled communities.

(Sherman 1997, 1)

According to the National Crime Prevention Council (1989), a neighborhood's crime problems begin with physical decay and public nuisance offenses such as vandalism. Crime prevention and improvements of the neighborhood's quality of life are tied together. Neighborhoods must not only target crime directly but also address the underlying causes of their crime problem. A wide variety of programs can be implemented: they can include improved housing, education, and employment opportunities, to name only a few.

It has been estimated that approximately 10–20 percent of neighborhood residents may, at any one time, be involved in crime prevention activities. Obtaining their involvement may require a great deal of effort. Further, even when crime decreases, crime prevention participation by citizens needs to be continued so that crime will not take an upward turn. Most citizens can muster enough energy for the short term but long-term involvement is needed to keep crime under control.

Crime Prevention and Community Policing

Crime prevention and community policing have six major features in common:

1. Each deals with the health of the community. Both community policing and crime prevention acknowledge the many interrelated issues that generate crime.
2. Each seeks to address underlying causes and problems. Looking behind symptoms to treat the causes of community problems is a strategy that both, at their best, share in the full measure.

3. Each deals with the combination of physical and social issues that are at the heart of many community problems. Community policing and crime prevention both acknowledge that crime-causing situations can arise out of physical as well as social problems in the community.

4. Each requires active involvement by community residents. Crime prevention practitioners—law enforcement and civilians alike—have acknowledged that their chief task is to enable people—children, teens, adults, senior citizens—to make themselves and their communities safer by helping them gain appropriate knowledge, develop helpful attitudes, and take useful actions. The very essence of community policing requires overt participation of residents in what has been termed the "coproduction of public safety."

5. Each requires partnerships beyond law enforcement to be effective. Crime prevention efforts involve schools, community centers, civic organizations, religious groups, social service agencies, public works agencies, and other elements of the community. Experience in community policing documents the need for similar partnerships both to reach people and to solve problems.

6. Each is an approach or philosophy, rather than a program. Neither community policing nor crime prevention is a "program"—that is, a fixed model for delivery of specific services. Each involves the development of an institutional mindset that holds community paramount and values preventive and problem-solving efforts in all of the organization's business. Each can involve a wide range of programs and other initiatives.

("Crime Prevention" 1996a, 3–4)

There are five basic arguments for linking crime prevention and community policing:

1. Crime prevention and community policing have a common purpose making the public safer and making communities healthier.

2. Crime prevention offers information and skills that are essential to community policing.

3. Crime prevention and community policing have great potential for enriching each other.

4. Crime prevention responsibilities may be repositioned within the department as it moves to community policing, but successful departments have found a need for a clear focus of responsibility for crime prevention and a driving necessity for the capacity to apply and teach crime prevention knowledge and skills.

5. Thoughtful, planned action that carefully nurtures a core of crime prevention expertise while making the skills and knowledge available to all officers, especially those working at the street level, can substantially benefit the transition to community policing as well as its practice.

("Crime Prevention" 1996a, 4–8)

The state of Oregon's board of public safety and training believes so strongly that crime prevention is a key ingredient of community policing that it provides an 80-hour course in crime prevention specifically designed for community-policing officers. The course was designed because state administrators realized that crime prevention officers had been doing the work described by the community-policing philosophy, including problem solving, citizen empowerment, and forming a partnership with the community. Under the Oregon program, crime prevention officers function as mentors, resources, catalysts, and troubleshooters for community-policing officers who are responsible for the day-to-day community-policing activities. The crime prevention officers instruct community organizations in conflict resolution, volunteer management, and program development ("Crime Prevention" 1996b, 3).

The integration of crime prevention and community-policing operations can only strengthen the security and safety of neighborhoods and the community as a whole. Crime prevention programs have discovered that neighborhood associations and individuals can play a successful part in ensuring their own security and safety. Programs such as block watches, Neighborhood Watch, business and security surveys, and security training have all proven useful in involving citizens in crime prevention. These programs have often involved the citizens in problem solving and the initiation of a police–citizen partnership. They also have given citizens a greater sense of empowerment with respect to their own safety. They are discussed in depth in the next section of this chapter.

Crime Prevention Strategies

According to the National Crime Prevention Institute (1986), setting up a crime prevention program involves three main tasks: "designing the organization; defining the crime problems and priorities; and developing crime prevention program objectives" (150). As Paul Whisenand (1977) has argued, all these tasks require community input and commitment if a program is to be successful. Therefore, police crime prevention specialists or community-policing officers must work with the community to develop and implement the crime prevention program.

In some areas, like Knoxville, Tennessee, police have established community advisory boards to help draw up the area's crime prevention plan. In Knoxville, board members included representatives from neighborhood associations, Neighborhood Watch groups, and business associations, as well as numerous civic leaders ("Crime Prevention" 1996c, 4–8). The section later in this chapter on Seattle's Community Crime Prevention Program provides more detail on this kind of planning.

Crime Analysis

Crime analysis is a process of collecting, analyzing, and disseminating information so that it can be put to use by the crime prevention specialist and community police officer. Police officers and investigators have always conducted crime analysis informally, but in the last several decades, some larger police departments have established formal crime analysis units to assist crime prevention specialists in preventing and controlling crime. The crime analysis unit uses information collected from reported criminal offenders to prevent crime, apprehend, and suppress criminal offenders.

The criminal analysis unit receives information from the patrol, detective, communications, administration, and special units. The primary source of information is police reports. The information collected from within the police department consists of preliminary investigative reports, supplementary reports, arrest reports, field contact reports, statistical data, and various other department reports. Usually, police reports include the type of incident, the location of the incident, information about the victim, the suspect's description, and any unique characteristics of the incident—the type of weapon used, verbal expressions, facial features, and so forth. The analysis unit also collects information from outside agencies such as corrections, probation, state agencies, private organizations, and other law enforcement agencies. Information collected from external agencies includes status and records of known offenders and crime problems in other law enforcement agencies.

The purpose of crime analysis is to provide practical information about crime patterns, crime trends, and possible leads of possible suspects. For crime analysis to be useful, information about suspects should be forwarded to crime prevention specialists, community-policing officers, and beat patrol officers, who generally have the primary responsibility for crime prevention.

Contemporary crime analysis units are using computerized mapping to solve crimes and to aid in the investigation of crime. According to the National Institute of Justice (Rich 1988), mapping software has many crime control and prevention applications. In addition to the location of crime, geographic data that can be helpful in crime control and in efforts to apprehend a perpetrator include the perpetrator's last known address, the location of the person who reported the crime, the location of the recovered stolen property, and the locations of persons known or contacted by the perpetrator. Geographical information valuable in planning, conducting, and evaluating crime prevention programs includes the locations of crimes committed during the past month; the locations of abandoned houses, stripped cars, and other "broken windows" conditions in a neighborhood; and the locations where persons who could benefit from crime prevention and other social programs actually live (15).

The potential uses for computerized mapping software are numerous. Computer-aided dispatch (CAD) and record-management systems that store and maintain service calls, incidents, arrests, and mapping data are commonly used in large police departments. Geocoding, a CAD feature and a record-management system, can verify addresses and can associate other geographic information, including police reporting areas, beats, and districts. The crime analysis unit can use mapping software to prepare crime bulletins and to assist crime prevention specialists by informing them of the geographical areas in the community that should be targeted.

The use of crime analysis and computerized mapping in crime prevention assists in developing victim profiles that can be used in crime prevention programs. Crime analysis can provide specific modus operandi information (offenders' methods of committing crimes) that can be used to prevent crime. The crime prevention specialist or community-policing officer can be expected to provide strategies and inform residents and businesses of actions that can keep them from becoming victims of crime.

Neighborhood Watch

Neighborhood Watch programs have received a great deal of national media attention, and students studying community policing should be familiar with them. Neighborhood Watch programs are instituted in neighborhoods to reduce crime as well as the fear of crime. They are based on the concept that citizens of a neighborhood where crimes occur play an important part in controlling crime in their neighborhood. Watch members can be either homeowners or apartment dwellers who band together to establish a sense of security and safety. The association works to create a genuine neighborhood and to exchange information among members on crime prevention techniques. The community police officer or crime prevention specialist should function only as a supportive advisor to the Neighborhood Watch. If the community police officer runs the meeting, residents will feel that they should not be actively involved in the association. The success of Neighborhood Watch depends on residents' active involvement to make their neighborhood safe and secure.

Community policing officers should be vigorous in looking for ways to improve the security and safety of residents and businesses in their assigned neighborhood, particularly by eliminating criminal opportunities. They should look for poor or inadequate locks and recommend that owners replace them. Owners who leave their establishment open or unlocked need to be informed of the dangers of this action. Officers should check the exterior of buildings while on patrol—specifically fire escapes, doors, locks, windows, ladders, boxes, and equipment left out (Perry 1994, 38). They should have the knowledge to perform an inside security check as well.

One rural police department that used its Neighborhood Watch program to introduce community policing at the block level was Caldwell, Idaho, a city with a population of 22,000. The Neighborhood Watch was expected to identify three problems and come up with possible solutions. Neighborhood Watch captains were kept informed of criminal activities and civic events.

A study sponsored by the National Institute of Justice (Garofalo and McLeod 1988) concluded that Neighborhood Watch has the potential to reduce crime but that police need to find ways to ensure continuing citizen participation in existing programs and to make Neighborhood Watch more attractive for low-income, high-crime neighborhoods.

Citizen Patrols

In addition to Neighborhood Watch, communities can have citizen patrols that patrol a specific neighborhood. Citizen patrols can assist police by providing additional eyes and ears for the geographical area they are patrolling, since the police cannot be expected to patrol every city street or to know when every crime or neighborhood problem is occurring. Citizen patrols can be either on foot or in an automobile. Unlike the police, patrol members do not intervene physically or become involved in suspicious situations. Instead, they primarily offer surveillance and notify the police of any unusual or suspicious incidents. Usually, a citizen patrol consists of residents who volunteer to patrol their neighborhood for a specific time period. These patrols generally operate in the evenings or on weekends when the neighborhood volunteers are not working at their full-time jobs.

Business Watch

The National Sheriffs' Association (NSA) launched a Business Watch program in 1987. Various studies have uncovered that nearly a third of business failures are the result of losses from crime. Usually, small businesses are deficient in maintaining security systems or are unable to afford security personnel. Business owners, like residents, need to know about crime prevention strategies. Only when they become familiar with prevention tactics can they play a key role in the protection of their businesses. The National Sheriffs' Association championed a vicinity approach whereby merchants assisted each other, specifically in city blocks where many small shops and shopping malls were located.

Merchants involved in Business Watch used target-hardening tactics (installing physical barriers to prevent crime, such as locks, alarms, and fences) and were counseled through security checks by crime prevention specialists on how to make their shops less vulnerable to victimization. Police crime prevention specialists met with business owners and managers regularly to inform merchants about potential crime issues pertaining to their businesses, such as burglary prevention, bad check passing, robbery, and credit card fraud, and about various approaches they could put in place to avoid becoming crime victims. Close cooperation and communication between the crime prevention specialist and the businesspeople were extremely important for Business Watch to become a success (Cantrell 1988, 3).

Beep-a-Beat Program

The Beep-a-Beat Program (BBP) was developed by the Chicago Police Department to enhance communication between business merchants and members of the Chicago Police Department who were assigned to foot posts. Through BBP, preauthorized business merchants provide pagers for foot patrol officers so that citizens can contact foot patrol officers and relay messages. Foot patrol officers who receive a pager message requiring a response notify the police dispatcher that they are responding to a BBP message. They then give the business caller an appropriate response, record their resolution of the caller's message on their daily incident report form, and give the police dispatcher the appropriate code when they return in service. BBP keeps the lines of communication open between the merchants and the foot patrol officer. In a number of situations, BBP has helped in apprehending criminal offenders. For example, following a store robbery, a merchant contacted the foot patrol officer, who then had the merchant get into a squad car to canvass the geographical area. The victim spotted the offender, who was immediately arrested and charged with robbery. Cooperation between merchants and patrol foot officers contributed to a 25 percent reduction in robberies in 1995. The BBP program also led to foot patrol officers breaking up a ring of smash-and-grab robberies. Crime prevention programs like BBP can only enhance the image of the police in the eyes of citizens and should lead to greater cooperation and a reduction of crime. Programs like BBP make the citizen a partner in crime prevention (Officer J.A. Alcanter, Chicago Police Department, personal communication, 1998).

Police Station Automatic Teller Machines

In 1995, the Anne Arundel County Police Department in Maryland became the first police department to operate automatic teller machines (ATMs) in all of its county police stations. The idea developed after a series of ATM robberies. Because ATMs are open 24 hours a day and the locations of some ATMs leave customers prone to being robbed, the placement of ATMs in county police stations should provide greater security to citizens using ATMs, particularly in the wee hours of the morning and in some sections of the city. Los Angeles and Philadelphia have ATMs located in police stations, but only in a few areas. One key advantage of placing ATMs in police stations is that it provides opportunities for positive citizen–police contact so that citizens do not interact with police only in unpleasant situations such as receiving a traffic citation. This program should work to the advantage of both the community and the police.

Auto Theft Protection

Automobile thefts in America have been a growing problem to the police, insurance companies, and to victims of this criminal offense. The theft of automobiles is costly financially and emotionally and an inconvenience to the victim. Auto thefts are not only committed by joyriders but by professionals as well. The quick recovery of an automobile theft is extremely important. If the theft is not recovered within a few days the vehicle has almost no chance of being recovered.

Auto theft protection devices can deter vehicles from being stolen. There are two categories of theft protection devices: those that deter thieves from stealing vehicles and those that recover stolen automobiles. The professional auto thief knows how to disarm alarms, clubs, smart keys, and satellite tracking systems (Street Smarts, n.d., 9).

The LoJack Corporation offers a frequency-based recovery system that is used by police agencies and provides a 90 percent recovery rate. The LoJack system employs radiofrequencies, which are covert and almost difficult to locate and disengage. This system is tied to police agencies in 21 states. Although recovery systems are not designed to deter thieves, the most effective systems provide theft prevention. In most situations, stolen automobiles are recovered within a few hours with minimum damage (Street Smarts, n.d., 12).

Another auto theft recovery device is OnStar. The OnStar device has a similar goal as the LoJack device that cooperates with policing agencies in locating and recovering stolen vehicles. When a vehicle equipped with OnStar is stolen, Global Positioning System (GPS) satellite and wireless cellular technologies attempt to locate the vehicle and notify the police of the location of the stolen vehicle, even if the vehicle is being driven on the highway (GMability, 2004).

OnStar is placed in General Motors vehicles when owners subscribe to the service. OnStar is available to owners of General Motors vehicles in all 50 states. The OnStar service includes notification of air bag deployment, stolen vehicle location assistance, emergency services, and roadside assistance (GMability, 2004).

Both Lojack and OnStar are valuable devices in recovering stolen automobiles. In the future, it may be expected that these devices will be used more frequently as a prevention tool for automobile thieves.

Crime Stoppers

In 1976, an Albuquerque, New Mexico, police officer developed the Crime Stoppers program as a joint effort by which law enforcement agencies, the media, businesspeople, and community residents could increase citizen involvement in solving crimes. Crime Stoppers is a crime control mechanism that pays for information leading to the indictment of felony offenders.

Crime Stoppers provides anonymity and monetary rewards as inducements to obtain information from the general population regarding specific crimes. Those who associate with offenders and become privy to needed information are given the chance to exchange that information for cash while remaining protected from retaliation.

A program coordinator generally provided by a police agency runs the daily operations of the Crime Stoppers program. The coordinator's responsibilities include interacting with an established board of directors to determine the amount of all rewards; maintaining and operating a round-the-clock telephone hotline; preparing crime synopses for distribution as news releases; selecting and videotaping "Crime of the Week" simulations for showing on local television; and interacting with an established finance committee for fund-raising efforts.

Monetary awards for information relating to specific offenses generally range from $100 to $2,000, with the maximum amount normally paid only for capital crimes. As calls are received on the hotline in response to Crime Stoppers publicity, information is immediately forwarded to the appropriate police agency, with follow-up written reports distributed once each week. To collect a reward, tipsters must contact the Crime Stoppers program coordinator and submit a claim, citing their private alphanumeric code.

As community service efforts, Crime Stoppers programs are generally dependent upon the business community for financial support and, to a great extent, upon the local news media for publicity. As mechanisms to assist in crime control, these seem to be very worthwhile. A study by the National Institute of Justice (Rosenbaum et al. 1986) found Crime Stoppers "a highly productive program from the taxpayer's point of view." The study found that on a national average, "Each crime solved recovered more than $6,000 in narcotics and stolen goods, and each felony arrest cost only $73 in reward money."

Innovative ideas such as Crime Stoppers can stimulate participation in crime control by all segments of the community and have a tremendous impact on reduction of crime rates and apprehension of offenders.

Operation Identification

Most of us want to mark our belongings for identification. As a crime prevention tactic, the identification of items was first used in Monterey Park, California, in 1963. To deter a rash of hubcap thefts, the police chief recommended that residents engrave their license numbers on their hubcaps for identification purposes and eventually recommended that they engrave their household items as well.

When implementing an operation-identification program, the crime prevention specialist should require that the numbers selected be permanently engraved on the property marked. The numbering system used should be a standardized system that is acceptable to the National Crime Information Center (NCIC). The crime prevention specialist has to establish a record system that will provide for an inventory and description of the property that also includes serial numbers if they are available. In addition, the crime prevention specialist has the obligation to make the community aware that property that cannot be engraved should be photographed. All the rooms of a house should be photographed to show the items that are in them (Chuda 1990, 4–8).

Operation CLEAN

Since the mid-1980s, the crack cocaine drug epidemic has had a devastating impact on our nation's cities. Neighborhoods have been taken over by drug dealers. To check the deterioration of city neighborhoods, the Dallas Police Department initiated a program called Operation Community and Law Enforcement Against Narcotics (CLEAN) to reclaim neighborhoods from drug dealers and users. With the curbing of the neighborhood's drug problem, it was hoped that the crime rate attributed to the drug environment would decrease substantially. This operation required the support not only of the entire Dallas Police Department but also of the city's administration and a variety of other city agencies (Hatler 1990, 22–23). The CLEAN team was composed of several municipal departments with specific responsibilities.

Operation CLEAN demonstrated that police departments can work with other city departments to enhance the quality of life of residents living in drug-infested neighborhoods. Strategies like Operation CLEAN are excellent examples of programs that can be used to decrease crime in a specific geographical area. The cooperation, respect, and support of law-abiding citizens can be gained when police agencies implement strategies that assist in improving the quality of life of a neighborhood's residents.

Security Surveys

Security surveys are conducted to discover existing physical and procedural deficiencies and to recommend security devices, procedures, and methods that can either eliminate or reduce potential criminal opportunities. A good security survey allows the crime prevention specialist to inform apartment and housing residents and businesses about the tactics and strategies they can use to keep from becoming crime victims. Even if no major security problems are found, the crime prevention specialist may find ways to increase the security of the premises. Two types of security surveys can be conducted, business surveys and residence surveys. The National Crime Prevention Institute (1986) has developed security survey guidelines for business establishments and for residences.

Programs for the Elderly

In some communities, crime prevention specialists may have to develop and manage crime prevention strategies aimed specifically at the elderly. National studies have found that the elderly have a smaller chance of becoming victims of a crime than any other age group. However, when the elderly are victimized, they are more likely to be the victims of property crimes than any other age group.

Older citizens may become victims of crimes because of either their poor physical health or their isolation from family, friends, and acquaintances. Many elderly live in high-crime areas where they are statistically more likely to become victims of a crime. Despite some of these problems, the elderly can still be involved in crime prevention strategies. The crime prevention specialist can work with senior citizens to instruct them on how to deter crimes such as muggings and purse snatching. The crime prevention specialist has the responsibility to instruct the older citizens concerning the precautions they can observe when they take public transportation or walk in public, their personal safety at home, safety on the telephone, and how to protect money and valuables. The crime prevention specialist can give valuable advice on confidence games and consumer fraud, because senior citizens are frequently the victims of unscrupulous individuals and their scams.

Police departments that serve a substantial senior citizen population should initiate crime prevention strategies for the elderly. When senior citizens become aware of crime prevention techniques and strategies, they can make an excellent contribution to crime prevention.

Cellular Watch Programs

In 1994, the Metro-Dade Police Department in Florida initiated the Neighborhood Cellular Watch program in 11 county neighborhoods, according to a plan that won the acceptance of the police department and of the neighborhoods. The neighborhoods provided volunteers who were issued cellular telephones to report instantaneously any crime observed or any other behavior in their neighborhood that led to the deterioration of the "quality of life" in their neighborhood. Neighborhoods were selected on the basis of their cultural diversity, degree of crime problems, involvement in other community programs, and, most important, the willingness to participate in the program. Cellular One of Florida underwrote equipment and airtime for the cellular telephones. At the end of nine months, an evaluation by Florida International University's College of Urban and Public Affairs found that crime generally decreased substantially in most neighborhoods for such crime as burglaries, robberies, thefts, and auto thefts (Ellison 1995, 14).

The neighborhood that was most successful in reducing crime was in a high-crime area, an apartment complex. Crime decreased in three of the four categories, increasing only in auto theft. Cellular Watch may have contributed to a reduction of 69 burglaries, or 35 percent. Robbery decreased by 14 percent, and theft decreased by 17 percent. Auto theft increased by 57 percent (Ellison 1995, 21).

Generally, Cellular Watch volunteers believed that crime had decreased in their neighborhood. According to volunteers, the in-progress calls were responded to faster by the police. Also, the volunteers reported that because of their involvement in the Cellular Watch program, they were more willing to telephone the police about suspicious persons and other situations. The cellular telephones were considered to be beneficial because residents could have instant contact with the police. The cellular telephone had "taken Crime Watch out of the house and into the streets" (Ellison 1995, 16).

The use of cellular telephones for neighborhood improvement can only be as effective as the participants in the program. However, Cellular Watch programs can be another method of developing a police–neighborhood partnership in crime prevention.

Crime Prevention Electronic Bulletin Board

A computerized bulletin, like other bulletin boards, gives users the opportunity to post messages, but instead of using pins placed on a corkboard, it uses a computer, modem, and host system. The purpose of a crime prevention bulletin board is to provide information and keep users up to date on events occurring in the neighborhood and community. In addition, mail files can be transferred, and questions can be answered. One of the key uses of a crime prevention bulletin board is to provide updated crime information and to cover crime prevention concepts relevant to a specific crime. Because many young people are familiar with computers, the computer is an excellent way for the crime prevention specialist to reach young people. Crime prevention tips relevant to young people can be provided in cyberspace.

Defensible Space

The term defensible space can be traced back to a conference held in 1964 at Washington University in St. Louis, Missouri, where two sociologists and two architects, along with police officers from the St. Louis Police Academy, discussed physical features that produced security for public housing (Newman 1973a, 1). It was defined in terms of a range of security mechanisms, including "real and symbolic barriers, strongly defined areas of influence, and improved opportunities for surveillance" (Newman 1973b, 3).

According to Newman (1973b), who coined the term, defensible space is a model for residential environments, which inhibits crime by creating the physical expression of a social fabric that defends itself. All the different elements which combine to make a defensible space have a common goal—an environment in which latent territoriality and a sense of community in the inhabitants can be translated into responsibility for ensuring a safe, productive, and well-maintained living space (3).

For residents of public housing, defensible space is a milieu of security that includes areas other than residents' individual apartments, such as lobbies, hallways, playgrounds, and adjacent streets.

To a great extent, public housing in the late 1980s and 1990s, with grants from the Department of Housing and Urban Affairs, incorporated the four elements of defensible space. In a joint effort with their local police departments, residents of public housing reclaimed their territory—their living environment—from drug dealers, drug users, and other criminal offenders. Their ability to survey the area from their apartments helped them to identify the legitimate residents and distinguish them from law violators. Playgrounds were reclaimed so that children could again play on them. This led residents to have feelings that are more positive about their place of residence. Graffiti was removed from walls, and grass was planted where none had existed. Finally, in some projects, public housing sites were dispersed across safer, middle-class neighborhoods. Such environmental techniques for preventing crime have since been used for residential areas, commercial businesses, schools, and parking garages.

Crime Prevention Through Environmental Design

Like Oscar Newman, J. Ray Jefferies, the theorist who developed the concept of crime prevention through environmental design (CPTED), believed that crime prevention involved the physical design of buildings along with citizen involvement and the effective use of police agencies. According to Jefferies (1977), the physical environment of each building and each room in a building should be examined. Jefferies correctly claimed that usually only a small area of the city is responsible for the majority of crime, so that analysis of crime must scrutinize house-by-house or block-by-block variations in crime rates. He advocated that for the purpose of crime prevention, crime data should be used to determine in what areas of a community crime generally occurs.

The CPTED model suggests that the physical environment be orchestrated to prevent potential offenders from committing crimes as well as to improve the quality of life. It involves creating a physical environment in which people can be free from the fear of crime and in which individuals prone to criminal activity can be checked in this inclination by physical barriers. The CPTED model draws on not only architecture but also sociology, psychology, and law enforcement.

Timothy D. Crowe (1991), an authority on CPTED, outlined three overlapping strategies in CPTED: "natural access control, natural surveillance, and territorial reinforcement" (30). The purpose of access control is to reduce the opportunity to commit a crime. Methods used to control access to an area can include gates, guards, locks, and shrubbery. The aim of this strategy is to create an illusion that the risk of attempting a criminal act is greater than the opportunity. The purpose of natural surveillance is to maximize opportunities to observe outsiders or intruders into the neighborhood. When strangers are under surveillance, the risk of being caught while committing an offense increases. Strategies of surveillance include police and security guard patrol, lighting, and strategic placement of windows. The third strategy, territorial reinforcement, creates a sense of ownership or influence through better design of the physical environment. Potential offenders can recognize the residents' ownership or influence over a geographical area. Natural access control and natural surveillance also contribute to a feeling of territoriality (30–32).

CPTED, to be successful, must be practical and be understood. Residents, storeowners, school officials, and parking garage owners must visualize the benefits of CPTED before they will be able to implement it. Crowe (1991) advocated a "three D" approach to space assessment to be used as a guide for the nonprofessional. This approach is based on the three functions or dimensions of human space:

1. All human space has some designated purpose.
2. All human space has social, cultural, legal, or physical defini- tions that prescribe the desired and acceptable behaviors.
3. All human space is designed to support and control the desired behaviors.

(33)

Situational Crime Prevention

Situational crime prevention, like the earlier approaches developed by Newman and Jefferies, is about reducing opportunities for crime. It is

(1) directed at highly specific forms of crime [in ways] (2) that involve the management, design, or manipulation of the immed- iate environment in as systematic and permanent way as possible (3) so as to reduce the rewards as perceived by a wide range of offenders.

(Clark 1992, 4)

Techniques used in situational crime prevention can include a wide variety of crime prevention measures, such as burglary alarms, fenced yards, graffiti cleaning, street lighting, baggage screening, closed-circuit TV systems, identification cards, and credit card photographs.

Situational crime prevention holds that specific crime situations have unusual features that can be appraised and examined for solutions. The focus is on finding solutions to specific problems (Brantingham and Brantingham 1990, 25). Crime analysis is the first step in this process. The following questions are asked: "What are the detailed characteristics of the problem? Who might be committing the offenses or causing the difficulty and why? What elements in the socio-physical background environment could be contributing, in an immediate way, to the observed crime pattern?" (Brantingham and Brantingham 1990, 26).

One retail company that employs many of the 12 situational crime prevention techniques is L.L. Bean, a nationally known retail outlet. Shoplifters who have obtained merchandise by theft frequently attempt to obtain cash refunds without ever leaving the store. L.L. Bean has a special coding system to detect this scam. An extensive CCTV monitoring system is in place in the outlet store that allows cameras to zoom in anywhere in the store and parking lot. This system can produce instant photographs from an image on a video screen. It allows store detectives to have photos of a shoplifter within minutes so that a store detective can make an apprehension. Also, to keep internal thefts at a low rate, L.L. Bean offers its employees anywhere from 50 to 90 percent off its merchandise. The idea behind such a liberal reduction policy is the belief that it would be foolish for employees to steal merchandise when they can get it for almost nothing. It appears that this policy has worked: L.L. Bean does not have an internal theft problem (Hoffmann 1994, 94–96).

Another organization that has employed situational crime prevention is the Downers Grove, Illinois Police Department. The department determined that the best strategy to prevent residential burglaries was to offer homeowners a home security survey conducted by a crime prevention specialist. The police department was able to have included in the water bill to residents a notification that a free home security survey was available from a crime prevention specialist. Then the police department initiated a telemarketing approach to reach residents who had not volunteered for the survey. The survey, which took approximately one hour, allowed the crime prevention specialist to evaluate home security risks, such as exterior lighting, locks, doors, windows, and landscaping, and to give the homeowner advice that would make his or her property and possessions less vulnerable to burglars. The home security survey was inexpensive and required no special equipment (Rechenmacker 1991, 8–9).

One problematic aspect of situational crime prevention is that crime may merely be displaced to an adjacent geographical area. When opportunities to commit crime are blocked in one area, criminals may simply shift their activity to another area. However, some studies of situational crime prevention have found no resulting displacement effect to nearby areas (see the section below, "Seattle's Community Crime Prevention Program").

Specific Community Crime Prevention Programs

Seattle's Community Crime Prevention Program

In 1972, the City of Seattle's Law and Justice Planning Office initiated a crime prevention program with a project to identify which crimes the program would do best to target. Three variables were taken into consideration:

1. Frequency of occurrence. Data were taken from Seattle Police Department's reports of crime incidents.
2. Severity and level of public fear and tolerance. This element was added to allow the rating plan to weigh an aggravated assault more heavily than a shoplifting incident. Data were collected through interviews with city residents.
3. Potential for crime reduction. Priority crimes must also be amenable to prevention strategies. For example, homicide is not a priority crime. Although it scores high on other measures, research indicated that the bulk of homicides occurred between acquaintances and that the crime is not particularly amenable to reduction strategies.

(Lindsay and McGillis 1986, 47)

Priority was given to burglary, rape, and robbery as serious crimes that have the greatest opportunity of being prevented.

This section will discuss only the burglary prevention program. The program selected the area with the highest burglary rate and overall crime rate. Civic organizations and church organizations were invited to assist in the project. The staff developed a community profile that included demographic data and crime information about the residents. The first contact with citizens was by mail and the second by canvassing the neighborhood. The prevention program included block watch organizing, property identification, and security inspections. Forty percent of the area's residents ended up participating.

The block watch was the most important aspect of the burglary prevention program. A block watch consisted of a group of approximately 10–15 neighbors who would keep a watch on their neighbors' homes to prevent burglaries. Each block watch was provided with an engraving instrument to mark property. Members of the block watch were given window decals to warn intruders that property on the premises was marked. Finally, each block watch home was inspected for burglary vulnerability.

Seattle's community crime prevention program benefited from a single focus—residential burglary. An evaluation of the burglary prevention program reveals that those involved had a lower burglary rate than those not involved in the program. Although not conclusive, the evaluation of adjacent areas indicated that displacement, or the transfer of crime to adjacent neighborhoods, did not occur.

Marketing Crime Prevention

The crime prevention specialist and/or community-policing officer have to know and understand the community—its socioeconomical makeup, its crime problems, and its needs. Do robberies, burglaries, and other serious crimes occur there? Does the community have a domestic violence problem, a child abuse problem, or a drug problem? Once this information is obtained, crime prevention programs can be developed that meet the community's needs.

As any knowledgeable police officer knows, the police cannot succeed in solving or preventing crime without the community's assistance. Crime prevention programs have to involve the community and deal with community-identified problems to be effective. When crime prevention programs are successful, they usually have the full support and participation of the community. The crime prevention specialist must sell prevention programs to the police department and to the citizens of the community. The police prevention specialist must work to overcome any resistance to crime prevention programs by educating the community on how the program works. The crime prevention specialist is an extremely important link between the police and the community.

The success or failure of mass media campaigns rests with the willingness of mass media programmers to disseminate crime prevention announcements and of local police officials to support crime prevention efforts. Findings indicate that both police officials and media programmers support crime prevention media campaigns (O'Keefe et al. 1996, 58).

At the local level, crime newsletters can provide specific crime information targeted for certain neighborhoods. A newsletter can supply detailed news about crime problems and offer measures that people can take to avoid becoming victims. The crime newsletter can include the classes of crime committed, where the offenses were committed, and descriptions of offenders if available. Another use of media has been the Crime Stoppers program, which has already been discussed in this chapter. In this program, the media inform the general public about a specific crime, and persons who have knowledge of the crime are encouraged to phone in information on the individual or individuals who may have committed the offense. The caller can remain anonymous and can receive a reward if an offender is arrested.

In the 1990s, television shows re-creating a crime have been successful in apprehending fugitives. We are familiar with many of these shows, including *America's Most Wanted* and *Unsolved Mysteries*. At the local level, the sheriff of Sedgwick County/Wichita, Kansas, announces on cable television his "Ten Most Wanted" list. A picture of the wanted person along with a physical description is provided to the viewing audience. The Wichita Police Department on cable television announces the names of individuals having warrants for their arrest. The local cable network of Sedgwick County/Wichita also places on television the names and ages of those offenders convicted of drunk driving.

As we can see, the news media, though they cannot be expected to provide all the information needed by citizens to keep from becoming a crime victim, can play an influential role in crime prevention strategies.

Summary

One of the key objectives for the police when Sir Robert Peel implemented the Metropolitan London Police in 1829 was crime prevention. But police researchers have found that many of the strategies incorporated into policing are not necessarily effective in preventing crime. Reactive strategies, such as the use of 911 by citizens to call the police after a crime has been committed, do not prevent crime and must be supplemented by proactive strategies. All police officers should be knowledgeable about crime prevention techniques. Especially in those departments adopting the community-policing philosophy, an understanding of crime prevention is essential.

There are many views about how the responsibility for crime prevention should be distributed. The approach most consonant with community policing is that the police, neighborhoods, and individuals share this responsibility. Obviously, the police have an obligation to concentrate on crime prevention, but they cannot do it alone; they need the cooperation of the neighborhood and its citizens. Crime prevention cannot be successful unless it involves the participation of all formal and informal structures and the willingness of all neighborhood residents to learn about how to avoid becoming victims of crime.

No other component of the criminal justice system has the vantage point that the police possess in working with the community. The police are the first to know if a crime has been committed. They have to investigate crimes, solve crimes, arrest criminal offenders, and recover stolen property. By the nature of their positions, they also know how offenders commit crime—knowledge that can be used to prevent crime from occurring.

Crime prevention and community policing are closely related. A number of police agencies have integrated their crime prevention efforts into community policing. Crime prevention specialists can give the community information on techniques and strategies to reduce and prevent crime. Both physical and social aspects of the neighborhood must be addressed by crime prevention.

Successful crime prevention strategies and programs involve police–community cooperation. The police crime prevention specialist or community-policing officer works with the community to develop and implement crime prevention programs. The crime prevention specialist has to be involved in security surveys, crime analysis, neighborhood watches, operational identification, and a multitude of other crime prevention strategies.

Situational crime prevention refers to reducing opportunities for crime. It can employ a wide variety of crime prevention measures, including burglar alarms, fenced yards, graffiti cleaning, street lighting, baggage screening, closed-circuit TV systems, identification cards, and credit card photographs. Situational crime prevention focuses on specific crime situations in order to come up with specific solutions for them.

The police can neither solve nor prevent crime without the assistance of the community. Even when crime has been reduced, crime prevention participation by citizens needs to continue if crime is not to take an upward turn.

KEY TERMS

- Beep-a-Beat Program (BBP)
- Business Watch
- Cellular Watch
- citizen patrols
- computer-aided dispatch (CAD)
- computerized mapping
- crime analysis
- Crime Stoppers
- defensible space
- direct control of crime
- electronic bulletin board
- indirect control of crime
- Neighborhood Watch
- Operation CLEAN
- operation identification
- police station automatic teller machines
- security surveys

REVIEW QUESTIONS

1. Explain the meaning of crime prevention.
2. Explain the police role in crime prevention.
3. Explain how crime prevention and community policing are interrelated.
4. Describe some crime prevention strategies.
5. Explain what is meant by situational crime prevention.
6. Explain what is meant by community crime prevention.
7. Describe how the media have been used in crime prevention.

8

PROBLEM-ORIENTED POLICING

CHAPTER OBJECTIVES

1. Be familiar with the concepts of problem-oriented policing and the aspects of traditional policing that it was reacting against.

2. Be familiar with SARA.

3. Be familiar with the value of problem-oriented policing for community policing.

4. Be familiar with the various aspects of implementing problem-oriented policing.

Introduction

Problem-oriented policing is an approach to policing that encourages all members of a police agency to engage in proactive problem solving (Eck and Spelman 1988, 5). For all practical purposes, the philosophy of community policing has as its foundation the problem-oriented police design. The primary idea behind problem-oriented policing is police accountability to the community and a focus on addressing community concerns. Community-oriented policing draws on this idea but takes it even further by emphasizing full community participation in the problem-solving process.

Background of Problem-Oriented Policing

Problem-oriented policing first emerged in the late 1970s out of dissatisfaction with policing under the professional (traditional) model.

It can best be understood by examining critiques of traditional policing by the first problem-oriented theorists.

The professional model of policing, as described in detail in Chapter 1, was characterized by a centralized police structure, top-down transmission of orders, a mission of crime fighting, a code of secrecy, adherence to written policies and procedures, close supervision over patrol officers, and separation of the police from citizens. In many police departments, patrol officers would be assigned a different beat each day or night they worked so that they would not become too familiar with the residents and business owners of a particular beat and possibly be corrupted by local influences. This approach placed a heavy emphasis on new operating technologies, such as "(1) patrol forces equipped with cars and radios to create an impression of omnipresence and to respond to incidents of crime and (2) investigative units trained in sophisticated methods of criminal investigation, such as automated fingerprint identification and the use of criminal histories," as means of solving and preventing crime (Moore and Trojanowicz 1988, 5).

In 1979, Herman Goldstein laid the groundwork for the concept of problem-oriented policing. He claimed that attempts to improve policing had for decades been focusing primarily on administrative improvements, such as recruiting better personnel, modernizing equipment, and incorporating business practices into police operations. These improvements were necessary: police departments in the earlier decades of this century were often disorganized, poorly trained, and inefficient (238–239). But under the professional model, the means of efficiency and routinized procedures had become ends in themselves, and police agencies had lost sight of the effectiveness of organizational improvements in reducing crime and meeting community needs. Police were devoting most of their resources to responding to calls from citizens, reserving too small a percentage of their time and energy for acting on their own initiative to prevent or reduce community problems. Further, they were failing to draw on the resources of the community, which had "an enormous potential, largely untapped, for reducing the number and magnitude of problems that otherwise become the business of the police" (Goldstein 1990, 15). And within the agencies themselves, they were ignoring "another huge resource: their rank-and-file officers, whose time and talent [had] not been used effectively" (Goldstein 1990, 15).

In 1988, Eck and Spelman offered a similar critique of professional-model policing that focused on its reactive approach to problems. In that approach, the job of the police was simply to respond to service calls. A citizen would call the police dispatcher, and an officer on patrol would be sent to address the citizen's complaint. When officers were not busy answering calls, they were expected to do random preventive patrol, but they could not leave their beat without authorization from a supervisor, and they were not expected to take initiative to solve problems of crime or public disorder. Thus, patrol officers were slaves to 911. The professional model of policing is so ingrained in police culture that many police officers and citizens are still convinced that answering calls is the most important aspect of police work. Citizens also may expect the police to respond to every call for police service, and police departments respond to these expectations. But, as discussed earlier, there is no need for the police to respond to every call: many calls can be handled over the telephone, or the citizen can be encouraged to come to the police station to make a complaint.

Eck and Spelman coined the term incident-driven policing to describe the traditional reactive approach of police patrols. They asserted that incident-driven policing had four characteristics: First, it is reactive. Incidents that have already occurred control the workloads of patrol officers and detectives. Most of these incidents are reported by citizens, though some are first detected by the police. There are some exceptions; the work of vice officers and crime prevention officers, for example, is usually proactive. However, these exceptions make up a small portion of police work. Second, patrol officers and detectives gather information primarily from victims, witnesses, and suspects. The goal of information gathering is to resolve the incident, sometimes by leading to the identification and arrest of suspects. Third, the threat of enforcing laws by invoking the legal system is the primary tool of incident-driven policing. Although people call the police to resolve a wide variety of difficulties, the responding officer's primary authority rests with the criminal law. If a solution to the difficulty is found, it is often because the presence of the officer is an explicit threat that the criminal law can be applied. Although efforts have been made to give officers non-criminal law alternatives for resolving certain types of disputes, the criminal law remains their single most important tool. Finally, the performance of incident-driven police agencies is gauged primarily by aggregate statistics, which group a variety of incidents over wide geographic areas. These performance measures include the FBI Index Crimes, clearance rates, arrest rates, drunken driving arrests, and many other sets of numbers (2).

According to Eck and Spelman, incident-driven policing had several undesirable consequences. Generally, the calls that patrol officers responded to took up a great deal of time with few results. Thus, they caused frustration on the part of patrol officers, who often handled the same calls repeatedly without noticing any progress. In addition, the public would become frustrated because they did not see any changes, even though officers had answered the same call on numerous occasions. Incident-driven policing had very limited objectives, and it could only have limited results if police agencies were not involved in problem solving (2).

The Problem-Oriented Approach

The new problem-oriented approach set forth by both Goldstein (1979, 1990) and Eck and Spelman (1988) was an attempt to go beyond the limitations of the professional model by focusing on the ends of policing rather than the means; encouraging police initiative in addressing community problems; attempting to solve persistent problems by analyzing their causes; assessing the appropriateness of current strategies; developing new solutions and monitoring their effectiveness; and engaging community resources and input. Goldstein (1990) has described problem-oriented policing as resting on the following assumptions:

- Policing consists of dealing with a wide range of quite different problems, not just crime.
- These problems are interrelated, and the priority given them must be reassessed rather than ranked in traditional ways.
- Each problem requires a different response, not a generic response that is applied equally to all problems.
- Use of the criminal law is but one means of responding to a problem; it is not the only means.
- Police can accomplish much in working to prevent problems rather than simply responding efficiently to an endless number of incidents that are merely the manifestations of problems.

- Developing an effective response to a problem requires prior analysis rather than simply invoking traditional practices.
- The capacity of the police is extremely limited, despite the impression of omnipotence that the police cultivate and others believe.
- The police role is more akin to that of facilitators, enabling and encouraging the community to maintain its norm governing behavior, rather than the agency that assumes total responsibility for doing so.

(179)

Exhibit 8–1 lists Eck and Spelman's guidelines for what a problem-oriented policing agency should do. According to Eck and Spelman (1988), a problem can be solved in five ways:

1. A problem can be solved by totally eliminating it. In this case, effectiveness is measured by the absence of the type of incidents that this problem creates. It is unlikely that most problems can be totally eliminated, but a few can.
2. A problem can be solved by reducing the number of incidents it creates. A reduction of incidents stemming from the problem is a major measure of effectiveness.
3. A problem can be solved by reducing the seriousness of the incidents it creates. Effectiveness of this type of solution is demonstrated by showing that the incidents are less harmful.
4. A problem can be solved by designing methods for better handling the incidents (treating participants more humanely, reducing costs, or increasing the effectiveness of incident handling). Improved victim satisfaction, reduced costs, and other measures can show that this type of solution is effective.
5. A problem can be solved by removing it from police consideration. The effectiveness of this type of solution can be measured by looking at why the police were handling the problem originally and the rationale for shifting the handling to others.

(6)

EXHIBIT 8-1: WHAT A PROBLEM-ORIENTED POLICING AGENCY SHOULD DO

1. Focus on problems of concern to the public.

2. Zero in on effectiveness as the primary concern.

3. Be proactive.

4. Be committed to systematic inquiry as the first step in solving substantial problems.

5. Encourage use of rigorous methods in making inquiries.

6. Make full use of the data in police files and the experience of police personnel.

7. Group like incidents together so that they can be addressed as a common problem.

8. Avoid using overly broad labels in groupings.

9. Encourage a broad and uninhibited search for solutions.

10. Acknowledge the limits of the criminal justice system as a response to problems.

11. Identify multiple interests in any one problem and weigh them when analyzing the value of the different responses.

12. Be committed to taking some risks in responding to problems.

Source: Reprinted from J.E. Eck and W. Spelman, *Problem-Solving: Problem-Oriented Policing in Newport News*, p. 3, 1988, United States Department of Justice.

Obviously, problem solving involves input and cooperation from various individuals, groups, organizations, and agencies. Eck and Spelman (1988) list five principles that should guide the development of a problem-solving process (Exhibit 8–2).

The SARA Model

Eck and Spelman (1988) have outlined a problem-solving process for police agencies that they call the SARA model. Before problem solving can be initiated, the problem or problems have to be defined. This process, which the authors tested in Newport News, Virginia, has been recommended ever since as the process to be used for solving problems in a problem-oriented policing agency. The acronym SARA refers to four stages of problem solving:

EXHIBIT 8-2: A GUIDE TO THE DEVELOPMENT OF THE PROBLEM-SOLVING PROCESS

1. The final process must involve all department members—all ranks and units, all sworn officers, and nonsworn department members—in the identification, study, and resolution of the problems.

2. The final process must foster the use of a wide variety of data sources—from internal records and officers' knowledge to other government agencies and private individuals and organizations—to understand the causes and consequences of the problem.

3. The final process must encourage police departments to work with members of other public and private agencies to obtain diverse, effective, and long-lasting solutions to problems.

4. The final process must be capable of becoming an integral part of police decision making, without creating special units or requiring resources.

5. The final process must be capable of being applied to other law enforcement agencies.

Source: Reprinted from J.E. Eck and W. Spelman, *Problem-Solving: Problem-Oriented Policing in Newport News*, p. 6, 1988, United States Department of Justice.

---

1. Scanning—identifying the problem.
2. Analysis—learning the problem's causes, scope, and effects.
3. Response—acting to alleviate the problem.
4. Assessment—determining whether the response worked.

(43)

Scanning

The problem-solving process begins with scanning, or identifying a problem. A problem can be defined as "a group of incidents occurring in a community, that are similar in one or more ways, and that are of concern to the police and the public" (Eck and Spelman 1988, 42). The Savannah (Georgia) Police Department (1994) requires that a problem have four attributes before it will be considered for problem-oriented policing:

1. The problem must involve a group of incidents.
2. The problem must involve two or more issues similar in nature.

3. The problem is causing harm or has the potential to cause harm.

4. The public expects the police agency to handle the problem.

(5–6)

Herman Goldstein (1990) listed four characteristics that the police commonly use to cluster incidents and thereby identify a problem:

1. Behavior. Behavior is probably the most frequently used organizing theme for clustering incidents, especially when the focus is on a citywide problem: e.g., noise, theft of vehicles, sale of drugs, sexual assault, drinking drivers, spousal abuse, and runaways.

2. Territory. A collection of different behavioral problems, concentrated in a given area, will typically result in the problems being identified by the place name of the area: e.g., Crown Heights neighborhood, Bryant Park, the intersection of Main Street and 2nd Avenue, Garden Village Apartments, Joe's Tavern, the residence at 2458 23rd Street. The problem at the intersection may involve merchants and pedestrians who are bothered by alcoholics, panhandlers, prostitutes, or individuals who are mentally ill and/or homeless. The most frequent problem identified in territorial terms is the low-income housing project, for the obvious reason that it is a convenient, umbrella like way of describing collectively the wide range of interrelated behavioral problems (burglary, theft, vandalism, arson, truancy, child neglect, assault, liquor violations, drug use, and sale) commonly found in such housing complexes. . . .

3. Persons. A problem may be identified in terms of offenders, complainants, or victims (e.g., the elderly); in terms of a large class of people (e.g., shoppers), a group (e.g., a gang), a family, or an individual (e.g., an identified repeat offender or a person who persistently harasses a neighborhood); or in terms of a condition that distinguishes the individuals, as would be true in describing a problem as the alcoholics, the homeless, the mentally ill, or the developmentally disabled.

4. Time. Both the public and the police tend to define some regularly recurring, predictable problems primarily in terms of an event or by the season, the day of the week, or the hour of the day in which they most often occur: e.g., an annual rock concert, Halloween party, or ethnic festival (any one of which may involve a subset of problems such as assaults, injuries, traffic congestion, sexual harassment, excessive consumption of alcohol or drugs, or potential racist conflict); thefts from parking areas in shopping malls prior to Christmas; burglaries in student housing when unattended in vacation periods; or drunk driving in the period immediately after the closing of bars on weekends.

(67–68)

The problem should be described by everyone who is affected by it. The various viewpoints should be reviewed so that the problem description can be as complete as possible, and a collective (community) description should be developed.

Analysis

The next step is analyzing the problem. Data and information should be collected from a variety of sources other than just police records. An analysis asks the questions of who, what, how, when, where, and why. It identifies the people involved: the offenders, the victims, and the parties that should respond. It defines the scope of the problem and pinpoints when and in what locations the problem occurs. It attempts to trace the sequence of events that produces the problem and to identify factors that might precipitate or contribute to the problem: location, individual, and group interests, agency and government policies and procedures. Finally, it examines the current community and institutional responses to the problem and the effects of those responses (Savannah Police Department 1994, 5–7).

Exhibit 8–3 provides a list of questions that can be used as a tool for the scanning and analysis phases of the problem-solving process.

EXHIBIT 8-3: SCANNING AND ANALYSIS CHECKLIST

The following questions will guide you through the scanning and analysis phase of the problem-solving process.

Scanning

- What actions or events constitute the problem?

- Has the problem been described by all affected persons or groups?

- Has the problem been scrutinized for unforeseen elements?

- Has the problem been identified by more than one person or group? How do others describe the problem?

- Does your description contain all the observed elements or components?

- After you have reviewed the problem from a variety of viewpoints, what are the common elements that can be used to develop a collective (community) description of the problem?

Analysis

- Who are the people involved or affected by the problem? Who are the victims? Who are the offenders? Who should respond to the problem?

- To what groups do the persons involved in the problem belong? What are the likely motivations of the action (committing crime, destroying property)? What activities of others contribute to the victims' vulnerability?

- What is the scope of the problem? How large a problem is it?

- Why did the problem develop? How did the problem develop? What is the sequence of events that produced the problem?

- When and where does the problem occur? What is the physical setting in which the problem is taking place? Does the location contribute to the problem?

- What underlying conditions precipitate the problem? Have you examined the problem's causal relationship to agency or government policies, procedures, and practices? What is the current community and governmental response to the problem? How do persons and agencies react to the actions or problems? What have they done about the problem? What results have they had?

- Has all available information or data on the problem been collected and analyzed?

Source: Reprinted from Savannah Police Department Community Policing and Problem Solving Workshop, Participants' Handbook, pp. 5–8, 1994, United States Department of Justice.

Response

The third step in the problem-solving process is responding to the problem. The Savannah Police Department (1994) defined a problem response as "an action taken that directly and appropriately addresses the issue, event, or condition in question. The response takes into consideration resources, external support, and planning requirements. It seeks to eliminate the problem or reduce it to manageable size" (5–8). The first step in responding is conceiving the response. This requires the cooperative labor of all those affected by the problem. Eck and Spelman (1988) emphasized that "it is extremely important that those who participated in the scanning and analysis of the problem be key collaborators in designing an appropriate response. After all, they know, in critical detail, the element, and causes of the problem" (5–9). Community meetings should be held that give the residents or business owners the opportunity to provide input on what they think will work to solve the problem. The goal of this effort should be to develop a workable consensus about a solution.

Several factors should be considered when responding to a problem:

- the potential that the response has to reduce the problem
- the specific impact that the response will have on the most serious aspect of the problem (or those social interests deemed most important)
- the extent to which the response is preventive in nature, thereby reducing recurrence or more acute consequences that are more difficult to handle
- the degree to which the response intrudes into the lives of individuals and depends on legal sanctions and the potential use of force
- the attitude of the different communities most likely to be affected by adoption
- the financial costs
- the availability of police authority and resources
- the legality and civility of the response and the way in which it is likely to affect overall relationships with the police
- the ease with which the response can be implemented

(Goldstein 1990, 143)

Response planning, or action planning, takes place following the conception of the response. This involves developing procedures for putting into place the precise response to solve the problem. It includes drafting goals and objectives and listing the steps needed to accomplish them. It also involves determining how the effectiveness of the plan will be measured so that assessment data can be collected on an ongoing basis.

Next, the plan will be implemented. Implementations of plans require flexibility.

The checklist in Exhibit 8–4 can be a useful tool for completing the response stage of the problem-solving process.

Assessment

The final stage in the problem-solving process is assessing the results and the effectiveness of the plan placed into action, identifying potential improvements, and revising the plan as necessary. According to Goldstein (1990), evaluating the police response to problems requires:

- a clear understanding of the problem
- agreement over the specific interest(s) to be served in dealing with the problem and their order of importance
- agreement on the method to be used to determine the extent to which these interests (or goals) are reached
- a realistic assessment of what might be expected of the police (e.g., solving the problem versus improving the quality of the police management of it)
- determination of the relative importance of short-term versus long-term impact
- a clear understanding of the legality and fairness of the response (recognizing that reducing a problem through improper use of authority is not only wrong, but likely to be reproductive because of its effects on other aspects of police operation)

(145–146)

The assessment stage involves process evaluation, impact evaluation, and new problem assessment. The process evaluation examines how the response was implemented and whether it was carried out as planned. Also, it looks at how people and policies functioned in carrying out the

EXHIBIT 8-4: RESPONSE CHECKLIST

The following questions will guide you through the response phase of the problem-solving process.

- Involve the persons involved in or affected by the problem (including residents) in a brainstorming session to identify potential responses.

- Has the response been tried before? What were the results?

- What action does the response include? What agencies need to be involved? Are representatives from those agencies present to discuss feasibility of action?

- What other resources are available for the response?

- What is the time frame for implementing the response?

- What barriers exist to implementing the response?

- What results can the stakeholders realistically expect?

- Using the collective description and the analysis of the problems and response (done above), obtain consensus on a response to be implemented.

- Set an action plan for implementing the response.

- Set response goals and objectives.

- Identify the action steps necessary to implement the response.

- Identify key stakeholders involved in or affected by each step.

- Assign individual responsibilities for carrying out each action step.

- Determine how the impact of the plan will be measured:

- What will be measured and how? (e.g., problem: eliminate graffiti on school and recreational center buildings. Will you measure the number of artists arrested for vandalism or the amount of new graffiti that has appeared?)

- What will the time period for assessment be? How long should the response remain operational to give it a fair opportunity to show success or failure?

- How will you collect data? Will you use a citizen survey, examine police statistics, etc.?

- How will you analyze data?

Source: Reprinted from Savannah Police Department Community Policing and Problem Solving Workshop, Participants' Handbook, pp. 5–11, 1994, United States Department of Justice.

plan. The next element, the impact evaluation, examines how effective the response to the problem was in obtaining the intended results. The last element of assessment, new problem assessment, should be viewed as an ongoing part of problem solving. The purpose of new problem assessment is to determine if the problem has changed or even if it has created a new problem. The checklist in Exhibit 8–5 can be a useful tool for evaluating the process and impact of a problem-solving response.

EXHIBIT 8-5: ASSESSMENT CHECKLIST

The following questions will guide you through the assessment phase of the problem-solving process.

Assessment: Process Evaluation

- Was the response implemented as intended? What problems were encountered, and how were they overcome?

- What specific action steps were implemented? Were all action steps implemented? Were steps implemented according to the timetable?

- Did these action steps lead to the attainment of specific objectives? Were objectives revised? Were any objectives added?

- To what extent were successes or failures a result of factors other than the response?

- What was the level of cooperation and participation among team members? Were the lines of communication between individuals and groups adequate?

- What changes in policies, procedures, or practices occurred or should have occurred during the implementation?

Assessment: Impact Evaluation

- Were the overall goals of the plan achieved?

- What were the expected results of the response?

- Were there any unintended effects?

- Was the response cost-effective?

- Did the response make a substantial difference?

- Will you replicate the response in other areas with the same problem?

Source: Reprinted from Savannah Police Department Community Policing and Problem Solving Workshop, Participants' Handbook, pp. 5–14, 1994, United States Department of Justice.

Implementation of Problem-Oriented Policing

Successful implementation of problem-oriented policing requires the complete support of the head of the police organization—not just verbal support but also full comprehension and action. Every member of the police organization, regardless of his or her rank or specific job assignment, should be trained in the problem-oriented policing concept. Performance evaluations of officers must be thoroughly revised. Numbers of arrests, traffic citations, and parking citations can no longer be the main criteria for determining whether an officer has been doing a good job. "Bean counting" must be replaced by evaluation of the officer's problem-solving role. If supervisors and managers claim to support problem-oriented policing but continue their traditional performance evaluation methods, police officers will continue to rack up high arrests and traffic citations at the expense of a problem-solving strategy in order to meet evaluators' expectations.

A study of the implementation of problem-oriented policing in the Newport News, Virginia Police Department (Eck and Spelman 1988) discussed two sets of concerns, internal and external, that must be addressed in the implementation process. Internal concerns include leading, directing, supervision, decision making, cooperation, coordination, and communications within the police department, as well as the police role in the community and police administrative and operational procedures. External concerns include obtaining the support of local government agencies, private businesses and organizations, churches, and schools and universities so that they can assist the police in problem solving. See the problem analysis model in Exhibit 8–6.

As Goldstein (1990) and Vaughn (1992) have pointed out, problem-oriented policing requires major organizational changes in police agencies. For example, police administrators, instead of micromanaging their line officers, must trust them to make decisions pertaining to a problem in their sector. They must also give officers time to solve problems and arrange for crime analysis units to give officers the necessary information on trends and patterns of community problems. Further, the police must become more open to public input and criticism. For example, if a citizen calls the police chief to ask why the officer assigned to his neighborhood is being transferred, the chief, instead of getting angry and saying that it is his department and he does not want any citizen telling him

EXHIBIT 8-6: THE PROBLEM ANALYSIS MODEL

Actors	Incidents	Responses
• Victims	• Sequence of events	• Community
– Lifestyle	– Events preceding	– Neighborhood
– Security measures	act	affected by
taken	– Event itself	problem
– Victimization history	– Events following	– City as a whole
	criminal acts	
• Offenders		• People outside the
– Identity and physical	• Physical	institution
description	– Time	– Criminal justice
– Lifestyle, education,	– Location	agencies
employment history	– Access control and	– Other public
– Criminal history	surveillance	agencies
• Third parties	• Social context	• Mass media
– Personal data	– Likelihood and	– Business sector
– Connection to	probable action of	
victimization	witnesses	
	– Apparent attitude of	
	residents toward	
	neighborhood	

Source: Reprinted from W. Spelman and J. Eck, *Newport News Tests Problem-Oriented Policing*, p. 5, 1987, National Institute of Justice.

how to run it, should be pleased that the citizen supports problem-oriented policing.

Resistance to Problem-Oriented Policing

Although Goldstein and Eck and Spelman have made many valid arguments for the implementation of problem-oriented policing and the abandonment of the professional model of policing, the professional model still has many supporters today. Some police administrators consider problem-oriented policing, along with community-oriented policing, to be merely the latest buzzword or fad that will not survive the long haul. Others believe that they support new approaches to policing such as problem-oriented policing, but their actions indicate otherwise. Their management style is rigid, and they emphasize "bean counting" over problem solving. Often, these administrators believe that a rigidly managed police department will present a positive image of the police to the community. Other factors as well have contributed to resistance to problem-oriented policing and the persistence of a focus on means over ends:

- The diverse, poorly defined, and sometimes overwhelming character of the police job makes it difficult to establish what, precisely, is the end product of policing [i.e., the type of service that the public should receive]. Appeals to focus on the end product therefore understandably meet with some confusion and apprehension.
- Police are commonly viewed as palliators—as being concerned primarily with meeting immediate, emergency needs. It follows that greater rewards are attached to alleviating problems than to solving or curing them.
- Many of the problems that police deal with are unsolvable. This is the very reason they come to the attention of the police. The potential for doing anything about an age-old problem like prostitution or shoplifting is limited. Improving a communications system or establishing a new operating procedure, in contrast, is much more satisfying. Nonsubstantive matters are more self-contained within the agency, and the police are therefore less dependent on outside forces for their success in dealing with them.
- The constraints under which police operate in a democracy make police reluctant to take the initiative in addressing problems. Many officers view their function as simply doing what is formally required of them, even if it is widely recognized that this may be ineffective.

(Goldstein 1990, 16–17)

Factors Encouraging a Shift to Problem-Oriented Policing

Goldstein argued in 1979 that various new trends would end up forcing the police to reexamine their philosophy of policing:

1. The Financial Crisis. The growing cost of police services and the financial plight of most city governments, . . . are making

municipal officials increasingly reluctant to appropriate still more money for police service without greater assurance that their investment will have an impact on the problems that the police are expected to handle. . . .

2. Research Findings. Recently completed research questions the value of two major aspects of police operations—preventive patrol and investigations conducted by detectives. Some police administrators have challenged the findings; others are awaiting the results of the application. But those who concur with the results have begun to search for alternatives, aware of the need to measure the effectiveness of a new response before making a substantial investment in it.

3. Growth of a Consumer Orientation. Policing has not yet felt the full impact of consumer advocacy. As citizens press for improvements in police service, improvements will increasingly be measured in terms of results. Those concerned about battered wives, for example, could not care less whether the police who respond to such calls operate with one or two officers in a car, whether the officers are short or tall, or whether they have a college education. Their attention is on what the police do for the battered wife.

4. Questioning the Effectiveness of the Best-Managed Agencies. A number of police departments have carried out most, if not all, of the numerous recommendations for strengthening a police organization, and enjoy a national reputation for their efficiency, their high standards of personnel selection and training, and their application of modem technology to their operations. Nevertheless, their communities apparently continue to have the same problems as do others with fewer advanced agencies.

5. Increased Resistance to Organizational Change. Intended improvements that are primarily in the form of organizational change, such as team policing, almost invariably run into resistance from rank-and-file personnel. Stronger and more militant unions have engaged some police administrators in bitter and prolonged fights over such changes. Because the costs in terms of disruption and discontent are so great, police admin-

istrators initiating change will be under increasing pressure to demonstrate in advance that the results of their efforts will make the struggle worthwhile.

(239–241)

All of these developments are still affecting policing today. First, although police agencies today may not be in a financial crisis, public officials are increasingly holding police agencies accountable and are requiring that programs be effective in meeting their stated goals. Second, since the 1970s, when police research first received initiatives from governmental grants, research has increased substantially, and much of it is challenging the effectiveness of traditional practices. Third, consumer advocacy today is stronger than ever, as shown by the victims' rights movement and initiatives to change how police handle spousal abuse and child abuse cases. Fourth, massive infusions of money and effort into managerial and technological improvements have made it even clearer that these improvements will not, in themselves, solve community problems. Finally, endless organizational changes without results other than disruption have made both managers and line officers skeptical about changes and made it more necessary for initiators of change to enlist broad support and focus on practical projects that are likely to be successful.

Problem Analysis in Policing

Herman Goldstein, the father of problem-oriented policing, had the following to say: "The problem-oriented approach calls for developing— preferably within the police agency—the skills, procedures, and research techniques to analyze problems and evaluate the police effectiveness as an integral continuing part of management" (Goldstein 1990, 49). Goldstein indicates that an in-depth analysis of a specific problem and factors that contributed to the problem must be evaluated. He states:

Analysis requires the acquisition of detailed information about defenders, victims, and others who may be involved in a problem, the time of occurrence, location, details about the physical environment, the motivations, gains and losses of all involved parties, and the results of current responses.

(Goldstein 1990, 36–37)

What has been previously been discussed by Goldstein has become known as problem analysis. Problem analysis can be defined as:

An approach/method/process conducted within the police agency in which formal criminal justice theory, research methods, and comprehensive data collection and analysis procedures are used in a systematic way to conduct in-depth examination of, develop informed responses to, and evaluate crime and disorder problems.
(Boba 2003, 2)

Problem analysis differs from problem solving which occurs on the beat level. Officers involved in beat-level problem solving attempt to identify and resolve minor problems. Problem analysis takes a general approach to investigate, respond to, and assess the impact of responses to problems. Problem solving at the beat level usually involves incident-driven calls involving a few individuals while problem analysis involves interviews of individuals and data analysis. Problem analysis may evaluate residents' perceptions of the problem (Boba 2003, 11–12).

The success of problem-solving programs relies to a great extent on those who have a stake in solving the problem playing a key role. There exists a need for a police–community partnership. There must be collaboration or a partnership not only in problem solving but also in problem analysis. In problem analysis, the community or neighborhood can play a major role by participation in developing the questionnaire, gathering data, conducting surveys, and observation of activities related to the problem. A good analysis of the problem could improve the understanding of it and the major factors that are contributing to it (Bynum 2002, 47–49).

Problem analysis utilized for problem solving should be structured and systemically conducted. Also, successful analysis starts with listening to what must be implemented to solve the problem. Problem analysis should be viewed as much as an art as a craft. Problem analysis involves taking a panoramic view of a problem. This means involving individuals, groups, and organizations in a collaborative effort to analyze and solve neighborhood and community problems. Problem analysis involves not only an effective problem solver but a creative one as well (Bynum 2002, 51–52).

Problem-Oriented Projects

Problem-oriented projects can range from fighting fear of crime, as Baltimore County did in the 1980s, to controlling prostitution, as Wichita, Kansas, did, to holding a community safety fair, as the Sedgwick County Sheriff's Department in Kansas did. They can focus on anything from minor community problems to very serious community problems: for example, gangs, curfew violations, drug dealing, crack houses, graffiti on buildings, burglaries, robberies, or malicious mischief. This section will review a number of problem-oriented projects that police officers in various departments have worked on and solved.

Citizen-Oriented Police Enforcement

One department in the early 1980s that was willing to be innovative and use the problem-oriented approach to policing as advocated by Herman Goldstein was the Baltimore County Police Department. In 1982, the Citizen Oriented Police Enforcement (COPE) unit was created in response to several murders as an attempt to combat citizens' fear in the county of Baltimore, which includes the surrounding areas of the city of Baltimore. The COPE unit began attacking fear by confronting the social problems that were the cause of the fear. The police officers assigned to the COPE unit developed skills in social research, community organization, and problem solving (Taft 1986).

COPE officers conducted surveys to determine the major concerns of a neighborhood's residents. The emphasis was on what the community considered to be a problem and not on what the COPE officers considered to be problems. The officers then used the problem-solving approach to address these concerns. They solicited the community's input, they researched the problem through such techniques as crime analysis, brainstormed with other officers, and networked with other public and private agencies to come up with solutions.

In one neighborhood, Garden Village, the officers in surveying the community concluded that the citizens were troubled by the lack of recreational facilities for their children and by the physical deterioration of the neighborhood. The COPE officers got the electric company to repair broken streetlights, convinced the county road department to repair potholes and cracked pavements, and got the county park and recreation officials to build a new park with basketball courts and playgrounds (Taft 1986, 14–15).

In addressing the issue that COPE officers were performing social work, one lieutenant responded by saying:

> Yet COPE may be closer to 'real policing' than patrol itself—and more successful as well. For years, people have called the police for any service they want, and the traditional response has been to send a car and solve that problem, whether it satisfied the community or not. . . . COPE's response makes much more sense: We're solving problems from the community perspective, not from the police perspective.
>
> (Taft 1986, 8)

Oaklawn/Sunview Community Fair

In July 1997, community policing officers of the Sedgwick County, Kansas, Sheriff's Department who were assigned to the Oaklawn/Sunview community conducted a brainstorming session with community residents to identify various methods that could improve the quality of life, enhance communication, and bring citizens of the Oaklawn/Sunview neighborhood together. Historically, the Oaklawn/Sunview community had been viewed negatively by other communities in the Sedgwick County/Wichita area because of its crime problem, particularly its reputation of having drug dealing and gang activity. As a result of the meeting, the sheriff's department and the community decided together to hold a community safety fair in Oaklawn/Sunview. The general public and residents from other areas in Sedgwick County and Wichita would be invited to attend the fair so that they would have a positive experience in the Oaklawn/Sunview community. The fair would feature games for children and refreshments and soft drinks sold at a nominal fee. The fair included information booths for parents, staffed by social service and governmental agencies, on such topics as substance abuse prevention. In addition to the sheriff's department and the Oaklawn Neighborhood Association, cosponsors for the fair included the Driving Under the Influence (DUI) Victim Center of Kansas and Big Brothers and Sisters of Kansas. Money made from the fair was donated to the DUI Victim Center (Lt. Michael Birzer, Community Policing Coordinator, Sedgwick County Sheriff's Department, personal communication, 1998).

The purpose of the fair was to foster a sense of community, pride, and security among residents of the Oaklawn/Sunview neighborhood. The event was a success, and the first step was made in getting Oaklawn/Sunview to function as a community. If Oaklawn/Sunview can work together on a fair, then it should be able to work together to solve some of its other problems, such as drug dealing and gang activity.

Sound Amplification Systems in Vehicle Violations

In 1996, an officer of the Wichita, Kansas Police Department began a project to change the way that violations involving loud music in vehicles were handled.* At that time, such incidents required making a brief report of approximately two to three sentences. Officers who observed this violation being committed by a juvenile were required to complete an incident and arrest report, notify, and wait for the juvenile's parent(s) to arrive, and enter the case through the case desk. This entire process, from initial contact with the juvenile to entering the case, took about 55 minutes. Given that most offenses were committed by juveniles, the arrangement took an exorbitant amount of an officer's time.

The proposal recommended that when officers observed this violation, they issue a moving citation to any violator who was 14 years of age or older. This would reduce the amount of time spent by officers on this type of violation by approximately 3 minutes for adult violators and 43 minutes for juvenile violators.

The benefits of this proposal included:

1. The significant reduction in officers' time spent on this type of violation, thereby freeing officers to perform other tasks
2. The significant reduction in costs of paying officers to take action on this type of violation
3. The reduction of paperwork and cost of paperwork associated with processing this type of violation
4. The resolution of a community concern, predominantly involving juveniles that had been only minimally addressed under departmental protocol

---

* The project was completed by Sergeant Ken McMillian of the Wichita Police Department for a community policing class assignment for me.

The author based his proposal on the following findings:

- A crime analysis showed that from September 1, 1995, to September 1, 1996, there were 147 adult violations involving sound amplification systems in vehicles.
- An attorney in the law department stated that the ordinance could be changed from Chapter 5 to Title 11, allowing violators 14 years of age and older to be issued a moving citation. The law department attorney stated that process could take place as soon as the department's command staff approved the proposed action and sent a Blue Letter to the law department requesting the change. The necessary change in the ordinance would then be made, and the new ordinance could be presented to the city council.
- The city attorney of Bel Aire (a suburb of Wichita) stated that it would be possible to change the ordinance to a traffic ordinance. He stated that Bel Aire had been issuing traffic citations for loud music in cars for a couple of months.
- Police departments of three suburbs of Wichita were contacted about their handling of the problem. All of them had changed their loud music ordinances, making it possible to issue moving citations to violators, and all had had good results.
- A Bel Aire judge stated that he had been presiding over cases in which moving citations were issued for loud music in vehicles and that he had been finding violators guilty.

On December 1, 1996, the chief of the Wichita Police Department signed a special order changing the departmental policy on sound amplification systems in vehicles. The city council changed the ordinance, and the new ordinance allowed officers to cite any operator of a vehicle who was 14 years of age or older on a moving violation.

This project shows how the initiative of one police officer was able to cut the paperwork for an entire department. It provides a good example of how to obtain information from other governmental units within the city and in areas adjacent to the city. Through his efforts, this officer was able to get the city council and police chief to change a city ordinance and police policy that would allow police officers to handle a minor situation quickly, thereby freeing them to perform other tasks.

Wichita Police Department South Central Prostitution Project

When the Wichita Police Department implemented community-oriented policing in specific high-crime target areas of the city, problem solving was initiated. Four Wichita police officers were assigned to the South Central Wichita area to implement problem-oriented policing. These police officers received two weeks of problem-solving training. They were also equipped with take-home vehicles, radios, pagers, and bicycles. The police chief and the city manager encouraged the officers to address the problems in the South Central neighborhood. The officers working on problem solving were allowed to work a flexible schedule so that they had more opportunity to meet the needs of the neighborhood.

In meeting with members of the South Central community, the officers quickly learned that the residents considered prostitution the biggest problem of their community. Therefore, the officers and neighborhood leaders developed a plan to combat prostitution. Support for the plan was obtained from the political leaders of Wichita, who included the mayor, the city council, the city manager, and police administrators. The officers obtained the service of Wichita State University professors to conduct a study of the ethnic composition, employment, education, and general characteristics of the South Central neighborhood. The study found residents concerned with the adverse appearance of the areas, the high crime rate, and prostitution. Another study conducted by the Wichita Chamber of Commerce found four major concerns: illegal activity, poor communication with the police, poor access to government services, and deteriorated neighborhood appearance. Also, two surveys conducted by the community policing officers assigned to the area found that residents identified prostitution and drug dealing as major problems. More than 50 percent of area businesses attributed the loss of customers to the prostitution traffic, drug activity, and crime. The officers also surveyed the prostitutes working the area in order to obtain another perspective on the neighborhood's problems. The survey resulted in prostitutes providing information about drug use, frequency of sexual contact, and the length of time they had been on the street.

A crime analysis for the period between January 1993 and December 1994 showed that the Wichita Police Department recorded 418 arrests for prostitution. Sixty-one percent of these arrests were made in the South Central neighborhood. Seventy-five percent of the arrests of johns occurred in the South Central neighborhood. A review of court records showed that the average fine for both prostitutes and johns was $200, with very few offenders receiving jail time. The officers also found a direct relationship between prostitution violations and other types of crimes. During the summer months, complaints about prostitution increased substantially.

Traditionally, the Wichita Police Department had emphasized enforcement when it received a complaint from the neighborhood, but it had not developed a strategic plan to control or eliminate prostitution, and there was no emphasis on crime prevention. Patrol officers indicated that there were insufficient ordinances to control prostitution and that the courts were too lenient in dealing with prostitution cases.

The problem-oriented trained officers worked with the South Central neighborhood association to solve the problems facing the neighborhood. Together, the police and the community established three goals: reduce prostitution and the crime associated with prostitution; improve police–community relations; and improve the neighborhood's appearance. Six recommendations were made to solve the prostitution problem in the South Central neighborhood: develop city ordinances, develop enforcement strategies, work with the courts, encourage community efforts, improve the environment, and work with the media. Each of these recommendations will be discussed.

City Ordinances

The officers assigned to the South Central neighborhood developed prostitution ordinances with assistance from the city's municipal court and law department. An ordinance was revised to allow police officers to arrest males who were loitering with the intent to solicit a prostitute. Prior to this ordinance, only females could be arrested with the intent to commit an act of prostitution. Another ordinance established an "Anti-Prostitution Emphasis Zone," which increased fines and jail time for anyone who was arrested within the major streets where prostitutes roamed. Arrest data on prostitution were used as the basis for creating boundaries for the zone.

Enforcement

The problem-solving officers met with supervisors, who approved the development of a 20-week strategic plan for weekly law enforcement actions. The plan was in place from May 1995 to August 1995, because prostitution increased during the summer months. The police actions taken included foot patrol, bicycle patrol, traffic enforcement, motel register checks, and sting operations. A "10 Most Wanted List" was created for the prostitution zone. It included prostitutes, drug dealers, pimps, and other criminal offenders who were active in the area. When those on the most-wanted list were arrested, the officers would request high bonds from prosecutors and judges. They also spoke to parole officers, probation officers, judges, and prosecutors about the offenders' actions in the neighborhood and requested longer jail sentences upon conviction. The problem-solving officers developed a "Reference Guide" that listed known offenders who frequented the area. The guide included photographs, which were placed in area patrol cars.

The officers provided other services as well. They left information brochures in every neighborhood business on how to document illegal activity. Communication channels were opened with the neighborhood so that, for example, officers were able to track down children abandoned by their prostitute mothers.

Courts

The problem-solving officers followed up every prostitution arrest and were able to get the prosecutors not to plea-bargain cases. Officers videotaped prostitutes and used the information to educate prosecutors on those involved in prostitution.

Community

Billboards were placed in the prostitution area warning potential offenders that prostitution would not be tolerated. The signs depicted a stop sign using the acronym STOP, which stood for "Stand Tough on Prostitution." A neighborhood action group was established that acted as a neighborhood steering committee. The problem-solving officers worked closely with the group.

In 1995, a citizen patrol group began patrolling the neighborhood. Citizen involvement was encouraged by police officers, who assisted in developing operational procedures, training curriculum, and program guidelines. Those involved in the citizen patrol groups were trained by the Wichita Police Department and received instruction on Neighborhood Watch programs and patrolling techniques.

Officers were able to hold a meeting with 30 motel owners. This meeting led to the development of a motel association that was formed with the intent to provide a networking system to warn motel owners of known prostitutes working in the area. The goal would be to keep the prostitutes from moving from one motel to another. The local police substation also kept a list of convicted prostitutes that was made available to motel owners.

Environment

To improve the appearance of the neighborhood, the problem-oriented police officers organized cleanups of vacant lots, alleys, homes, and businesses. Improving the environment was an important aspect of the anticrime strategy for the South Central neighborhood, because prostitutes and drug dealers would make contact with customers on city streets and move to alleyways to conduct their business. Residents of the neighborhood, along with Boy Scouts and inmates from the local community corrections halfway house, were involved in the cleanups. City trucks were used to haul the debris away. Neighborhood businesses donated equipment and food for the workers involved in the cleanups. Areas that needed to be painted to improve the neighborhood's appearance were completed.

Housing inspectors trained a neighborhood residents group known as Neighbor-to-Neighbor to detect city housing code violations. This neighborhood group would identify housing code violations and tell the homeowner to correct the violations. If the homeowner ignored the warning, the group informed the city housing inspector, who had the legal authority to take corrective action. Officers with problem-solving responsibilities had a close working relationship with the Neighbor-to-Neighbor volunteers and the Clean Team city code inspectors. These groups met to share information concerning housing code violations. The Neighbor-to-Neighbor volunteers would attend court trials to monitor cases pertaining to housing code violations. Clean Team inspectors were called by the police officers whenever a search warrant was executed in a criminal case. The Clean Team would perform an inspection and, where appropriate, would use the building code to close businesses that were used for criminal activities.

Media

The media highlighted the changes in the neighborhood. The city newspaper reported the improvements taking place, the electronics media reported ordinances changes, and one local television station ran a special news report on the cleanup of the neighborhood, and another aired reports on the effects of the community policing officers' problem-solving approach on the neighborhood.

Evaluation

The strategies for controlling the major problems of the South Central Wichita neighborhood were evaluated at the end of 20 weeks. Although prostitution was lower in the winter months, revisions could be made in the strategy for the summer months. The evaluation led to the maintenance program for the summer of 1996. To determine the project's effectiveness, surveys were conducted of business, residents, court personnel, and patrol officers who patrolled the neighborhood. The surveys found that 75 percent of the businesses reported a decrease in prostitution and that 90 percent felt that community policing (problem solving) had had a direct effect on the prostitution problem. A residents' survey indicated that residents in general felt better about their neighborhood and its appearance. The improvement in the appearance translated to a feeling of safety for residents. Crime statistics were compiled and evaluated for the 20 weeks of the project. An examination of the statistics found an 11 percent decrease in crime. There was a 41 percent decrease in drug law violations, a 47 percent decrease in prostitution, and a 16 percent decrease in 911 calls to the neighborhood.

Court documents showed that 26 people were charged with the new Anti-Prostitution Area Ordinance and that eight of those charged pled guilty. Seven prostitutes were mapped out under the new mapping ordinance along with two johns. Four prostitutes were arrested by patrol officers for violating the mapping ordinance. The mapping ordinance helped to reduce prostitution in South Central Wichita. Prostitutes learned the street boundaries for the enforcement zones and mapping areas and took their business out of the area. The physical appearance of the neighborhood improved as a result of the police and neighborhood working together (Sgt. K. McMillian, Wichita Police Department, personal communication, 1998).

The South Central Prostitution Project reduced crime and the fear of crime, improved the physical environment of the neighborhood, and improved police–neighborhood cooperation. The problem-solving efforts of the police officers in this project were a success. This award-winning project can be duplicated in other neighborhoods.

Summary

Problem-oriented policing is an approach to policing that encourages and assists all members of a police agency to engage in proactive problem solving. For all practical purposes, the philosophy of community policing has as its foundation the problem-oriented policing design. The primary idea behind problem-oriented policing is police accountability to community and a focus on addressing community concerns. Community-oriented policing draws on this idea but takes it even further to emphasize full community participation in the problem-solving process.

Problem-oriented policing emerged in the late 1970s out of dissatisfaction with the professional (traditional) model of policing. Herman Goldstein claimed that attempts to improve policing had for decades been focused primarily on administrative improvements, such as recruiting better personnel, modernizing equipment, and implementing business practices into police operations. Although these improvements were necessary, they had become ends in themselves, and police agencies had lost sight of the effectiveness of organizational changes in reducing crime and meeting community needs. Eck and Spelman (1988) similarly argued that the professional model of policing was incident driven, consisting of routine and limited responses to calls for service, instead of being problem driven. All these authors advocated an alternative style of policing that would focus on the ends of policing—what the public wanted—rather than the means; attempt to solve persistent problems by analyzing their causes; monitor the effectiveness of solutions; encourage police initiative; and engage community resources.

Before problem solving can be initiated, the problem or problems have to be defined. A problem can be defined as a group of incidents occurring in a community on several occasions that are similar in one or more ways and are of concern to the police and the public. The similarities could refer to people or types of people involved in incidents, whether they are victims (e.g., the elderly) or offenders (e.g., gangs or the homeless); behaviors (e.g., drunk driving, sexual assault); time (e.g., at an annual rock concert, before Christmas); or place (e.g., a public housing project).

The SARA model developed by Eck and Spelman is a model for solving police problems that has been widely used by departments that practice problem-oriented policing. SARA stands for the four stages of problem solving: scanning (i.e., identifying the problem), analysis, response, and assessment.

Successful implementation of problem-oriented policing requires the complete support and understanding of the head of the organization; training in problem-oriented policing for every member of the police organization, sworn personnel, and civilians; and the replacement of "bean-counting" evaluations of officer performance (e.g., counting arrests) with evaluations that emphasize officers' problem-solving role.

KEY TERMS

- analysis stage
- assessment stage
- Herman Goldstein
- incident-driven policing
- problem-oriented policing
- problem solving
- response stage
- SARA model
- scanning stage

REVIEW QUESTIONS

1. Describe the problem-oriented policing approach.
2. Who developed the problem-oriented policing approach, and what were his criticisms of professional-model policing?
3. What are five trends that have encouraged the adoption of problem-oriented policing?
4. What does the term incident-driven policing mean?
5. What are five ways that problems can be solved?
6. Describe the SARA model.
7. What are four ways that incidents in a community can be clustered to frame a problem?
8. Describe some of the problems that can be encountered when implementing problem-oriented policing.

9

COMMUNITY-ORIENTED POLICING

CHAPTER OBJECTIVES

1. Have an understanding of community-policing philosophy.
2. Have an understanding of the value of community policing.
3. Have an understanding of the potential pitfalls of community policing.
4. Have an understanding of obstacles to implementing community policing.
5. Be familiar with the Community Patrol Officer Program in New York City.
6. Be familiar with how community policing works in Seattle.

Introduction

Public officials, from the president of the United States to local chiefs of police, herald community policing as the long-awaited solution to violent crime. In his 1994 State of the Union address, President Clinton prods the nation to "take steps to reduce violence and prevent crime, beginning with more police officers and more community policing." A local police chief unabashedly proclaims that community policing and precinct patrolling "have gone a long way toward preventing crime. . . . They have worked" (Holland 1994, 12). Both proponents and detractors of community policing agree that it constitutes a revision of the police role, away from that of crime fighter to that of planner, community organizer, problem solver, and broker of governmental services. Currently, scores of police departments not only in America but also throughout the world claim to be implementing community policing. Although community policing is the newest policing model, this approach cannot be considered completely new. In 1900–1910, Arthur Woods, the New York City Police Commissioner, instituted a number of policies that could be described today as community policing. Woods believed that the rank-and-file police officer should be in a position of social importance and public value. He also was convinced that the public would benefit if they were informed of issues affecting the community and the local police precinct and would have more respect for the police once they realized the complexities and difficulties of police work (Skolnik and Bayley 1988, 37).

Woods placed into operation within the New York City Police Department what today would be termed community-oriented policing. Captains were directed to establish junior police leagues. Young people were provided with junior police badges and were trained to report violations of law that they observed in their neighborhoods. Sergeants were assigned to visit schools and to educate the students that policing was more than just making arrests. Officers' duties included working to improve neighborhoods and make them safer places for people to live. Woods emphasized that every police officer was responsible for the social conditions of the neighborhood he patrolled. Because unemployment, according to Woods, was a major cause of crime, police precincts were used to distribute employment information and beat officers were expected to help the unemployed in their neighborhood to find employment (Skolnick and Bayley 1988, 37–38).

Woods is credited with creating "play streets" for youngsters in neighborhoods that had no playgrounds, parks, or open places to play in. The police would close a street for several hours by placing barricades that prevented traffic from entering the street. In addition, Woods communicated with ethnic newspapers, Greek, Italian, and Yiddish, and encouraged them to publish city ordinances and laws in the newspapers so that immigrants could read about the laws in their own language. Teenage males who were involved in acts of delinquency were placed in contact with such social service agencies as Big Brother and YMCA. Woods' policing philosophy was widely accepted in New York City and praised by the news media (Skolnick and Bayley 1988, 38). A journalist of Woods' time commented on Woods' policing philosophy that for too many persons, and particularly the foreign-born population, the law stands for a vast machine of menace. The new police idea is wholly different. It aims to do something that in America seems never to have been tried as an angle of police duty—to strive for the inculcation of the thought that the law is an engine of mutuality, of good will, of positive influence; that it is constructive. The new police idea is to present it as a protector (MacCulloch 1915).

When Woods left his position as police commissioner, the philosophy he espoused fell by the wayside. As discussed in Chapter 1, police departments from the 1930s or 1940s through the 1960s or 1970s were largely dominated by a professional model of crime control through making arrests, expanding strategies of surveillance, and deploying technology and professional expertise. Close community relations were not considered important or were even discouraged.

The shift away from the crime control model can be traced back to the 1960s. The social, political, and civil turmoil of the 1960s created unprecedented changes in American policing. These changes affected the thinking, tactics, and resources of the police and forced police to focus on relations with the community (Skolnick and Bayley 1988). Two governmental reports of that era, *The Challenge of Crime in a Free Society* (President's Commission 1967) and the *Report of the National Advisory Commission on Civil Disorders* (National Advisory Commission 1968), underscored, in particular, the marked hostility of African Americans toward the police and the failure of police to cultivate and maintain constructive relationships with the African American community.

Subsequent research in the 1970s investigating the efficacy of policing as a formal mechanism of social control showed that the usual policing strategies were having little impact on crime or public safety. Skolnick and Bayley (1986) summarized this research:

> First, increasing the number of police does not necessarily reduce crime rates or raise the proportion of crimes solved. The same is true for budgetary expenditures on the police. The most that could be said was that if there were no cops there would be more crime; however, once a certain threshold of coverage has been reached, presumably long passed in the United States, increments of money and personnel are no longer efficacious. Variations in

both crime and clearance rates are best predicted by social conditions such as income, unemployment, population, income distribution, and social heterogeneity. We have learned that you cannot simply throw money at law enforcement and expect proportionate results.

Second, random motorized patrolling neither reduces crime nor improves chances of catching suspects. Moreover, it does not reassure citizens enough to affect their fear of crime, nor does it engender greater trust in the police. Regular patrols by police officers on foot . . . [have been] shown to reduce citizens' fear of crime, [but] they have no demonstrable impact on the crime rate.

Third, two-person patrol cars are no more effective than one-person cars in reducing crime or catching criminals. Furthermore, injuries to police officers are not more likely to occur in one-person cars.

Fourth, saturation patrolling does reduce crime, but only temporarily, largely by displacing it to other areas.

Fifth, the kind of crime that terrifies Americans most—mugging, robbery, burglary, rape, homicide—is rarely encountered by police on patrol. Only "Dirty Harry" has his lunch disturbed by a bank robbery in progress. Patrol officers individually make few important arrests. The "good collar" is a rare event. Cops spend most of their time passively patrolling and providing emergency services.

Sixth, improving response time to emergency calls has no effect on the likelihood of arresting criminals or even on satisfying involved citizens. One recent and very large study showed that the chances of making an arrest on the spot drop below 10 percent if even one minute elapses from the time the crime is committed. Only instantaneous reaction, in other words, would be effective in catching criminals. Yet that cannot reasonably be expected unless a cop is put on every corner. Speed of response makes so little difference because victims delay an average of four to five and one-half minutes before calling the police, even when they have been victims of confrontational crimes.

Rapid response also does not satisfy citizens, surprisingly, because what most victims of crime want is predictable rather than quick response. Victims seem to recognize that in most crimes the criminal will be long gone whenever the police arrive. What they want is a police response they can count on as they go about reordering their stricken lives. They would rather wait forty-five minutes, the research shows, for an assured reaction from the police than [experience] the uncertainty of waiting for an unpredictable response. They do not want to sit around waiting.

Seventh, crimes are not solved—in the sense of offenders arrested and prosecuted—through criminal investigations conducted by police departments. Generally, crimes are solved because offenders are immediately apprehended or someone identifies them specifically—a name, an address, a license plate number. If neither of those things happens, the studies show the chances that any crime will be solved fall to less than one in ten. Despite what television has led us to think, detectives do not work from clues to criminals; they work from known suspects to corroborating evidence. Detectives are important for the prosecution of identified perpetrators and not for finding unknown offenders.

(Skolnick and Bayley 1986, 4–5)

Klockars (1985) pointed out, in the same vein, that the patrol officer's typical tour of duty does not result in any arrests; the typical New York patrol officer, for instance, makes only three felony arrests per year. What makes a difference in apprehension rates is the cooperation of witnesses and neighborhood residents in providing information to the police. This research resulted in a resurgent interest in experimenting with forms of policing that would improve police–community interaction. Goldstein's innovative problem-oriented policing article, published in *Crime and Delinquency* in 1979, and Wilson and Kelling's seminal article "Broken Windows," which appeared in the *Atlantic Monthly* in 1982, combined with police research published in the Perspectives on Policing Series sponsored by the National Institute of Justice and Harvard University, specifically the Moore et al. publication "Crime and Policing" in 1988, provided a strong impetus for policing strategies organized around the principles of service decentralization, neighborhood focus, and close interaction between citizens and police as co-producers of public safety. The stage was set for the development of community policing.

What Is Community Policing?

A review of the community-policing literature reveals that the concept has a variety of definitions and meanings. Some police administrators believe that community policing has always occurred in small towns where the police officer knows everyone on a first-name basis. Others equate problem-oriented policing with community policing. Some even believe that community policing is having specialized units work in a high-crime area. In addition, many give lip service to community policing because they consider it to be the latest fad and claim that they have instituted community policing for public relations purposes. Community policing has become so fashionable that a majority of police departments claim to be doing it or, at least, planning to do it.

As one police scholar has pointed out, community policing "is one of those terms that simultaneously suggests so much that is general and so little that is specific that it risks being a barrier rather than a bridge to discourse about development in policing" (Wycoff 1988, 104). Although the term can cause confusion, several researchers have offered useful working definitions. A good brief definition was provided by Stipak (1994): "Community policing is a management strategy that promotes the joint responsibility of citizens and police for community safety, through working partnerships and interpersonal contacts" (115). Trojano-wicz and Bucqueroux (1994) provide an expanded definition:

> Community policing is a philosophy and an organizational strat-egy that promotes a new partnership between people and their police. It is based on the premise that both the police and the community must work together to identify, prioritize, and solve contemporary problems such as crime, drugs, fear of crime, social and physical disorder, and overall neighborhood decay, with the goal of improving the overall quality of life in the area. Com-munity policing requires a department-wide commitment from everyone, civilian and sworn, to the community policing philos-ophy. It also challenges all personnel to find ways to express this new philosophy in their jobs, thereby balancing the need to

maintain an immediate and effective police response to individual crime incidents and emergencies with the goal of exploring new proactive initiatives aimed at solving problems before they occur or escalate. Community policing also rests on establishing community policing officers as decentralized "mini" chiefs in permanent beats, where they enjoy the freedom and autonomy to operate as community-based problem solvers who work directly with the community—making their neighborhoods better and safer places in which to live and work.

(2–3)

Skolnick and Bayley (1988), who studied community policing in police departments throughout the world, concluded that there are some common elements to all the community-policing approaches:

- A growing reliance on "community-based crime prevention" through the use of citizen education, neighborhood watches, and similar techniques, as opposed to relying entirely on police patrols to prevent crime
- The reorientation of patrol from being primarily an emergency-response force ("chasing calls") to using "proactive" techniques such as foot patrol
- Increased police accountability to the citizens they are supposed to serve
- Decentralization of command and police authority, with more discretion allowed to lower-ranking "generalist" officers, and more initiative expected of them

Brown (1989) came up with a similar list of components:

- A problem-solving, results-oriented approach to law enforcement
- Articulation of police values that incorporate citizen involvement
- Accountability of the police to each neighborhood
- Decentralization of authority
- Police–community partnership and sharing of power

- Beat boundaries that correspond to neighborhood boundaries
- Permanent assignment of patrol officers
- Empowerment of patrol officers to show initiative
- Coordination of investigations at both neighborhood and citywide levels
- New roles for supervisors and managers, as supporters of patrol rather than evaluators of patrol officers
- Changes in the content of training at all levels
- New systems of performance evaluation, placing much less emphasis on "production" of quantified activities
- New approaches to "demand management," the response of the agency to calls for service

(5–6)

Bayley (1994), who described community policing as "the most serious and sustained attempt to reformulate the purpose of and practice of policing since the development of the 'professional' model in the early twentieth century" (104), claimed that it rests on three insights. First, the police cannot solve society's crime problems alone. They need the public's assistance to deter crime and to apprehend criminal offenders. Second, the resources of the police have to be deployed proactively against crime and criminals. This approach addresses the circumstances that cause crime. Third, routine police patrol is too passive; it does not deter crime. Police patrol should create a moral order with a respectable public appearance, and behavior should reflect the standards of the local community (102–104).

To understand what community policing is, it pays to review what community policing is not. According to Trojanowicz and Bucqueroux (1990):

- Community policing is not a technique. . . . The entire department must be infused with the community policing philosophy, with CPOs [community police officers] as the department's direct link to average citizens. Community policing is not something to be used periodically, but it is a permanent commitment to a new kind of policing that provides decentralization and personalized community problem solving.

- Community policing is not public relations. . . . Community policing instead enhances the department's image because it is a sincere change in the way the department interacts with people in the community. It treats law-abiding people as partners, a new relationship based on mutual trust and shared power. The traditional system often makes people feel that the police do not care about their wants and needs. In traditional departments, officers often see the people in the community as them, those nameless and faceless strangers whose reluctance to cooperate and share what they know makes them indistinguishable from the criminals. Community policing instead treats law-abiding people in the community as an extension of us.

- Community policing is not anti-technology. . . . Many people erroneously assume that community policing rejects technology because it refuses to lock the officer into a patrol car and handcuff him to the police radio. CPOs can make tremendous use of new technologies, such as hand held computers, remote telephone answering machines, and cellular telephones. Yet community policing also recognizes that no technology can compete with a fully functioning, creative human being, whether the person is a police officer or a law-abiding citizen willing to help.

- Community policing is not soft on crime. . . . Critics suggest that community policing's broad mandate and its focus on using tactics other than arrest to solve problems detract from a proper focus on serious crime. CPOs often face derision within the department from fellow officers who call them lollicops or the grin-and-wave squad. The reality is that CPOs make arrests just like any other officer does, but CPOs deal with a broader variety of community concerns in addition to crime, not as a substitute for addressing serious crime. . . .

- Community policing is not flamboyant. . . . The media reinforces the image of the macho police officer whose job is glamorous, tough, and often dangerous. That hero myth also appeals to police officers themselves, which is part of why many police officers refuse to volunteer for duty as a CPO. For community policing to succeed, however, the entire department must embrace the wisdom of this approach. All officers must focus on working together among themselves and with people in the community on solving community concerns.

- Community policing is not paternalistic. . . . Community policing threatens those who enjoy the traditional system, because it says that police superiors must stop treating line officers like children who must be watched constantly. It also says that police officers must stop acting like parents to people in the community and must begin treating them like respected partners. . . .

- Community policing is not an independent entity within the department. . . . Departments launching a new community policing effort can use war stories from elsewhere to educate everyone in the department about how community policing benefits the entire department. Police officials should also make a special effort to make sure that any initial successes are touted within the department in ways that do not seem to set CPOs apart from their fellow officers. Integrating the community policing philosophy into any day-to-day operation of the entire department is a challenge, one that requires care and feeding over time.

- Community policing is not cosmetic. . . . Community policing not only broadens the agenda to include the entire spectrum of community concerns relating to crime and disorder but also offers greater continuity, follow-up, and accountability. Important as well is that community policing goes far beyond handing out brochures, making speeches, talking with community leaders, telling people how to guard against crime, and urging fellow officers to treat people with respect. As line officers directly involved in the community, CPOs have the opportunity to make far-reaching changes.

- Community policing is not a top-down approach. . . . Community policing decentralizes decision-making, opening up departments so that new ideas can surface. Community policing provides the department grass roots input from both community residents and line officers, which can help overcome a bureaucracy's inherent tendency to become more stodgy and stagnant over time.

- Community policing is not just another name for social work. ... The fact is, social work has always been an important element of police work. When line officers talk about the use of police discretion, they mean that the job requires doing more than just sticking to rules and procedures. It also means allowing police officers the freedom to make immediate decisions on their own, including the freedom to solve problems in ways that have nothing to do with arresting bad guys. Though it conflicts with the superhero myth, good police officers have always tried to encourage youngsters to live within the law and help the elderly feel less vulnerable.

(20–27)

Watson et al. (1998) have also contributed to our understanding of what community policing is not by describing four myths and misconceptions that opponents of community policing expound:

The first myth is that community policing is so radically different from traditional law enforcement practices that it requires a complete restructuring of a law enforcement agency. . . . Organizational restructuring is not the first step in implementing community policing. It may not always be necessary even as the last step. The second myth is that community policing involves an enormous increase in officers' workload, especially for patrol officers, who are suddenly required to "interact with the community" in addition to all of their ordinary duties of preventive patrol and responding to calls for service. The truth is that many officers will spend part of their time in different activities, depending on their assignment and the nature of the community in which they are deployed. Patrol officers and their supervisors will be expected to take the initiative in establishing a partnership with the community. However, their ability to perform these new duties will depend on their being relieved of some of the burden of "chasing 9-1-1 calls," plodding through administrative paperwork, or laboring on tasks that either do not need to be done at all or can be done just as well by someone else.

Ultimately, if community-policing lives up to its promise of making neighborhoods safer, most patrol officers should be able to spend most of their time on productive, "proactive" duties without being in any way overburdened. The third myth is that community policing distracts police officers from their main responsibility of enforcing the law, and therefore leads to an increase in the incidence of crime. Evidence is sometimes offered to support this myth, in the form of crime rate statistics from some of the cities that have implemented one or another form of community policing. . . .

The first duty of a police officer is to enforce the law by identifying and arresting offenders and gathering evidence to secure a conviction. That is just as true in a community-policing agency as in a traditional agency. The question is not what police officers should do, but why and how they do it. Perhaps the most pernicious myth of all is that community policing turns patrol officers into "social workers." This myth is doubly damning. First, it implies that there is something demeaning about social work. . . . Second, the myth reflects a profound misconception about the nature of the criminal justice system and the role of police officers in the system. . . . The police cannot fulfill all of the roles by themselves. They do not have the resources to do so, and therefore must depend on other segments of the community (including social workers) to participate.

(54–56)

Finally, it may be helpful to scan a list of questions devised by Trojanowicz (1994) in a study sponsored by the Department of Justice to determine if a police department has in reality implemented community policing. The following questions should be answered "Yes" if community policing is being practiced:

- Do citizens nominate the problem?
- Do citizens work with the police to help solve the basis of the problem, and not just react to the symptoms?
- Does the officer have a defined beat area?
- Is the officer full service, both reacting to and preventing crime?

- Does the officer make arrests?
- Does the officer have a permanent assignment of at least 18 months in the defined beat area?
- Is it possible for the officer to interact with most of the people in the particular area within a six- to eight-month period?
- Does the officer work out of a decentralized office?
- Does the officer actively work as a member of a team with non-law-enforcement agencies?
- Does the officer, with help, conduct a long-term evaluation to determine if problems are solved and not merely interrupted on a short-term basis?

(38)

The Value of Community Policing

Benefits to the Community

The key question about community policing is whether it will produce safer communities. Although some anecdotal evidence suggests that it can, no definitive answer can be given at this point because community policing has not yet been sufficiently evaluated. Therefore, supporters of community policing have stressed other benefits to the community that are easier to demonstrate. Citizens' attitudes, particularly their fear of crime, their evaluation of the police, and their satisfaction with their neighborhood, have been surveyed before and after implementation of community policing strategies, such as distribution of police newsletters informing residents about crime prevention and police programs; community organizing to develop special projects (cleanup campaigns, property identification, "safe" houses for children); citizen contact programs in which police go door to door, introducing themselves to residents and businesspeople and asking if citizens have any problems they wish to bring to the attention of police; victim recontact programs in which patrol officers make telephone contact with victims to inform them of the status of their case, inquire whether they need assistance, offer to send crime prevention information, and ask whether victims can provide additional information; police community stations that provide a variety of services for the area; increased foot patrols; increased enforcement of disorderly conduct laws; and programs to reverse physical deterioration of neighborhoods (Wycoff 1988, 107–108). In a study conducted in Houston, Texas, and Newark, New Jersey, and sponsored by the National Institute of Justice (Wycoff 1988), such strategies were shown to reduce the fear of perceived social disorder in the area, reduce fear of personal victimization, reduce worry about property crime, improve evaluation of police, and increase satisfaction with the area (110). Other community benefits have been listed by Skolnick and Bayley (1988):

- Public scrutiny. Even when community policing is only rhetoric, an opportunity is created for legitimate public examination of police practices. If community policing minimally means greater involvement of the public in public safety, how can the police convincingly deflect public discussion of police strategies? Community policing is like a Trojan horse that attacks the pretensions of professional insulation from within. Even if community policing cannot do much in the way of preventing crime, it does offer the public a larger window into police activity.
- Public accountability. Community policing increases effective public control over the police. There are three primary ways in which the public can constrain what the police do: (1) by providing, or not providing, a framework of laws and money for police action; (2) by participating in policy-making with respect to the means of achieving desired objectives; and (3) by examining and possibly punishing errors in performance. . . . Community policing also makes civilian oversight of implementation more acceptable. . . . Community policing is a back door into comprehensible accountability. What could not be achieved by public demand through political channels may occur because the police believe wider community participation is essential to the achievement of organizational objectives. Accountability may occur under police auspices, where it could not under political ones.
- Recruitment. Community policing provides a double-barreled rationale for representative recruitment. On the one hand, it challenges the macho, martial model of policing. Traditional officers are being very acute when they distinguish "hard" from

"soft" policing. The tactics of community policing are indeed soft, even though the goal of deterring criminality is not. Those of community policing are geared toward soliciting, enlisting, inviting, and encouraging, whereas those of traditional policing are geared toward warning, threatening, forcing, and hurting. Community policing is less direct than traditional policing. It is a kind of policing that can be done as well by women as by men, by the short as by the tall, by the verbal as by the physical, by the sympathetic as by the authoritarian.

(67–70)

Benefits to the Police Organization and Police Officers

Skolnick and Bayley (1988) have listed seven benefits to community policing to police organizations and individual officers:

1. Political benefits. Politically, community policing is a game the police cannot lose. If coproduction through community participation leads to lower crime rates and higher arrest rates, the police can take credit as foresighted agents of change. If community policing fails to increase public security, the public is hardly likely to reduce support for policing because a new gambit does not work out. Moreover, even if the police cannot actually deliver on the large goal of crime reduction, a heightened police presence is reassuring. Thus, community policing reduces fear of crime—and, from the perspective of political benefits to the police, delivers the message that police care.
2. Grassroots support. Community policing offers a magnificent opportunity to build grassroots support for the police. It embeds the police in the community, giving them an opportunity to explain themselves, associate themselves with community initiatives, and become highly visible as concerned defenders with public safety. Community policing makes the population at large a "special interest group" supporting police-led programs.
3. Consensus building. Community policing is a means for developing consensus between the police and the public about

the appropriate use of law and force. The police have an obligation not only to catch criminals but also to maintain order in public places. There are sound crime-prevention reasons for this, quite apart from enforcement of standards of decency and propriety. Research has shown that people are made fearful and insecure by disorder and incivility, not just by criminal activity. In fact, criminal victimization is rare; most people's knowledge of crime comes secondhand through the media. Inability to curb public disorder—loud music, vandalism, drunkenness, uncouth behavior—generates further disorder, more serious crime, and diffuse feelings of insecurity. In order to maintain public decorum, the police use the authority of law and sometimes the reality of constraint or the threat of force. This is a delicate balancing: if police under-enforce, the "signs of crime" multiply, encouraging further depredations; if they over-enforce, the public becomes mis-trustful, worse yet hostile, and perhaps even violent. Community policing is a vehicle for undergirding police action with support. Through community liaison, the police can assimilate local standards of conduct and acceptable levels of perform-ance. . . .

4. Police morale. Community policing probably raises the morale of police involved because it multiplies the positive contacts they have with a community's supportive people, those who welcome police presence and activity. Traditional deployment concentrates police contacts on "difficult" people—criminals and incorrigibles as well as deserving but demanding claimants for police service, such as victims, incompetents, and mental cases. . . . Community policing leads to unemotional, non-emergency interaction with citizens, increasing contact with people who want nothing more from the police than their reassuring presence. Community policing increases the likeli-hood that the public's quiet regard will be displayed to individual officers. . . .

5. Satisfaction. Because effective community policing requires that subordinate ranks take more initiative and responsibility,

it makes the police job more challenging. Community policing cannot be managed in a quasi-military way, fulfilling easily measured norms and avoiding stipulated errors. Community policing may, in fact, be the operational strategy that is peculiarly fitted to the new breed of police recruit. Police managers report that today's more highly educated officers are less accepting of routine, more likely to question command, and more impatient with non-solutions to recurrent problems. Community policing may be the best program the police have devised for maintaining zest for the job.

6. Professional stature. Community policing raises the professional standing of the police by broadening the range of skills required. To be successful at community policing, police must be more than large, physical, and tough; they must be analytic, empathetic, flexible, and communicative. . . .

7. Career development. By enriching the strategic paradigm of policing, community policing creates more lines for career development. Because community policing encompasses and expands upon the traditional model, it provides more ways for personnel to be valuable. For community policing to work, police forces must reward a wider range of performance skills. This provides career opportunities to a more diversified group of officers.

(71–73)

Several other benefits can be added to this list. Officers engaged in community problem solving are putting their energy into productive use and are less prone to carry out pranks on their fellow officers than officers with free time on their hands. If they develop a closer attachment to their assigned neighborhoods and more familiarity with residents, they are more likely to be concerned about the welfare of the residents. This concern can lead to better rapport with residents, fewer complaints about police, fewer police abuses, and greater conscientiousness on the part of police in performing their duties, resulting in fewer accidents and damages to equipment and perhaps even fewer disciplinary problems. Further, data from Newark indicate that foot patrol officers who are satisfied with their jobs have lower rates of absenteeism (Wycoff 1988, 115–116).

Problematic Aspects of Community Policing Practice

Although community policing can produce many benefits, we need to recognize that it can have some problematic effects as well. Wycoff (1988) has discussed five possible pitfalls of community policing:

1. Illegal policing. This is possible in the event that community-based officers become more responsive to local norms than to legal constraints.

2. Inequitable policing. Many communities or neighborhoods are far from homogeneous, and it would be possible for some groups to benefit more than others from police service. We found this to be the case in Houston, where blacks and renters were much less likely to be positively affected by the fear-reduction strategies than were whites and homeowners.

3. Politicization of the police. Mayors and city managers have some reason to question the intent of community-oriented strategies. More than one politically ambitious chief has used the community link as a source of political clout—either in electoral or in bureaucratic battles. Officers might find it tempting to use their community organizing skills and good relationships with the neighborhood to mount a campaign to accomplish a political objective, whether it be a salary increase or the ouster of an unappreciated judge or chief.

4. Corruption. Close contact between police and businesspeople or residents always makes an anticorruption manager alert to possibilities for unacceptable behavior, especially in communities in which the civic culture does not dissuade corrupt practices.

5. Police intrusion into private arenas. Clearly, the better the police know us, the more they are able to know about us. In a democratic society, it is always appropriate to ask how effective we really want our police to be.

(116)

It is unfortunate that advocates of community policing have not sufficiently addressed these five potential problem areas. Rather than waiting for a crisis to occur, they should be developing strategies to prevent inequities, abuses of power, and corruption from occurring under community policing systems.

Problematic Contradictions in Community Policing Philosophy

Peter Manning (1997) has argued, "historical policing practices co-exist in variable amounts with 'community policing.' This suggests that it is not a definitive logical entity but a collection of ideas and concepts already present to some degree in many police departments" (13). Consequently, the community policing philosophy is full of ambiguities and contradictions:

1. The rhetoric of community policing positions it as customer oriented, yet this is patently impossible as a full role definition for police.
2. Community policing promises "co-production" with neighborhoods, but the police in various ways retain full control over every resource allocation decision, assignment, tactic and strategy, and type of "service" delivered to neighborhoods.
3. Despite emphasizing community integration, community policing has been used to rationalize street sweeps, harassing youths, drug crackdowns, and other "preventive" actions to reduce disorder.
4. "Neighborhood" and "community" are arbitrarily defined as isomorphic with police precincts or arbitrary political boundaries—not with natural social areas.
5. Community policing promises continuous area-based policing, but union contracts that privilege seniority in shift and beat assignments obviate this continuity.
6. Community policing promises a level of coordination of neighborhood service, but ... [often] ... dispatchers continue a division of labor that assigns crime and fast response calls to tactical units or special response teams and leaves routine and often boring work to the beat officer.
7. Community policing is generally symbolized as the first priority of the department, but officers are given no special training, rewards, perks, or promotional opportunities. Officers

are given little or no training in the new roles and routines they are to adopt or the skills they are expected to display, such as leading meetings, organizing talks, and making maps and other databased presentations. They are left to create strategies for serving the public as well as handling their calls.

8. Community police officers, or all officers in a community policing-oriented department, are to spend some time problem solving and working with the community, but they are given no recognized block of time to do so and continue to go where the radio leads.

(13–14)

Police administrators who are adopting a community-policing approach in their organization need to address all these other points to determine the extent to which each contradiction is manifested in their organization's practices and to reassess their own priorities. A department may proclaim that community policing is valuable, but does it back up its rhetoric with money and training, and does it structure patrol officers' work so that they have the time and discretion to perform their new duties? To what extent is the community really "empowered" in police–community collaborative projects, and to what extent do police keep the control? To what extent do police tactics disrupt a community instead of fostering unity? All these questions need to be openly discussed in every department that has incorporated community policing.

Obstacles to the Implementation of Community Policing

Internal Obstacles

If community policing is to be incorporated into a police organization, changes in that organization and its culture must occur. Nevertheless, given that police personnel resist change, community policing is not always easy to implement. Skolnick and Bayley (1988) identified ten obstacles to implementing community policing within police departments:

1. The traditional culture of policing. This includes the defensive attitude of suspicion that officers develop to deal with the public. Because citizens can be dangerous, police may not be

inclined to develop closer relations with them and may prefer to socialize with one another. The solidarity among police reinforces distrust of civilians.

2. Young police officers who exhibit macho attitudes. They may have bought into the crime-fighting image sold to them while they attended the police academy. A community policing system requires officers to have qualities of maturity.

3. Street cop culture. Street cops are generally more apt to be cynical and skeptical about community policing and more resistant to innovative policing concepts and strategies in general. Management cops are more likely to welcome policing innovations such as community policing.

4. The responsibility to answer emergency calls. An emphasis on responding to 911 calls as the highest priority of police officers is antithetical to community policing.

5. Limited resources. This factor is closely related to the preceding one. When the emergency response system has top priority, many police administrators do not believe they have sufficient resources to implement community policing. More resources will be needed if community policing and an emergency response system are in operation at the same time.

6. The inertia of police unions. These may see community policing as a threat to the traditional model of policing. Unions are more concerned with police salaries and benefits than with supporting community policing.

7. The two-officer patrol car. This policy creates a shortage of personnel for many police departments and further constrains the development of community policing by distancing officers from the community and limiting their social interaction to each other.

8. The reward structure of traditional policing. A "bean-counting" approach to evaluation encourages officers to focus on making large numbers of arrests or giving large numbers of citations instead of on solving problems.

9. The centralized, hierarchical, quasi-military command structure of traditional policing. Community policing requires a decentralization of authority and a reorganization of the

command structure to give lower-level officers more flexibility and initiative and to increase bottom-up communication.

10. Lack of coordination with crime detection. Often, when community policing activities are assigned to specialized units, such as crime prevention units or ministrations, these units do their own thing and are not integrated into the crime detection activities of the department, so that their effectiveness is reduced.

(49–66)

External Obstacles

The role of the community in community policing is crucial, but sometimes the cooperation and participation of the community can be difficult to obtain. One study, for example, reported "extreme difficulty in establishing a solid infrastructure on which to build their community programs" and concluded, "the most perplexing . . . [problem] was the inability of the police department to organize and maintain active community involvement in their projects" (Grinc 1994, 437, 442). There are many reasons for difficulty in obtaining community cooperation:

1. Many families today have both parents working, and there are a substantial number of single parents. In addition to having full-time jobs, parents have to spend time with their children, run errands, cook, clean their home, and attend school functions with their children; no wonder they do not have time for neighborhood activities.

2. In many communities, the police and citizens have a long history of confrontation and alienation. Residents may fear, mistrust, and feel hostile toward the police. They may perceive the police as brutal, arrogant, and nasty and may be more interested in monitoring police misconduct than in developing a close relationship with the police.

3. Low-income high-crime areas generally lack the organizational infrastructure required for people to become involved.

4. Residents of high-crime communities may fear retaliation by neighborhood thugs and drug dealers.

5. After decades of traditional policing being sold to the general public, it is rather difficult to switch to community policing and to expect the public to understand the concept or to readily buy in to it. The police have for decades informed the public that they are the crime fighters, the specialists who will control crime. Now they say they want to develop a "partnership with the community," but they cannot expect attitudes formed by decades of traditional policing to change overnight. Nor can they expect a community to be interested in a partnership with them unless community residents are persuaded that the police and the community have similar interests and goals.

6. Residents of high-crime areas are all too familiar with police anticrime programs. They have seen such programs come and go and are likely to be skeptical.

7. Studies reveal that citizens who have been personally victimized by crime are usually more dissatisfied with the police than those who have not. Victims of crime want service, and community policing may not seem to have much to offer the crime victim.

8. Police programs imposed upon the community can often create problems because of the diversity of communities. Race, class, and lifestyle differences can all contribute to suspicion and fear among residents. Various groups contending for various governmental services, such as housing and public sector jobs, often find themselves in battle with one another over police priorities. Communities can become polarized if it is perceived that the police are favoring one group over another or treating a particular group unfairly. Further, to protect the rights of a minority, the police may have to act contrary to majority opinions.

(Skogan 1996, 31–34)

Guidelines for Successful Implementation

Wesley Skogan (1996), in his evaluation of community policing in Chicago, offered several guidelines for police administrators who wish to implement community-policing programs successfully. First, the support must be won by the police and not assumed by the police. The police must respond to citizens' interests and deliver on community policing's strategy of problem solving. There must be an organizational framework for responding to citizens' concerns. There must be communication channels to allow the public to articulate their interests and priorities to the community policing officers. One mechanism that has been used in Chicago is beat meetings. Beat meetings are small groups of neighborhood residents and police officers who meet on a regular basis throughout the city to discuss and come up with solutions to community problems.

Second, citizens should be trained as well as the police. They need to know what they can expect from the police and what they can do to contribute to neighborhood problem-solving efforts. When citizens are trained along with the police, they are better able to make decisions about prioritizing problems. Trained citizens will have a better understanding of community policing and their importance to the community-policing philosophy.

Third, community organizations have to be actively involved in community policing. Organizations have agendas that keep their members focused on issues even when their leaders change. They provide social benefits to members, such as a sense of solidarity, that can bring people out to meetings even in inclement weather. They also can provide political support for community policing.

Evaluation of Community Policing

Community policing has evolved over the last several decades and for the most part seems to be accepted by police administrators and officers. Because of this acceptance when interviewing or dealing with police personnel they will as a rule say that community policing is a success. They seem to be the biggest supporters of community policing. However, there seems to be little or no evaluation to support the effectiveness of community policing. Gary Cordner (2005) advocates that this is due to four complicating factors that make it extremely difficult to determine the effectiveness of community policing:

- Programming complexity. There exists neither a single definition of community policing nor any universal set of program elements. Police agencies around the country (and around the world) have implemented a wide array of organizational and operational innovations under the label "community policing." Because community policing is not a consistent "thing," it is difficult to determine whether "it" works.

- Multiple effects. The number of intended and unintended effects that might accrue to community policing is considerable. Community policing might affect crime, fear of crime, disorder, community relations, and/or police officer attitudes, to mention just a few plausible impacts. The reality of these multiple effects, as opposed to a single bottom-line criterion, severely reduces the likelihood of a simple yes or no answer to the question, "Does community policing work?"

- Variation in program scope. The scope of community policing projects has varied from single-officer assignments to department-wide efforts. Some of the most positive results have come from projects that involved only a few specialist officers, small special units, or narrowly defined target areas. The generalizability of these positive results to full-scale department-wide implementation is problematic.

- Research design limitations. Despite heroic efforts by police officials and researchers, most community policing studies have had serious research design limitations. These include lack of control groups, failure to randomize treatments, and a tendency to measure only short-term effects. Consequently, the findings of many community-policing studies do not have as much credibility as we might hope.

(401)

The author of this book agrees with Cordner that these four points should not be used as excuses. They should make those individuals looking at community policing aware of the difficulty in obtaining reliable information about how effective are the activities of community policing.

Examples of Community-Policing Programs

The Community Patrol Officer Program in New York City

In 1982, the New York City Police Department began developing a demonstration project called the Community Patrol Officer Program

(CPOP) in the 72nd Precinct in Brooklyn. The Vera Institute of Justice, a New York City consultant firm, was invited to assist in developing the project and to study it to determine if it merited expansion to other precincts in the city. This project was designed to incorporate four elements of community policing—"(1) community based crime prevention, (2) proactive service as opposed to emergency responses, (3) public participation in the planning and supervision of police operations, and (4) shifting of command responsibility to lower ranks" (Bayley 1988, 266)—and to be guided by the following operational and organizational principles, which were considered to be common to all community-policing programs:

- continuous assignment of police units to specific neighborhoods or beats
- insistence that the unit develop and maintain a knowledge base regarding the problems, cultural characteristics, and resources of the neighborhood
- emphasis on the importance of the unit's reaching out to neighborhood residents and businesspeople to assure them of the presence and concern of the police
- use of formal and informal mechanisms to involve community people in identifying, analyzing, and establishing priorities among local problems and in developing and implementing action plans for ameliorating them
- delegation of responsibility to the community police unit for addressing both crime and order maintenance problems of the neighborhood, and expansion of the unit's discretion in fashioning solutions to those problems
- emphasis on increasing information flow from the community to the police and on using that information to make important arrests and to develop important intelligence on illegal enterprises in the community
- sharing with representatives of the community accurate information on local crime problems and the results of ongoing efforts to address them

(New York City Police Department 1987, 4)

In 1984, the project was initiated with the creation of a special unit within the 72nd Precinct. The unit consisted of ten CPOs and a sergeant who reported to the precinct commander. Upon acceptance as a CPO, each individual received 80 hours of training on the philosophy and aims of the CPOP program, tasks to be performed, ethical concerns, and city service agencies and community organizations in the precinct. Each CPO was permanently assigned to a beat ranging in size from 16 to 60 square blocks. Officers were expected to patrol their beats alone and on foot to enhance their accessibility to the people of their beat. They were relieved of the task of responding to 911 calls so that they would have sufficient time to proactively address crime, order maintenance, and serious quality-of-life problems within their beat. With the approval of their sergeant, they could decide the starting and ending times of their tour of duty so that their work schedule could coincide with the time frame in which the problems of their beat were occurring. CPOs were also allowed to determine what day they would have off, with the approval of their sergeant, to coincide with the time of fewest problems. They were expected to become knowledgeable about the community, identify with the community, and assist community residents and businesses. Each CPO was required to maintain a "beat book" that contained his or her monthly work plan and to record information on beat problems, priorities, collective strategies, implementation progress, community leaders/organizations, and businesses (McElroy et al. 1993, 8–9).

CPOs were described as having four major roles:

1. Planner. The first responsibility of the CPOs would be to identify the principal crime and order maintenance problems confronting the people within each beat area. Toward this end, the CPOs would be expected to examine relevant statistical materials, record their own observations as they patrolled their beats, and solicit and secure input from residents, merchants, and service delivery agents in the community. The problems identified would then be prioritized and analyzed and corrective strategies designed. These strategies would be reviewed with the Unit Supervisor and incorporated in the CPO's Monthly Work Plan, which would form the focus of the officer's patrol for the coming month.

2. Problem Solver. CPOs would be encouraged to see themselves as problem solvers for the community. This would begin with the planning dimension of the role described above and proceed to the implementation of the action strategies. In the implementation phase, the officer would be encouraged to mobilize and guide four types of resources against beat area problems: the CPO acting as a law enforcement officer; other police resources on the precinct and borough levels that could be brought to bear through the CPO sergeant and the precinct commander; other public and private service agencies operating, or available to operate, in the beat area; and individual citizens or organizations in that community. The strategies developed by the CPO would call for the application of any or all of these resources, and the CPO's success in resolving the problems identified would turn in large part on his or her success in marshaling them and in coordinating their application.

3. Community Organizer. Community resources cannot be brought to bear on crime and quality-of-life problems unless the community is willing to commit them for that purpose. Increasing the consciousness of the community about its problems, involving community people and organizations in developing strategies to address the problems, motivating the people to help in implementing the strategies, and coordinating their action so that they may contribute maximally to the solution are all aspects of the community organizing dimension of the CPO role. The CPOs would be required to identify potential resources and, where they were not adequate, to help in organizing and motivating the citizenry.

4. Information Exchange Link. Through his or her links to the community, the CPO would be in a position to provide the department with information about the problem conditions and locations, active criminals, developing gangs, illicit networks for trafficking in drugs and stolen property, information about citizens' fears, and insights into [citizens'] perceptions of police tactics. In turn, the CPO could provide citizens with information pertinent to their fears and problems, technical

information and advice for preventing crimes and reducing the vulnerability of particular groups of citizens, information about the police view of conditions in the neighborhood and strategies or addressing them, and information about police operations in the community. This information exchange aspect of the CPO role was expected to result in arrests that might not occur otherwise, greater cooperation between the police and citizens in addressing crime and order maintenance problems, and a heightened sense in the citizenry that the police were a concerned and powerful resource for improving the quality of life in the community.

(Farrell 1988, 78–79)

These four roles were the basis for a guide that instructed CPOs on how to carry out the activities connected with each role. Thus, the officers were not put out on their beats to fend for themselves without guidance. The project was well planned, and all CPOs were informed of what was expected of them.

CPOs' duties as planners included identifying the principal crimes and quality-of-life issues facing the people on their beat. To achieve this goal, the CPOs would review relevant statistical records, observe the conditions on their beat, and solicit information from beat residents and businesses. When a problem was identified, the officers were to give it top priority and solve it with the collective support and input for the people on their beat. The community was to play a key role in identifying problems and finding solutions to them. The vast majority of problems that the CPOs found were quality-of-life issues that were rarely addressed by traditional policing. Some of these issues, such as prostitutes doing business on a street without police interference, were not reported to the police by citizens. In a number of areas, CPOs found small-scale drug operations.

When the officers identified problems, the next step was problem solving. The CPOs had access to four types of resources that could assist in solving problems: (1) their own law enforcement role; (2) other police resources; (3) public or private service agencies; and (4) individual citizens or neighborhood organizations. Use of community organizing could involve enlisting existing community organizations to solve neighborhood problems or developing new community organizations, such as block watches. The CPOs were effective in using existing community resources, but they found it more difficult to establish new community organizations.

CPOs' role in information exchange involved: (1) providing the precinct commander with information from citizens about crime, order maintenance, and citizens' attitudes regarding police strategies and tactics; and (2) providing the citizens with information on police department activities and priorities. By working closely with citizens, CPOs were able to gain citizens' trust and thereby to gain access to information on criminal behavior in their beat areas that was unavailable to other patrol officers (Weisburd and McElroy 1988, 91–99).

The New York City Police Department implemented a number of preventive tactics to prevent misconduct by CPOs:

1. Careful screening and selection of personnel
2. Functional supervision by all patrol supervisors and the CPOP unit sergeant
3. Staff monitoring of the program by an inspectional unit of the chief of patrol's office
4. Weekly and monthly interviews of merchants and community residents within the CPO beat areas by the unit supervisor, precinct commander, and zone commander to determine the manner in which the CPOs were conducting themselves.

(Farrell 1988, 86–87)

The CPOP project was expanded in January 1985, and in September 1988, it became operational in all 75 of the city's precincts. By that point, 750 police officers and 75 sergeants were involved (McElroy et al. 1993, 11).

Support of the CPOP project came from citizens who sent thousands of letters to the department praising the efforts of the CPOs assigned to the precincts. Precinct commanders also supported the CPOP program, because the CPOs filled a void that had existed in police operations: precinct commanders now had a resource to deal with order maintenance problems in neighborhoods (Farrell 1988, 82–83).

Seattle Public Safety Action Plan

In 1988, the National Institute of Justice provided funding for the Seattle Police Department to conduct a crime prevention project that led to community policing in that city (National Institute of Justice 1992). The southeast area of Seattle was the section of the city selected for the project. The southeast was economically behind the rest of the city, with a large proportion of low-income minorities. The crime rate was high, and there was a crack cocaine problem. Commercial burglaries were a major concern. In a meeting of the precinct police commander with businesspeople, the police commander was able to convince the business leaders that the prevalence of crack houses and drug use was tied to the high rate of commercial burglaries. From this meeting, business leaders made a number of recommendations to the mayor about crime. These recommendations led to the creation of a Crime Prevention League that established a variety of crime prevention programs, including a criminal trespass program, in which property owners gave police advance permission to enter their property to investigate and arrest loiterers, and an antigraffiti program in which volunteers would paint over graffiti. These crime prevention programs eventually spread throughout the city.

In 1989, the police department brought in a management-consulting firm to recommend improvements in public safety. The city accepted the recommendations and placed them on the November ballot. The plan, known as the Public Safety Action Plan, was approved. It had several provisions to strengthen not only the police but a number of community organizations:

- Crime Prevention Councils. The plan authorized the city to allot $95,000 each year to increase citizen involvement in precinct work. This took the form of grants to South Seattle Crime Prevention Council (SSCPC) and other crime prevention councils to pay for record keeping, mailing lists, board support, and other expenses.
- Police Department Advisory Councils. Funds were also earmarked for the development of citizen-based councils that would advise the precinct commanders on community issues. Precinct commanders would provide input on the selection of board members as well as agenda items.

- Community-Police Teams. A key recommendation of the consultants' study that was incorporated into the Public Safety Action Plan was to introduce into each precinct of the city a community policing team composed of five officers and one sergeant. The team would give full-time attention to community policing and would be specifically excluded from the responsibility of answering 911 calls. The purpose of creating the specialty teams was to lock the concept of community policing into each precinct.
- Joint Parks Department and Police Guide Program. Funds were allocated to a program in which police union volunteers would work with older youth in an evening-hours recreational program.
- Youth Intervention Program. The plan called for a program to be jointly planned by the police, the department of human resources, the schools, and community agencies. The program's purpose was to prevent youth from getting involved in gangs and to intervene with youth who were already at high risk of involvement.

(National Institute of Justice 1992, 7–8)

The Seattle Public Safety Action plan placed the city and police department in the middle of community policing, because all of the above programs required the cooperation of police and community organizations. The Seattle policing philosophy was that traditional police methods were not incompatible with community policing. CPOs were expected not only to work proactively on community problems but to function as law enforcement officers by making arrests when appropriate.

Summary

The community-policing approach is not entirely new, but it represents a major break with the professional or crime control model of policing that dominated policing agencies for much of the twentieth century, and it is in large part a reaction to the failure of previous crime control methods to adequately prevent, solve, or reduce crime. The concept of community policing has a variety of definitions and meanings but in general can be said to include a problem-solving, results-oriented, consumer-oriented approach to law enforcement and an emphasis on partnership with the community in solving problems of crime, fear of crime, public disorder, and neighborhood decay. Although the effectiveness of community policing in preventing crime is not yet clearly proven, community policing can positively affect citizen attitudes such as fear of crime and satisfaction with the neighborhood. It also facilitates public examination of police practices, makes police more accountable to the community, and stimulates efforts to employ more women and minorities in police work. Benefits to police departments include a more positive image of police, more grassroots support for police, and raised police morale. Some potential problems with community policing are that police action to uphold local norms of order and respectability may go beyond legal bounds (e.g., in harassment of the homeless); that police strategies may selectively benefit the more well-to-do and powerful segments of the community at the expense of the others; that CPOs may use their close community ties for political ends or for their own gain (i.e., corruption); and that police may become too intrusive into residents' private lives.

The implementation of a community-policing program may face several obstacles. Many aspects of traditional police organization and culture are resistant to the changes that community policing involves. In addition, community involvement may be difficult to obtain, for reasons ranging from residents' lack of time, to residents' mistrust of police or fear of neighborhood criminals, to the lack of a neighborhood infrastructure in high-crime neighborhoods. Community support must be won by police and not assumed by police.

This chapter discussed two programs in detail: the Community Patrol Officer Program in New York City and the Public Safety Action Plan in Seattle. Both programs were initiated on a small scale and eventually expanded to the entire city. These programs were considered to be successful and provided many benefits to the community that traditional policing did not provide.

KEY TERMS

- beat book
- community policing
- CPO
- CPOP
- Arthur Woods
- Mary Ann Wycoff

REVIEW QUESTIONS

1. Define community-policing philosophy.
2. Discuss the benefits of community policing.
3. Discuss the potential pitfalls of community policing.
4. Discuss obstacles to implementing community policing.

10
PLANNING THE IMPLEMENTATION OF COMMUNITY POLICING

CHAPTER OBJECTIVES

1. Be familiar with the planning process.

2. Be able to define the term planning.

3. Be familiar with the value of strategic planning in implementing community policing.

4. Be familiar with the value of continuous assessment in implementing community policing.

Introduction

As Malcolm Sparrow (1982) remarked, those who accept the desirability of introducing community policing confront a host of difficult issues: What structural changes are necessary, if any? How do we get the people on the beat to behave differently? Can the people we have now be forced into the new mold, or do we need to recruit a new kind of person? What should we tell the public, and when? How fast can we bring about this change? Do we have enough external support? (2).

Before community policing can be implemented to any degree in a police organization, a plan must be established to address such questions and many others. A plan often will depend upon the size of the police organization and the number of qualified personnel who are familiar with the planning process. Large police organizations may have a planning section with trained planners, whereas small ones may not have any trained planning personnel or planning unit. Depending on whether there are planning personnel, a police organization may have either a very detailed strategic plan or a "plan as you go" approach. A "plan as you go" approach may have goals, objectives, and a mission for implementing community policing, but goals and objectives are not detailed, and there may not be any consideration of potential problems, issues, or impediments to implementing community policing. A strategic plan includes mission, vision, and values statements, goals and objectives, analysis of community and department needs and resources, analysis of potential obstacles, action steps for accomplishing goals, time frames and sometimes personnel assignments for action steps, and mechanisms of monitoring and assessment.

Police departments that have the capabilities to develop a strategic plan are advised to do so. A well-developed strategic plan can assist in knocking down barriers to the implementation of community policing. Both police personnel and members of the community should be involved in the planning process. A well-thought-out strategic plan should make community policing easier to implement and increase chances of obtaining the support of police personnel and community members.

The transition from traditional policing to community policing is not easy, and this must be taken into consideration by the chief executive of the police organization. Patience and understanding are important in implementing community policing.

What Is Planning?

Planning has been defined as "setting objectives and deciding how to achieve them" (Tansik and Elliott 1981, 33), or, in more detail, as

> a management function concerned with visualizing future situations, making estimates concerning them, identifying the issues, needs and potential points, analyzing and evaluating the alternative ways and means for reaching desired goals according to a certain schedule, estimating the necessary funds and resources to do the work, and initiating action in time to prepare what may be needed to cope with changing conditions and contingent events.
>
> (Mottley 1972, 127)

Planning entails decision making; it involves selecting a route that an organization will follow. There are various types of plans, ranging from the detailed to the broadly defined plan for getting organizational goals on track. Planning asks the basic questions, What to do? How to do it? When to do it? Who will do it? (Koontz et al. 1986, 35).

Plans to implement community policing vary a great deal in scope. Some are plans to set up a special community policing unit within a department that is free from responding to radio calls and is thus able to work on community problems full time. Others are plans to turn every officer in the department into a community policing officer. Some plans cover a specific neighborhood, others an entire city. The scope of the plan will generally depend upon the size of the agency, the number of police personnel who can be assigned to the plan, the ability of the police organization to accept innovation, the extent of changes required, and the expectations of the community concerning the police. But even agencies with ambitious plans tend to start out small and initiate community policing in a single neighborhood.

Why Plan?

Planning brings an organization's present situation into line with its goals for the future and lets members of an organization know what these goals are so that they can more effectively accomplish the organization's mission. By focusing on organizational goals, it allows the organization to concentrate its resources on goal-oriented priorities. It provides a blueprint and a process for achieving goals and makes clear who is responsible for what. It allows administrators to anticipate problems and to think about how to sidestep them or lessen their impact. It encourages long-range thinking. It cuts down on haphazard actions and makes possible better coordination of action so that different actions do not undercut each other or cancel each other out. Finally, it increases the chances of obtaining the external and internal support necessary for the plan to succeed (Whisenand and Ferguson 1989, 157–159). A plan should be considered as a specified outline of the format to be executed. A plan follows the following points:

1. The need for the plan must be recognized. An apparent need must be verified by a more intensive investigation and analysis.

2. The objective must be stated, and the general method of operation (the manner in which the objective is to be attained) must be determined.

3. Data necessary in the development of the plan must be gathered and analyzed. Included will be answers to the questions of "what," "where," "when," "who," and "how."

4. The details of the plan must be developed: personnel and equipment must be provided and organized, procedures developed or applied, schedules drawn up, and assignments made.

5. Planning reports must be prepared.

6. Planners should participate in a staff capacity during implementation, if this is requested by persons carrying out the plan.

7. Plans must be reviewed, and modified if necessary, to accommodate changes in need and technology.

(Fyfe et al. 1997)

Silverman (1995) has vividly described the chaos and confusion that result from insufficient planning:

1. We are not sure what the problem is. Definitions of the problem are vague or competing, and any given problem is intertwined with other messy problems.

2. We are not sure what is really happening. Information is incomplete, ambiguous, and unreliable, and people disagree on how to interpret the information that is available.

3. We are not sure what we want. We have multiple goals that are unclear or conflicting or both. Different people want different things, leading to political and emotional conflict.

4. We do not have the resources we need. Shortages of time, attention, or money make a difficult situation even more chaotic.

5. We are not sure who is supposed to do what. Roles are unclear, there is disagreement about who is responsible for what, and things keep shifting as players come and go.

6. We are not sure how to get what we want. Even if we agree on what we want, we are not sure what causes what.

7. We are not sure how to determine if we have succeeded. We are not sure what criteria to use to evaluate success. If we do know the criteria, we are not sure how to measure them.

(37–45)

In making the transition to community policing, planning is particularly important because community policing involves new concepts and strategies that may be unfamiliar to many people and that may conflict with many established police practices and organizational structures (see Chapter 9).

How Much Planning Before Implementation?

A key question facing police agencies is how far ahead and how extensively they should plan a community-policing program before putting it into operation. The Bureau of Justice Assistance (1994b) outlined three possible approaches, along with their strengths and weaknesses:

1. Plan, then implement. This method entails developing a detailed long-range plan, with tasks and timelines, and assigning officers to execute the plan. This approach clearly delineates a set of strategies and actions that impart a sense of direction to implementation efforts; however, and even a very detailed plan will be unable to predict the obstacles that will arise. In the absence of experienced-based feedback, some part of the implementation process may be miscalculated. Planning can also be complicated by the size of the staff involved. Keeping the planning staff relatively small may prevent the process from becoming unwieldy; however, it may not adequately represent all levels of command, function, and experience within the organization, thus creating the risk that the plan will not be implemented. Planning can also become excessive and may stifle enthusiasm.

2. Plan and implement. In this approach, planning and action occur simultaneously. While the planning process continues, the agency, to get started quickly, involves more personnel at the outset and permits further planning to benefit from

feedback. However, the agency risks false starts, confusion, and major blunders unless effective, rapid, and regular communication takes place between planners and implementers.

3. Implement with little planning. The third option is for an agency with little preparation or knowledge of the nature of community policing to quickly launch into the action phase and then, on the basis of feedback, to retool the effort and begin the cycle again. This process is continuous, with each reevaluation cycle advancing the idea of community policing a bit further within the organization. This approach assumes that a limited knowledge of community policing may prevent agencies from initially planning in a meaningful way. Advocates note that the almost immediate action will catch officers' attention at all organizational levels and will harness the existing enthusiasm to help mobilize support. However, the constant shifts in goals and actions can be highly unsettling to the organization and the community it serves.

(29–30)

According to the Bureau, none of these approaches is the "one right way." Police administrators will have to choose among them on the basis of agency priorities, resources, and support for change.

Who Plans?

All personnel in a police department should be involved in planning, but the expectations from personnel will vary. Kuykendall and Unsinger (1979) describe general planning responsibilities of each of the three levels of administration:

1. Top management is concerned with long-range considerations and general planning, and considerable time is invested in planning activities. In large police departments, top management is placing increasingly greater reliance on specialized planning and research units.

2. Middle managers participate in development of all ranges of plans in the agency, oversee the short- and intermediate-range

plans, develop many of the details in long- and intermediate-range plans, and usually play a key role in making adjustments in the execution phases of plans.

3. Supervisors participate in the planning process by overseeing operational plans, and in many small police departments may perform the functions of middle managers as well; they also assist in developing the specifics or details for translation of plans into action.

(105)

But as discussed in Chapter 9, community policing requires a more democratic management style, and this should begin in the planning for the transition to community policing. Therefore, all community-policing plans should include not only the three levels of management but also line, staff, and civilian personnel. Bottom-up thinking should be employed rather than top-down thinking. Command staff should have limited involvement in strategic planning. A police officer could be the leader of the committee, and it would not be a bad idea for the chief not to be on the committee.

Community policing especially needs the understanding and support of line personnel if it is to have an impact on their community. The gap between "management cops" and "street cops" can be closed if management shows a willingness to make the street cop an important component of community-policing planning, and this can make a big difference in the plan's success. A study sponsored by the National Institute of Justice of neighborhood-oriented policing of eight cities found that gaining police acceptance was a principal obstacle to implementing community policing and that officers who had limited or no knowledge about community policing or who felt that they had no voice in planning it did not support its implementation (Sadd and Grinc 1996, 7–11).

The participation of a cross-section of personnel—administrators, middle managers, supervisors, line and staff personnel, civilian personnel, and representatives from all department units and divisions—makes it possible to deal with and overcome resistance to community policing at an early stage—for example, claims that too much work will be required, that the plan will be used against employees at a later date, or that the plan limits officers' law enforcement powers. The more people who see that their input is solicited and incorporated, the more support the plan will have.

Planning for community policing should also involve the community.* A strategic plan created without soliciting the cooperation of the community is doomed to failure. The community must buy in to the plan for it to be implemented successfully. When a community-policing strategic plan involves the community, the process includes bringing together a community as a whole to plan the policing philosophy and practices in a specific geographic location and developing community consensus and political momentum to ensure long-term support and commitment to change (National Center 1997, 8).

Active community and neighborhood members, along with persons who reflect the diversity of the community, should be made members of the strategic planning team. Community team members should represent the interest of homeowners, apartment dwellers, and business owners. Planning should also involve other governmental and service agencies who are involved in communities and neighborhoods.

How to Plan

A precursor to making a strategic plan is developing a vision, a values statement, and a mission statement (see Chapter 9):

- Vision: a picture or image of where people want the organization to be
- Values statement: statement of the principles, standards, or qualities that are regarded as worthwhile or desirable by the organization
- Mission statement: a statement of the organization's purpose or what it is striving for

(National Center 1997, 17)

This is to ensure that whatever the organization plans will be in keeping with its values and will contribute to accomplishing its mission and fulfilling its vision.

---

* Source: These two paragraphs are adapted from National Center for State, Local, and International Law Enforcement Center on Strategic Planning and Implementation, STAR Manual, Federal Law Enforcement Training Center.

Then, constructing the plan involves answering three major questions:

1. Where do we want to be? This is the process of strategically setting goals.
2. Where are we now? Relative to the strategically set goals, what is the current position? What resources do we have? What limitations or barriers are we facing?
3. How do we get there from here? What programs, projects, and policies will allow us to achieve the goals?

(Tansik and Elliott 1981, 39; see also
Fyfe et al. 1997, 214–215)

The first step, defining realistic goals, is not easy particularly because goals of organizations are often contradictory. For example, the community-policing goal of proactive problem solving in the community might come into conflict with a goal of rapid response time to every call because there might not be enough officers or enough time for officers to accomplish both goals. In this case, it might be necessary to relinquish or modify the goal considered to be less important.

Goal setting, like every other stage of planning, requires community participation. Goals should be what both the police department and the community want to accomplish. Also, goal setting requires input, from both internal and external surveys, to gauge departmental and community views, priorities, needs, and concerns. Step 2 involves analyzing how far the department is from achieving its goals, whether the goals are realistically achievable, and the current circumstances that could help or obstruct goal attainment. Here, resources are a major issue, in the form of assistance and expertise (e.g., from community organizations) and in the form of manpower and material resources such as equipment and money. Are there a sufficient number of officers to establish community policing? Does the chief have to obtain new funding, take resources from, or even eliminate another policing activity? Attitudes of support or opposition are also crucial to recognize. They include:

- Leadership attitudes. Police administrators are often autocratic. They often feel personal ownership of the department and run it rigidly with a philosophy of "My way or the highway." The democratic style of community policing may threaten them.

- Rank-and-file attitudes. Adherence to the crime-fighting image of policing and a view of the citizen as the enemy are contradictory to the community policing philosophy. Also, concerns about changed workloads and responsibilities will have to be addressed. For example, if some officers are freed from responding to calls for service in order to do community policing, how will positive working relationships be maintained with officers who must take on their workload?
- Attitudes of elected officials. Policing is embedded in politics. Governmental officials provide the budget for the police department to hire more personnel, obtain more equipment, and institute pay raises. Therefore, these officials must buy in to the community policing philosophy for it to be successfully implemented.

(Rush 1992, 44–45; Bureau of Justice
Assistance 1994a, 57)

Finally, aspects of traditional organizational structure may interfere with the implementation of community policing. These are discussed extensively in Chapter 9. The third step involves developing a sequence of specific actions to achieve the goals. Alternative actions should be designed in order to give community policing the best chance of succeeding in a constantly changing environment (Tansik and Elliott 1981, 40).

Fine-tuning the Plan

Once planners have specified goals, assessed needs, resources, and barriers, and specified a sequence of actions to attain goals, they must work out more details of how the plan will be implemented. First, people must be assigned to work on each action and see it through to completion. Then realistic time frames for completing specific tasks should be established. It should be taken into consideration that if implementation moves too slowly, enthusiasm may be checked and any momentum that existed may be lost, but that moving too quickly may create confusion and chaos.

Training is an important aspect of implementing any community-policing program and will be discussed in detail in the next chapter. Planning for training involves four steps, each of which must be assigned an estimated time frame:

1. Developing a curriculum.
2. Identifying and possibly training the trainers.
3. Acquiring training materials (books, handouts, etc.).
4. Developing a training schedule and making arrangements for officers to attend.

(Bureau of Justice Assistance 1994a, 53)

The community-policing implementation plan should also describe how community-policing activities will be monitored. The monitoring function should be made as much a part of the normal activities of the police department as possible. For example, if command meetings are regularly scheduled, then the progress on the community-policing plan should be placed on the agenda and discussed. If department heads are required to provide activity reports, then community-policing-related information should be included in the report. Units or individuals responsible for the specific community-policing objectives should provide feedback about the progress being made toward achieving these objectives. The primary purpose of monitoring the progress of goals and objectives of the community-policing plan is to inform personnel responsible for specific programs if they are achieving their objectives. If they are not, the monitoring process will allow them to make corrections in their activities in order to achieve the objectives they were assigned (Meese 1991, 57).

Finally, mechanisms for assessing whether the objectives of the plan are being achieved must be established from the beginning, as part of the planning process, and assessment must be a continuing process. Continuous assessment can determine whether the plan is on track and, if not, can prompt the necessary decisions to get it back on track. The assessment gives the police personnel direction and helps to determine what procedures should be changed, eliminated, or altered. Assessment can help answer two questions: whether the project is proceeding as planned and whether it is having the desired impact. The first question can be answered through regular meetings of the chief executive of the police organization with those responsible for implementing the community-policing plan to find out about problems and how to correct them, and by regular reports submitted to the police agency's head on the progress in implementing community policing and any problems pertaining to the attainment of specific community-policing objectives and goals. In addition, the implementation team can periodically survey police personnel to obtain their input as to which community objectives and goals are working. This input can be used to correct any problems where appropriate. The second question, concerning the project's impact on the organization and the community, cannot be answered by using traditional methods of assessment. Measures such as the number of 911 calls served, number of arrests made, response time to calls, and number of arrests made and traffic citations issued are not useful for assessing the impact of community policing. Crime statistics can be a measure but should be only one of many used to assess community policing. Because the community-policing philosophy has as its goals eliminating the fear of crime, improving the quality of life in the community, and developing a partnership between the police department and the community, these must all be assessed as well.

Meese (1991) has suggested using criteria of effectiveness, efficiency, and equity to assess community policing (44–51). Effectiveness is important to measure because one outcome expected from the community-policing strategy is that it will be more effective than the traditional approach to policing. Dimensions of effectiveness here would include reducing neighborhood crime, decreasing citizens' fear of crime, and improving communities' quality of life. Also assessed is the success of the strategies used to solve neighborhood problems.

Efficiency involves whether the community-policing strategy has been obtaining the most results from the available resources. Are resources being used to their fullest possible extent to solve neighborhood and community problems? Use of technologies, use of community organizations, prioritizing of service calls, redefining of job descriptions, and coordination of problem-solving activities all fall under this head.

Equity, or fairness, criteria should be used to assess every community-policing program and its results:

- Equal access to police services. All citizens, regardless of race, religion, personal characteristics, or group affiliation, must have equal access to police services for a full and productive partnership with a community. The paramount commitment of community policing should be respect for all citizens and sensitivity to their needs. . . . Supervisors should help to ensure that police services are readily available throughout the community.

- Equal treatment under the Constitution. Police must treat all individuals according to the constitutional rights that officers are sworn to protect and enforce. Careful attention to the constitutional rights of citizens, victims, or perpetrators will help to engender bonds of trust between the police and community. Police must treat all persons with respect and impartially including the homeless, the poor, and the mentally or physically handicapped. They must reject stereotypes, ignore skin color, and use reason and persuasion rather than coercion whenever possible because inequitable or harsh treatment can lead to frustration, hostility, and even violence within a community. Such unethical behavior will imperil the trust so necessary to community policing.

- Equal distribution of police services and resources among communities. Because community policing customizes policing services to the needs of each community, services should be distributed equitably among poor and minority communities. Care must be taken, however, to ensure that this is the case. For equitable distribution of resources among communities, each community must articulate its needs and be willing to work with the police to ensure its share of police services. Each neighborhood officer must listen to the community members and be willing to work with the community members to meet those needs. Poor and minority neighborhoods can present particular challenges for some patrol officers, who may have to bridge differences of race and class before a level of trust and cooperation can be established.

(50–51)

Community policing needs to be continuously assessed and reevaluated to determine its successes and failures. Adjustments to ongoing programs should be expected and made where appropriate.

The Final Plan Document

Generally, the final plan document will contain a chief executive summary, an introduction to the plan, an overview of the community and police department, a vision statement, a values statement, a mission statement, an organizational table, internal and external analysis, goals, objectives, action steps, time frames and sometimes job assignments, and mechanisms of monitoring and assessment. Initially, a draft of the plan is developed, and a committee of team members is selected to review it. The team reviews the goals and objectives and works to eliminate redundancy and maintain the plan's focus. After review, the plan is finalized and presented to the police department, local government, and the community. It is recommended that all personnel receive a copy of the strategic plan.

A strategic plan is a living document that is flexible and open to change and adjustments. It provides a road map for the police department to use as a guide for operations and encourages strategic thinking and organizational learning. It should be noted that a strategic plan will not be etched in concrete and that it in no way substitutes for leadership.

Evaluation

Upon completion of the implementation of community policing, it may be a good idea to evaluate if community policing has been achieving its mission and goals. Community policing should be evaluated periodically to determine if adjustments or changes are required for community policing to meet its objectives. Evaluation can be defined as "the use of social research methods to systematically investigate the effectiveness of social intervention programs in ways that are adapted to their political and organizational environments and are designed to inform social action to improve social conditions" (Rossi, Lipsey, and Freeman 2004, 16).

There are numerous reasons why community policing should be evaluated. It could be done to provide information to police executives and commanders on what needs to be improved in community policing. The evaluation could provide specific information to supporters of community policing and answer critics of community policing. Evaluation of community policing will provide data on what is working. Do the line officers and the neighborhood residents support community policing? Do changes need to be made in community policing? If so, what are they?

Evaluations can provide police agencies with useful information concerning the efficiency and effectiveness of community policing. An evaluation of community policing can determine if problems are being addressed; has community policing been successful. By evaluating community policing support could be solidified, make adjustments in community policing where needed, and review the effectiveness of community policing. A national evaluation of the Community-Oriented Policing Services (COPS) took place several years after COPS was put into place. The national evaluation examined the success of five criteria as it pertained to COPS. The success of the criteria included: "client satisfaction; effect on the quality or level of policing in the United States; effect on agencies' transitions to community policing; effectiveness in stimulating technologies and organizational innovation and effect on crime" (Roth and Ryan 2000, 19).

Evaluation is considered compatible and valuable with community policing and problem-solving techniques. Evaluations should include involvement from stakeholders who can contribute to improving community policing. Obtaining input from the community and police professionals can enhance community policing and contribute to neighborhood improvements. A police–neighborhood partnership along with accountability can develop into citizens' satisfaction and support of the police. Although obstacles exist in evaluating community policing evaluation should be done to determine if it has value to the community and more importantly that the police are actually performing, supporting, and have community policing in place (Ward, Chibnall, and Harris 2007, 7–8).

The major push of the Community Policing Evaluation Survey (CPES) is to provide information in a short survey. The survey instrument should be able to be understood and scored by nonstatisticians. Also, the survey should be able to reveal evaluation of community policing. A short survey of 20 questions was divided into four sections with each section having five questions. The four sections were divided into quality of police contact, view of crime, fear factors, and community cohesion (McKee 2001, 200; 208).

In a study published by *Crime and Delinquency* an evaluation of the impact of community policing in six midsize North Carolina police departments evaluated the impact of how community policing officers view traditional policing and how they accept community policing goals and police officers satisfaction with their jobs (Adams, Rohe, and Arcury 2009, 422).

Community policing in all communities should be evaluated periodically. Only through evaluation can a police department determine the success of community policing in their city. Evaluation can provide information on the attitude of the officers of their department and the perceptions of the citizens about community policing, and need for new strategies and innovations to correct deficiencies of the philosophy of community policing.

Summary

Before community policing can be implemented by a police agency, the implementation must be planned. Planning is setting objectives and deciding how to achieve them. A complete strategic plan includes mission, vision, and values statements, goals and objectives, analysis of community and department needs and resources, analysis of potential obstacles, action steps for accomplishing goals, time frames, and personnel assignments for action steps, and mechanisms of monitoring and assessment.

Police departments that have the capabilities to develop a strategic plan are advised to do so. A well-thought-out plan gives a department direction, focuses its resources on agreed-upon priorities, allows administrators to anticipate and circumvent problems, encourages long-range thinking, cuts down any haphazard actions, coordinates agency actions, and increases the chances of obtaining internal and external support.

Planning should involve the community at all stages and should enlist the participation of all police personnel at all levels. The input of lower-level "street cops" should be especially encouraged. The planning process begins with statements of the agency mission, vision, and values, because any goals must be in keeping with them and help to fulfill them. Planners should then determine where they want to be (goals), where they are now (how far they are from achieving the goals and current circumstances that could help or obstruct goal attainment), and how they can get there from here (specific action steps to reach goals). The finished plan should not be regarded as unalterable or as a substitute for leadership. Its workability and its impact must be continually assessed as it unfolds so that it can be modified as changing circumstances require.

Evaluation of community policing is important to determine if it is working, being accepted by the community and by the officers in the police department. Changes in community policing may have to take place if there are difficulties to the community police approach adopted by the police department. Police administrators should want feedback from the neighborhoods where community policing has been initiated and obtain the attitude of the police officers where it has been established.

KEY TERMS

- assessment
- effectiveness
- efficiency
- equity
- mission statement
- monitoring

- planning
- strategic planning
- time frame
- values
- vision

REVIEW QUESTIONS

1. Describe the planning process.
2. Discuss the importance of strategic planning to community policing.
3. Discuss who should be involved in planning and why.
4. Discuss the various approaches to how much planning should be done before implementation.
5. Discuss why assessment is important to the implementation of community policing.

11

SELECTED APPROACHES TO TRAINING AND PLANNING

CHAPTER OBJECTIVES

1. Be familiar with new developments in community-policing training.

2. Be familiar with the Royal Canadian Mounted Police approach to training.

3. Be familiar with one small police agency's approach to community policing.

4. Be familiar with one midsized police agency's approach to community policing.

5. Be familiar with the Illinois State Police approach to community policing.

6. Be familiar with the elements of one strategic community-policing plan.

Introduction

The training of police officers in the community-policing philosophy is a key element for the successful transition from traditional policing to community policing. Police officers must understand the community-policing concept if they are expected to use it.

There are a variety of training programs and methods to teach the community-policing philosophy. Training can range from the traditional lecture method, with the instructor feeding the police student information, to computer-based instruction, role-playing, and adult-based learning. In the last several years, police training academies have been approaching training police officers using adult-based learning. It is believed that adult-based learning gives police officers a better opportunity to learn and retain information and holds them responsible for their learning. The first part of this chapter presents selected police agencies' approaches to training in community policing.

When police departments make a transition from traditional policing to community policing, they use different approaches to implement it depending on the demographic characteristics of the community being served, the major problems and needs of the community, the support of government officials, the availability of resources, the willingness of police command staff and officers to accept the community-policing philosophy, police administrators' managerial and policing philosophy, the progressiveness of the community, and the educational and training level of police personnel. The second part of this chapter showcases selected police departments' approaches to implementation.

New Approaches to Police Training

The training of police officers is going through a transition. Community policing will revolutionize both the content of police training and how police are being trained. According to Edwin Meese (1991), a former Attorney General of the United States, "The content of police training must go beyond merely preparing officers for the mechanical aspects of police work. . . . Training should help them understand their communities, the police role, police history, and even imperfections of the criminal justice system" (6). Meese's comments are especially true for training in community policing. Palmiotto et al. (1998) have advanced three guidelines for the content of such training:

1. Police officers should possess a sense of social history. An understanding of police history can contribute to an understanding of policing's current mission and objectives. For practitioners to prepare for and create the future of policing, it is imperative that they examine where policing has been. They need to know what has been tried, what has succeeded, and what has failed in police practice and why. They should know the characteristics of each era in policing history (prepolitical era, political era, and reform era). Only by understanding the past will police personnel be in a position to

understand and implement needed change in their organization and to improve interaction with the community.

2. Police officers should have a sense of how societies and communities function. Responding to community disorder is at the heart of community policing. Instruction should include social indicators of crime and disorder (e.g., crime rates, crime trends, jail and prison populations, victimization numbers, juvenile crime rates, poverty indicators, unemployment figures, and other economic antecedents and consequences of crime) as well as related indicators of "quality of life" and neighborhood wellness.

3. Police officers should be equipped with the skills and knowledge for incorporating community policing into their work. Before instructors teach any police training class, they should attend a training session on the value of incorporating the community policing philosophy into their courses.

(9–11)

A shift in training methods is also being recommended. The traditional method, referred to as the pedagogical technique, emphasizes information-based learning, primarily through the lecture-driven class. In this approach, learning is passive: the instructor dictates to students what they should learn, and students play no role in deciding what is important; they merely digest the information and give it back in the form of written examinations. In this model, students assume no responsibility for their learning.

The alternative to the pedagogical model is the andragogical model. Its supporters believe that the pedagogical approach is best fitted to children, whereas the andragogical approach is best fitted to adult learners. According to Malcolm Knowles, the leading proponent of andragogy:

Andragogy is premised on at least four crucial assumptions about the characteristics of adult learners that are different from the assumptions about child learners on which traditional pedagogy is premised. These assumptions are that, as a person matures, (1) his self-concept moves from one of being a dependent personality toward one of being a self-directing human being, (2) he accumulates a growing reservoir of experience that becomes an increasing resource for learning, (3) his readiness to learn becomes oriented increasingly to the developmental tasks of his social roles, and (4) his time perspective changes from one of postponed application [to one of immediate application], and accordingly his orientation toward learning shifts from one of subject centeredness to one of problem centeredness.

(quoted in Cross 1981, 222–223)

According to this approach, adults learn differently from children or people with no experiences or knowledge base to build upon. Knowles (1990b) described five characteristics of adults as learners:

1. The need to know. Adults learn more effectively if they understand why they need to know or be able to do something.
   . . .
2. The need to be self-directing. Adults have a deep psychological need to take responsibility for their own lives—to be self-directing. . . .
3. Greater volume and quality of experience. Adults, by virtue of having lived longer, accumulate a greater volume and a different quality of experience than children and youth. The greater volume is self-evident—they having done more things, and the longer they have lived, the more things they have done. . . .
4. Readiness to learn. Whereas youth have been well conditioned to be ready to learn what they are told or have to learn, adults become ready to learn those things that they perceive will bring them greater satisfaction or success of life.
5. Orientation to learning. Whereas children and youth have been conditioned to enter into a learning activity with a subject-centered orientation to learning, adults have a life-centered, task-centered, or problem-centered orientation.

(6.8–6.12)

With an andragogical approach, the instructor or teacher functions as a facilitator and resource: he or she guides and assists the students but does not necessarily make learning decisions for them. The learning environment created by the facilitator is characterized by mutual trust and respect between students and facilitator, the encouragement of student inquiry, and openness to learning (6.13–6.14).

According to Knowles (1990a), the primary purpose of schooling is to help individuals develop the skill of learning, with the final objective of becoming involved in self-directed inquiry in self-actualizing directions. Learning, in his view, should involve the following seven abilities:

1. The ability to develop and be in touch with curiosities. Perhaps another way to describe this skill would be "the ability to engage in divergent thinking."
2. The ability to perceive one's self objectively and accept feedback about one's performance nondefensively.
3. The ability to diagnose one's learning needs in the light of models of competencies required for performing life roles.
4. The ability to identify human, material, and experiential resources for accomplishing various kinds of learning objectives.
5. The ability to design a plan of strategies for making use of appropriate learning resources effectively.
6. The ability to carry out a learning plan systematically and sequentially. This skill is the beginning of the ability to engage in convergent thinking.
7. The ability to collect evidence of the accomplishment of learning objectives and have it validated through performance.

(174)

Royal Canadian Mounted Police

In 1990, the Royal Canadian Mounted Police (RCMP) reviewed their techniques of traditional training by interviewing graduates and trainers, interviewing top management, and reviewing evaluations, audits, and training practices of other police organizations. A major finding from this review was that the skills needed for policing were changing and that the process for learning police skills would consequently have to change as well. The RCMP were at the time making a transition to community policing that involved flattening the organizational structure, encouraging the use of problem-solving techniques, and developing partnerships with the community. They recognized that police officers, to fit into this new approach, would need to be innovative problem solvers with excellent people skills in such areas as negotiation and alliance development. The RCMP therefore introduced a new approach to training that incorporated many aspects of the andragogy model. Trainees were held responsible for their own training, with the instructor-trainer functioning as a facilitator (Himelfarb 1997, 33–34).

The RCMP developed a community-policing problem-solving model known as CAPRA and restructured their police training so that all officers began their careers committed to it. The purpose of CAPRA is to promote discussions in small groups of employees, clients, and community partners. The CAPRA model emphasizes the importance of

- developing and maintaining partnerships and trust within communities/the workforce to establish priorities for service delivery and preventive problem solving
- understanding clients' perspective on work-related matters for establishing priorities and potential partnerships in service delivery
- encouraging ongoing feedback for continuous improvement

(RCMP, n.d., 1)

The acronym CAPRA stands for:

- C = Clients. Police assess and define problems through understanding the needs and expectations of diverse clients. Starting with the client means that the police must step outside their own professional understanding, their own culture, and learn to see the world through the eyes of those they serve. . . . Effective policing requires an understanding of the diverse and changing needs of the full range of clients in any particular situation and the ability to integrate or balance competing interests.
- A = Acquiring and Analyzing Information. Key to preventing, defining, and resolving problems, especially in our information-driven society, is the ability to collect, organize, analyze, and

document information. . . . Effective community policing requires information beyond a specific case or incident. It requires information that helps police to understand their clients' concerns. New technologies provide unprecedented access to information on patterns of crime, community profiles, client/ community perceptions and expectations, services available, etc. . . .

- P = Partnership. . . . At a minimum, increasingly complex police problems require multidisciplinary teams that bring together various skills, often both police and non-police agencies. Additionally, partnerships now include more specific clients, community groups, and their representatives, for example, in the form of advisory committees. . . .

- R = Response. . . . Enforcement is one possible response. Service, crime prevention, and protection are also possible responses depending on clients' needs, and usually a combination of responses will be required. All police responses, including enforcement, fall within the CAPRA model. Thus, planning and implementing the appropriate response will require an understanding not only of police duties, responsibilities, and powers, but also [of] the principles that guide the use of discretion and, increasingly, the role of police in supporting non-enforcement responses.

- A = Assessment for Continuous Improvement. Increasingly, effective policing demands approaches and techniques for ongoing assessments that promote continuous improvement and learning. Complementing traditional approaches to audit, evaluation, and management review will be the commitment of each member to continually review and learn from each problem-solving process. Policing in modem society must build in processes of adaptation, promote flexibility, and instill continuous learning.

(Himelfarb 1997, 34–37)

The RCMP approach to police training is learner centered rather than instructor centered. The teaching of recruits involves problem solving through research, group problem-solving exercises, information gathering, case studies, and the use of scenarios. This kind of application of the andragogical model to teach police officers may be the wave of the future. Several police departments and academies in the United States have adopted the RCMP training approach. However, because this training approach is relatively new to policing, several decades may pass before we can determine whether it is an improvement over the traditional approach to police training.

Savannah Police Department Training

The Savannah Police Department, like most police departments, recognized that before they could implement community policing they had to train police personnel in its philosophy and principles. The department's training director and the deputy chief responsible for implementing community policing developed seven training modules to bring police personnel up to date on the philosophy of community policing.

The first module was for command staff. It was divided into two parts: the first previewed the next six, thereby giving administrators an overview of community policing and the content of instruction for personnel, and the second introduced total quality management (TQM) and the essential role of a TQM leadership style in the successful implementation of community policing.

The second module of training provided an overview of community policing. It began with an in-depth analysis of crime in Savannah and the conditions found in high-crime areas. Community policing principles were reviewed, and the goals of the Savannah Police Department were outlined. The specific roles and responsibilities of managers, supervisors, and police officers were addressed.

In module three, problem-oriented policing was examined. Because the Savannah Police Department considered problem-oriented policing to be a major component of community policing, officers were instructed on how to identify problems and go about solving them. The officers were informed that community resources could be focused on solving recurring problems.

The fourth module dealt with referrals and the specific agencies available in the city of Savannah. Officers were given city codes that could assist them in eradicating problems endemic to Savannah. In the fifth module, "Developing Sources of Human Information," the focus was on communicating with Savannah's residents in order to develop their trust. This module reviewed field interviews and investigative detentions in detail.

The sixth module discussed how to conduct neighborhood meetings, surveys of citizens' needs, and tactical crime analysis. The common thread in these subject areas was that each requires face-to-face contact between the police and citizens. The seventh module provided an understanding of crime prevention within the context of community policing. The emphasis of this module was that crime prevention is the responsibility of all police officers.

Los Angeles Sheriff's Department

As mentioned in previous chapters, supervisors and managers should receive training in community policing. Just as the Savannah Police Department developed a specific module to train their command staff on the community-policing concept, the Los Angeles Sheriff's Department developed a six-hour course specifically for supervisors and managers. This course defined community policing, provided a brief history of policing, discussed problem-oriented policing and the "broken windows theory," and covered various community-policing strategies, such as combining investigative and patrol functions, allowing lower-level flexibility in policy making, and permanently assigning patrol officers to specific neighborhoods. There were sections on "Why We Need Community Policing," "Problem Solving," "Surveying the Community," and "Solutions for Criminal Nuisance Activity." Additional sections covered strategic planning, managing organizational change, and supervising community policing.

Regional Community Policing Institute Training

The Office of Community-Oriented Policing Services (COPS) through its Regional Community Policing Institutes established throughout the country offers training on community policing. The various institutes offer community-policing training without cost to law enforcement officers, community residents, city employees, social service agencies, and private sector representatives. This training is available to government employees, business employees, community leaders and citizens, police personnel, probation officers, police officers, and campus police. Training provided by the institute can be adapted to the specific needs of an agency, business, or community. Course materials are also provided without charge. A brief list of courses available from the institutes located throughout the country follows:

- Introduction to Community Policing
- Coping with Workplace Stress
- Diversity in COP
- Ethics: Racial Profiling
- Homeland Security
- Introduction to Strategic Planning
- Mediation for Campus Law Enforcement
- Mediation for Supervisors
- Supervision & Management for the Problem Solver
- Conducting Complete Traffic Stops
- COP Response to Domestic Violence
- Early Identification & Intervention System
- Ethics for the Individual
- Intake & Investigation of Citizens' Complaints
- Racial and Profiling: Issues & Dilemmas
- State & Local Anti-Terrorism Training (SLATT)
- Use of Force Issues in COP Environment
- Volunteers in Police Services (VIPS)
- Cultural Awareness
- Response to Club Drugs
- Response to Drug Facilitated Sexual Assault
- Response to Gangs

Building Bridges

"Building Bridges: Police/Community Partnership" was a two-day conference developed and coordinated by the Regional Community Policing Institute at St. Petersburg Junior College in St. Petersburg, Florida, and attended by both police and 250 community residents. The chiefs of police and sheriffs of the St. Petersburg region participated in a panel discussion on the vision, philosophy, and future of community policing; residents were also afforded the opportunity to meet and network with their chiefs and sheriffs; and workshops were held on problem solving and community-policing partnerships that were co-facilitated by residents and community police officers.

P3 Probation–Police Partnerships

P3 Probation–Police Partnerships is CD-ROM training developed by the Regional Community Policing Institute of St. Petersburg Community College. The multimedia CD-ROM is geared specifically toward bridging the information gap between probation officers and community-policing officers throughout Florida. It outlines the steps that police and probation agencies must take to form a partnership. By sharing information on an offender, both officers better serve the community, as well as develop an understanding of each agency's mission, role, and scope as they relate to one another. The CD-ROM contains five instructional units, each with an interactive quiz. Topics covered include:

- importance and purpose of partnering community-policing officers with probation officers
- foundations for integrating community police officers and probation officers
- importance of using a zone approach to supervision with a probation officer
- methodology for implementing and managing zone supervision
- definitions and examples of community-oriented policing and SARA problem-oriented policing model
- how to administer and manage a partnership between probation and police officers

The training program also includes video simulations that depict real-life situations in which probation–police partnerships are used and that provide opportunities for user interaction.

Citizen Police Academies

As a facet of community policing, many police agencies in the 1990s have established citizen police academies. Citizen police academies originated in England. Shortly afterward, the Orlando, Florida Police Department conducted the first citizen police academy in the United States. The academies are open to citizens who volunteer to attend classes for approximately 12 weeks, usually meeting one evening a week for three hours.

The training program generally consists of classroom and "hands-on" instruction. The police departments provide comprehensive instruction that covers a different area of policing each week. Training topics include the responsibilities of patrol officers, criminal investigative skills, crime scene search, gang activities, communications, drugs, tactical operations, and community involvement. Citizens may spend time on patrol with officers and take a tour of police headquarters or a district police station. They may spend time on the firing range firing the exact weapons that officers are assigned. Classes may include lectures by the district attorney, judges, and other criminal justice personnel. Some police departments have conducted citizen police academies in Spanish for their Hispanic citizens.

Selected Approaches to Implementing Community Policing

Astoria Police Department

Generally, medium-sized and big police departments receive publicity on their community-policing approaches, but small police departments are neglected by the media and researchers. Small departments may not have the resources to do extensive planning to implement community policing. One such department is the City of Astoria Police Department, located in the state of Oregon.*

The Astoria Police Department is a small agency with 16 officers serving 10,000 people in a 5-square-mile area. The department has a chief who directly supervises a captain, an emergency communication manager, and a support services manager. The captain supervises four sergeants, who perform all the functions of patrol officers, and a detective and a community-policing officer. The emergency communication manager dispatches as well as supervises seven full- and part-time dispatchers, who provide regional 911 call-answering and dispatching services for 17 police and fire agencies. The support services manager is the department's administrative assistant and supervises two clerical personnel who provide records maintenance and evidence custody services.

In 1992, the department developed and published a plan to implement community policing, but because the city had limited financial resources,

---

* The information in this section was obtained from a letter from Chief Robert E. Deu Pree and from copies of memoranda of the Astoria Police Department.

very little was done to put the plan into action. In 1993, the plan was reviewed and revitalized. It called for one senior officer to be trained in community policing and to put into practice the philosophy of community policing in a particular neighborhood from one to two years. This officer would not be assigned radio calls. When it was determined that community policing was working, two additional officers were selected for community-policing activities. They were assigned radio calls but were expected to be involved in community policing when freed from service calls and other assignments. Two more officers will be assigned to community-policing activities once they have sufficient experience. Eventually, all police officers and sergeants will be community-policing officers and will be assigned to specific neighborhoods. It will take approximately ten years to implement community policing in Astoria if no additional police officers are hired. Astoria has one detective, who rotates from patrol every two years, and patrol officers perform most follow-up investigations. Therefore, incorporating the detective into community policing is not an issue. The department uses volunteers to conduct some community-policing activities, such as citizen surveys.

The Astoria Police Department has a simple plan for a small police agency that for all practical purposes should work. With city officials, business owners, neighborhood residents, and police personnel behind community policing, the plan should make for better and closer relations between the police and citizens.

Bellingham Police Department*

One department that developed a detailed strategic plan was the Bellingham, Washington Police Department. The information here was obtained from their strategic plan. The City of Bellingham is the county seat and major city of Whatcom County, which is located between the cities of Seattle, Washington, and Vancouver, British Columbia. Bellingham covers an area of approximately 26 miles. The department has 159 employees with 97 police officers. In 1997, the Bellingham Police Department published a strategic plan for adopting community policing as its organizational philosophy. The plan stated that community policing

---

* Source: Adapted from The Bellingham Police Department Strategic Plan: January 1997 to December 2001, 1997, Bellingham Police Department.

is based on the four principles of partnership, problem solving, participatory management, and progressive visionary leadership, which it described as follows:

1. Partnership. Partners enlighten and empower the community to solve their problems, concerns, and fear of crime. Partnerships bring together people from all parts of the community that are willing to work together to problem solve for the betterment of the entire community.

2. Problem Solving. Problem solving occurs in a community when there is a discernible combination of a cooperative effort, a comprehensive systematic model, and an environment that lends itself to equal input. Issues in a community can, and will, be dealt with in a more complete and successful manner when the problem-solving model is used as the structure for resolution.

3. Participatory Management. Ideas that are embodied in the concept of participatory management are the following: the integrity of the department will be maintained with as few levels of management as possible, all levels of the organization will participate in developing and organizing the efforts of the department, decision-making responsibilities will exist at the lowest levels possible, and, finally, the department will work to be as inclusive and supportive of one another as possible.

4. Visionary Leadership. Community policing employs the organizational structure of the inverted pyramid rather than the classic bureaucratic structure. Leaders within the department are committed to the future development of the department and personnel of the department. Leaders within the department will allow, and enhance, the change process.

The Bellingham plan is founded on the department's mission statement and values statement. According to the mission statement, the primary mission of the Bellingham Police Department is to coordinate and lead the efforts with the community to preserve the public peace, protect the rights of persons and property, prevent crime, and generally provide assistance to citizens in urgent situations. The department is responsible for the enforcement of all federal laws, Washington State laws, and city ordinances within the boundaries of the City of Bellingham. The department must enforce the law in a fair and impartial manner, recognizing both the statutory and judicial limitations of police authority and constitutional rights of all persons. It is not the role of the department to legislate, render legal judgment, or punish. The department serves the people of Bellingham by providing law enforcement service in a professional and courteous manner, and it is to these people that the department is ultimately responsible.

The values of the department are as follows:

- Individual members of the Bellingham Police Department are valued for their unique contributions. The department is strengthened through the creativity and participation of each member.
- The Bellingham Police Department is committed to close and constant contact with our community members to help maintain the quality of life enjoyed and expected.
- The Bellingham Police Department is committed to furthering democratic values. Every action of the department reflects the importance of protecting constitutional rights and ensuring basic personal freedom of all citizens.
- Honesty and integrity are essential qualities of all members of the Bellingham Police Department. These qualities foster an environment where members are supportive of each other and a "family-like" trust exists.
- The Bellingham Police Department is committed to maintaining our high level of professionalism.
- The Bellingham Police Department is committed to a problem-solving partnership with the community as the means to maintaining public peace and order.

As part of their implementation plan, the Bellingham Police Department conducted a random survey of citizens. The patrol officers who distributed it described it as a method for the department to evaluate the services provided by the department and encouraged citizens to give their honest opinions. Along with the survey instrument, a stamped addressed envelope was provided. Fifty-six percent of the citizens who received the surveys returned them. The survey covered citizens' opinions of the

Bellingham Police Department, the amount of contact citizens had with the police, and the major crime and disorder issues of concern. This survey helped a 40-member strategic planning team to establish department goals and objectives. The strategic planning team included businesspeople, school officials, citizens, and police personnel from all levels within the organization. Goals and objectives were developed for three different divisions—administration, operations, and services—under the headings of empowerment, partnership, organizational development, and organizational effectiveness. As an example, the goals and objectives of the operations division are outlined here:

1. Organizational Development
   - Goal: Assist employees in their efforts to perform problem-solving techniques while working in cooperation with community members.
   - Objectives: Develop and implement community policing resource/procedure manual for employees.

2. Organizational Effectiveness
   - Goal: Provide previous shift information to oncoming shift.
   - Objectives: Disseminate previous shift's activities to create broader base of knowledge for oncoming shift.

3. Empowerment
   - Goal: Empower employees to work within the philosophy of community policing.
   - Objectives: Allow employees the ability to have more input and affect their community policing neighborhoods.

4. Partnership
   - Goal: Integrate downtown foot beat/transit officer position with existing COP program.
   - Objectives: Recruit and assign officers to downtown foot beat/transit duty with the intention of fully meshing these responsibilities with the establishment goals of the COP program; enhance the COP attention to growing downtown business community.

The strategic plan also devised strategies on how the goals and objectives were to be established.

Eugene Police Department*

The City of Eugene, Oregon, has a population of approximately 180,000 within 47 square miles. In early 1990, a study done by the City of Eugene found that the city's population was growing and that the number of calls for service was increasing much more rapidly than the resources available to meet this need. The department's incapacity to handle service calls was diminishing the quality of life in the city and was a direct threat to life and property. Major root causes of public safety problems were determined to be drug abuse and unemployment. Because of the city's problems and the limited resources to deal with them, the city's planning team determined that fundamental changes in the community's approach to its public service needs were required—specifically, increased cooperation of human service agencies, neighborhood groups, and individuals with public safety agencies. The City of Eugene therefore adopted a new approach called the partnership model, which stressed the need for outreach and networking to address underlying social problems that contributed to criminal behavior and unsafe neighborhood conditions. It was believed that this approach would enable the department to have a more positive and consistent presence in the community and would allow for more productive use of personnel, equipment, and public facilities. The primary goal of the partnership model was to promote a modern, competent, and service-oriented department accessible and answerable to the community it served. The planning team developed a 20-year, long-range plan that allowed for regular review, amendments, and refinements. It included policies, goals, and strategies that addressed public safety needs. To allow for a timely transition, the partnership model established eight key strategies:

1. Community-Oriented Policing. The existing program, concentrating the combined resources of the Department of Public Safety, the Parks, Recreation, and Cultural Services Department, the

---

* Source: Adapted with permission from Partnership for Public Safety: Long Range Public Safety Plan, 1991, City of Eugene.

White Bird Clinic, and other community agencies on quality-of-life concerns—particularly street-level crisis intervention and referral as opposed to traditional enforcement measures—needs to be continued and expanded.

2. Prevention and Education. In addition to the department's current efforts in this area, resources should be added allowing fire crews to participate in presentations to local schools and community groups, citizens to receive training in organizing and conflict resolution, more crime prevention presentations [to be held] and [opportunities for] positive, regular interaction with the community's young people [to be provided].

3. Community Service Specialist. Greater utilization of this non-certified paraprofessional classification will provide support needed to maintain existing service levels by supplementing the work of certified police officers and fire fighters and will help to address some of the community policing and prevention/education needs noted above. Cost saving also will be realized as these employees assume some of the duties now being performed by certified personnel.

4. Fire/EMS Redeployment. To maintain an adequate level of fire protection citywide, while recognizing changes in the nature of the fire and emergency medical service (decreasing fire suppression activity, increasing requirements related to hazardous materials, fire prevention, and medical emergencies), the plan recommends redistribution of fire stations in the community. Another key advantage of this redeployment is that it will bring the Eugene community closer to citywide availability of a four-minute emergency response capability.

5. Public Safety Stations. The plan proposes establishing a presence in neighborhoods with facilities that would include community meeting rooms, note taking and referral services, public safety resource materials, and fine and bail collection capabilities. This could be done, at least in part, in conjunction with the Fire/EMS redeployment plan.

6. Metro Coordination. In view of the success of regional public safety programs, such as 911, Emergency Medical Services, etc., the city should participate in examining the potential for the creation of

a Metro Public Safety Board, as well as in the formulation of a regional plan for public safety programs, possibly to include fire prevention and suppression, purchasing, training, and other programs and services.

7. Training and Employee Development. New strategies will be required to attract and retain high quality public safety employees to perform effectively in a community-oriented public safety environment. Changing community demographics will require a more culturally diverse work force.

8. Planning, Evaluation, and Amendments. The long-range plan should be reviewed annually, with a full evaluation and amendment procedure every five years, by the Public Safety Advisory Committee (PSAC), supported by the department's planning, research, and development staff. This process will include abundant opportunities for citizens' participation, in accordance with the fundamental principles of the partnership model.

This plan, at the time it was developed and implemented, might well be considered innovative. It provided an opportunity for a variety of governmental and community agencies to become involved in public safety issues, and it recognized that public safety involves development of a partnership among fire fighters, emergency teams, and police.

In 1997, the Eugene Police Department developed what they referred to as a Community Involved Policing (CIP) Action Plan for their community-policing philosophy. (The next three paragraphs (and lists) are adapted with permission from Community Involved Policing (CIP) Action Plan: October 1, 1997–December 31, 1997, Eugene Police Department, 1997.) The CIP Action Plan was based on the 1991 partnership model plan. It defined community-involved policing as

officers who know their beats. Residents and business who know their beat officers. No graffiti, gang presence, or broken streetlights and windows. No blighted neighborhoods. Streets that are cared for, clean, and safe. Quick response to emergencies, thorough follow-ups, complete, high quality, tough-on-crime investigations that lead to arrests. Police are there to help through close partnerships with social services, victims' services, neighborhood groups, business associations, other city departments, charitable associations. Or just [to help citizens] feel safer.

(3)

The new action plan had seven components:

1. Interdepartmental Cooperative Action Team (ICAT). The purpose of ICAT is to identify, prioritize, and refer crime and neighborhood safety issues within the city organization and to our community partners. The ultimate objective of this activity is to make neighborhoods look safe, feel safe, and be safe.
2. Differential response. The objective of this action item is to redirect the need for officers to respond to certain categories of incidents and investigations, so that more time is available for police to provide neighborhood interaction, problem solving, and other activities that are being requested.
3. Area coordinators, crime analysis, and beat health. The concepts of beat health and area coordinators are integral to a successful long-range community involved policing philosophy. . . . Beat health and the area coordinator are just two components to reduce crime and increase the livability of Eugene's diverse neighborhoods.
4. Youth strategies. The objective of this action is to collaborate with community agencies to develop and implement a regional crime prevention strategy. Public safety personnel will provide intervention, alternative actions, skill building, and role models for youth at risk.
5. Community involvement. To accomplish this objective, meaningful citizen input will be encouraged and considered in policy development and evaluation of police performance.
6. Recruitment, diversity, training, and promotion. The objectives of this action item are to select diverse recruits interested in community policing; to increase the quality of training provided to our recruit officers; to reduce the training time necessary; to make the training more community oriented; to provide department supervisors and managers with the training necessary to assist them in implementing and managing CIP;

and to foster success in community policing into promotion for supervisors and managers.

7. Regional coordination and automation. This action item will develop and implement strategies to improve coordination and cooperation among regional criminal justice stakeholders, including social services and the private sector, while minimizing the possibility that efforts in one part of the criminal justice system will have unanticipated adverse impacts on other parts.

(14–31)

A review of the CIP Action Plan in 1998 made recommendations to enhance the community-police partnership:

- Beat-level citizen/police groups: As much as possible, use preexisting groups in each beat rather than creating new ones. Where necessary, set up new structures consistent with city plans for neighborhood group revitalization that allow people in the beat to communicate with the beat officer and the police department on an ongoing basis about issues and concerns in that beat. For some beats, a neighborhood group will be the answer. For others, a neighborhood advisory board or a preexisting business group will be the key. Many beats should coalesce into one group, both to recognize shared issues, to cut down on the number of groups and meetings, and to save staff time. The exact structure involved needs to remain flexible so that people in each beat are best able to define what they need and change these structures over time. Beat officers will attend all meetings of the beat groups and will be able to call upon whatever resources are relevant to helping people in the beats to resolve public safety concerns through the development of partnerships, proactive approaches, and collective efficacy. . . .
- Police Forum: The focus of the Police Forum will be to work on communitywide issues, with a special focus on community policing efforts. The forum will help the department by reviewing its plans; acting as advocates for revenue measures;

and providing a forum for people to bring their issues. The forum can refer issues to beat groups, the Police Advisory Committee, the Human Rights Commission, or the complaint/commendation process, as appropriate. . . .

- Police Advisory Committee: Create a standing Police Advisory Committee by ordinance. This group will be advisory to the city council and the chief of police regarding police policy issues and will replace the Council Public Safety Committee. Again, details will need to be worked out with the group itself, but the broad charge will be to review police policies, practices, and priorities and mesh them with community values; to review revenue measures and alternative strategies; to take on council projects; and to provide a sounding board for public concerns. Membership will need to include representatives from education, social services, seniors, youth, minority committees, businesses, the city council, and at-large public seats. . . .
- Complaints/commendation process: If the voters so choose, an External Review Board will be added to this process.

(Eugene Police Department 1998)

The Eugene Police Department is continuously revising and updating its approach to community policing. The beat-level citizen/police groups, Police Forum, Police Advisory Committee, and complaints/commendation process are all indicators that a concentrated and committed effort has been made by the Eugene Police Department to implement community policing. The department is continuously working toward developing a police–community partnership and empowering its officers to deal with issues on their beats by making the beats small enough so that the officer assigned to a particular beat can not only function as a community police officer but also be the crime prevention officer and investigate minor crimes.

Illinois State Police

Generally, state police agencies are not involved in community policing, because they have statewide police jurisdiction and are not assigned to populated areas that would have a police agency. However, several state police agencies are involved in community policing either as community-policing trainers or as resource centers. Students of community policing should be aware that several state police agencies are involved in community policing. The Illinois State Police were selected for this chapter because they are one of the more advanced state agencies involved in community policing.

The Illinois State Police implemented community policing in 1993 by deploying six state police officers in a pilot Statewide Community-Oriented Policing Effort (SCOPE). State, municipal, and county police agencies usually have relied on the state police for support services such as crime scene services and data system information, but by adopting community policing, the Illinois State Police expanded this service role to include the full range of policing responsibilities, including patrol, traffic, and investigation. From six state police officers involved in community policing in 1993, the number has increased to 350 in 1999. These officers have been involved in over 800 problem-oriented projects throughout the state (Illinois State Police, n.d.).

The Illinois State Police community-policing philosophy led to the development of Resource Support Centers. These centers collect, process, and analyze information about major crimes and incidents. Their databases are accessible to all state law enforcement agencies and are backed up by a centralized mapping unit that provides valuable analytical and mapping assistance to police departments' patrol and investigative units. The Resource Support Centers allow police departments to deal efficiently with crime trends (Illinois State Police, n.d.).

The Illinois State Police refer to their community-policing strategy as geographically oriented community oriented policing (GEOCOM). According to the Illinois State Police, GEOCOM is a breakthrough in community policing in that it broadens the definition of community beyond neighborhood-oriented, beat-walking, and bike-riding strategies. One Illinois state police GEOCOM officer is assigned to each Illinois county. GEOCOM state police officers are required to reside in their GEOCOM area (county) and become part of the community. They act as liaisons between the state police and local police agencies. They patrol the state and local highways and network with citizen advisory councils and state, county, and municipal agencies to target and identify specific crime problem areas. The goal of GEOCOM is to decrease duplication efforts and direct resources to problem areas (Illinois State Police, n.d.).

The Illinois State Police initiative in establishing community policing on a statewide basis is exemplary. Although community policing on a statewide level is in the early stages in Illinois, the attempt at a minimum indicates that the Illinois State Police are innovative risk takers.

Madison Police Department

The Madison, Wisconsin Police Department can trace its involvement in community policing to the mid-1980s. Community policing in Madison is referred to as quality policing and is based on the system of total quality management (TQM), which was discussed earlier.

The Madison Police Department, when establishing "quality policing," drew on Deming's Fourteen Points to create five points:

1. A clear and understandable mission statement.
2. A commitment to engaging in teamwork and problem solving in each and every unit.
3. The creation of a community orientation and customer focus on the part of each and every employee.
4. The full utilization of the important resources of the organization by recognizing employee worth and the untapped resources and potential of employees.
5. An overall focus on quality.

(Couper and Lobitz 1991, 64)

The police department rewrote its mission statement to reflect the principles of "quality policing" and drew up "Principles of Quality Leadership" as well. Thus, the concepts of "quality policing" have been fully integrated into the department. The experience of the Madison Police Department illustrates several key ingredients in organizational change:

- a strong vision of the future
- a strong unyielding commitment from the chief executive
- a commitment to developing the skills and abilities of leaders as well as employees in the organization and continually training them
- a patient and persistent focus on the long-term operations of the organization

(Couper and Lobitz 1991, 87)

Portland Police Bureau

In the late 1980s, the City of Portland, Oregon, had a sharp increase in crime, gangs, and drug problems that severely affected the quality of life for citizens, neighborhoods, institutions, and businesses and placed a severe strain on limited police resources. At that time, the police bureau made the traditional response to an increase in crime when resources are limited. Because the city government decided that police resources would not or could not be increased, the bureau removed police officers from support functions to patrol activities, demoted detectives, eliminated crime analysis, scaled back crime prevention and planning and research units to skeleton crews, and eliminated tactical units. Civilian positions were reduced so that more funding would be freed up to put more patrol officers on the street. But even with more patrol officers on the street, radio service calls continued to increase, and response time to priority calls averaged over nine minutes. The numerous service calls allowed the patrol officers little time to develop community relations with citizens. The gap between the community and the police was not closing; rather, it was widening. Citizens viewed police merely as responders to problems, and police viewed citizens as complainants who wanted the police to fight crime without their help.

During this period, there was a growing awareness of community policing. The mayor, upon hearing about the success of the community-policing concept in other cities, directed the police chief to adopt the community-policing philosophy. The police chief placed in action the events that led to the development of the Community Policing Transition Plan (Portland Police Bureau 1990, 4).

The Portland Police Bureau has periodically revised its strategic plan over the years to meet the needs of the community. When the plan was last revised in 1998, strategies were given with detailed descriptions, listings of the police units involved, applicable work plans, and partner agencies used to carry out the specific strategy. All the versions of the strategic plan have included a vision statement, mission statement, values statement, priority issues, goals, objectives, and work plans. Since the implementation of community policing, the bureau has continued to look for feedback from its officers and the community to improve the department's approach to community policing.

The history of the bureau's strategic planning process is as follows:

1988
- A policy is drafted proposing that the bureau make a transition from being a traditional policing agency focusing on arrests and crime rate to being a community-policing agency focusing on community problem solving and results.
- The mayor directs the police bureau to prepare a strategic management plan incorporating a community-policing philosophy.
- The community-policing planning process is initiated; the Community Policing Working Group is created from police, the Office of Neighborhood Associations, the community, and the mayor's office.

1989
- A community-policing concept paper is created with a vision statement definition of community policing, an outline of the strategic planning process, and five-year goals; it is distributed to community members for comment.
- A critical path chart (with timelines and benchmarks) is created. The critical path has four stages: definition phase to define community policing; design phase to create recommendations for realignment of services and functions; planning phase from various committees and their action; and implementation phase to create an operational strategy/action plan for FY 1990–91.
- Five committee meetings, with surveys, are conducted by the Office of Neighborhood Associations. It is attended by the mayor, the chief, precinct captains, and members of the community.
- Community-policing transition committees are formed with community members, representatives from other agencies, and bureau employees. The committees are Menu (to respond to issues raised in the five community meetings); Media/Education; Evaluation; Productivity/Workload Analysis; Information and Referral; Legal/Legislative; Training and Recruitment; Grants/Finance; and Criminal Justice.
- Resolution No. 34627 is passed by unanimous vote of the city council. This resolution includes a definition of community policing that was created from community meetings.

1990

- Resolution No. 34670 is passed by the city council, adopting the Community Policing Transition Plan. The plan outlines a mission statement and one-, two-, and five-year goals and objectives. Each strategy is analyzed to determine if its implementation would require additional resources.
- Three demonstration projects are selected, one in each precinct: Iris Court in North; Central Eastside in East; and Old Town/Chinatown in Central.
- The Citizens' Crime Commission funds an analysis by the Institute of Law and Justice on law enforcement climate; organizational structure and resource deployment; staffing levels; management practices; service demand and workload; human resources management; management; communication; and budget process.
- The Chiefs Forum, a policy advisory group, is created.

1991

- A Citywide Community Policing Workshop and survey is conducted.
- The Year 1 Report on Community Policing Implementation is adopted by the city council. The report contains Year 1 strategies employed, highlights of activities, and Year 2 strategies. Adopted with this report are the bureau's attributes and success factors for community policing. The attributes are a set of qualities desired in a bureau that has fully implemented community policing. Success factors are a set of factors that measure how the qualities have been achieved.

1992

- The Portland city auditor surveys Portland residents to gauge the performance of city government, which includes the police, and publishes the Service, Efforts and Accomplishments (SEA) baseline report.
- The Human Goals Statement is adopted as a bureau general order. The statement defines the human resources and work environment goals for the bureau as a whole.
- A National Institute of Justice $366,000 evaluation grant to create community policing performance measures is awarded to the police bureau.

1993

- The second SEA report is published by the city auditor. It compares response on police services and overall perception of safety from 1992 to 1993. Data collected are used by the police bureau as performance measurements in its 1994–1996 budgets and are reported on three times a year in budget monitoring reports.
- Work begins on creating the second strategic plan. Initial research is conducted by the bureau on the transition plan to determine what has been working and what has not been working, what obstacles exist, etc. The bureau mission statement is revised to include the aspect of maintaining and improving community livability. Bureau goals of the previous strategic plan are restated as values. New goals are adopted: reduce crime and fear of crime; empower the community; develop and empower personnel; and strengthen planning, evaluation, and fiscal support.
- A draft of the 1994–1996 strategic plan is reviewed by RU managers, the budget advisory committee, the precinct advisory committees, the Chiefs Forum, and internal advisory committees. The draft is distributed to neighborhood associations, community groups, and individuals; more than 600 are distributed for review. The draft is reviewed by the mayor and the city council. Employee job satisfaction survey results are released. The survey measures bureau employees' assessment of job satisfaction, supervision support, autonomy, recognition, teamwork, fairness, and problem-solving support. Surveys were distributed to all 1,200 employees, with a 46 percent rate of return.

1994

- The city council adopts the bureau's 1994–1996 strategic plan, with an updated mission statement, five values, and the goals of reducing crime, empowering the community, empowering personnel, and strengthening planning and fiscal support.
- The first integrated work plan reports, incorporating progress reports and performance measurements on the 1994–1996 strategic plan, are released to the city council and citizen advisory council.
- The Portland Police Bureau 1994 Community Assessment Survey, based on interviewing from July to August 1994, is released. The

analysis is based on questions regarding crime, livability, victim-ization, satisfaction with police services, familiarity with police and crime prevention specialists, and recommendations on how to improve services.

1995

- The results of the second employee job satisfaction survey results are released. The survey measures bureau employees' assessment of job satisfaction, supervisor support, autonomy, teamwork, recog-nition, fairness, and organizational culture. The report released compares the 1995 with the 1993 results. Surveys were distributed to all 1,250 employees, with a 43 percent rate of return.
- The final report on Community Policing Performance Measures, supporting the National Institute of Justice grant to the City of Portland, is released. The report contains findings from a partner-ship agreement survey and assessment, interagency focus groups, an implementation profile analysis of bureau managers, a dis-affected youth survey, a youth in school survey, and a domestic violence reduction unit evaluation.
- Work begins on the 1996–1998 strategic plan, with a review of the assessment information and recommendations gathered to date and a review of the current integrated work plan process. The 1996–1998 strategic plan is connected to individual division work plans and contains performance measurements for the first time.
- The Police Bureau conducts its second National Community Policing Conference, focusing on the area of organizational development to support the transition to community policing and other contemporary policing topics. More than 600 attendees from 35 states and five countries participate.

1996

- Performance measurements corresponding to the four program areas in the budget are developed and included in the 1996–1998 budget submission. Reports on the city council benchmarks are also included in the budget submission.
- The second Portland Police Bureau Community Assessment Survey is conducted and released in 1996. The analysis is based

on questions regarding crime, livability, victimization, satisfaction with police services, familiarity with police officers and crime prevention specialists, and recommendations on how to improve services.

- For the City's Comprehensive Organizational Review and Evaluation (CORE) efforts, the bureau produces a report outlining recommendations made to the bureau from outside agencies or major task forces for the last ten years, along with the changes made as a result of those recommendations.
- An extensive review of all bureau programs and services is performed to assess the response to requests for budget cut packages due to the passage of property tax limitation Measure 47.
- The bureau applies for, and receives, federal grant support from the U.S. Department of Justice Office of Community-Oriented Policing Services (COPS) to fund 60 officer positions for three years, with a commitment from the city council to fund the positions after the grant period ends. This assists in bringing the bureau up to strength after 47 officer positions were cut after Measure 47.

1997
- The results of the third employee job satisfaction survey are released. The survey measures bureau employees' assessment of job satisfaction, supervisor support, autonomy, teamwork, recognition, fairness, and organizational culture. The report compares the 1997 with the 1995 and 1993 results. Surveys were distributed to all 1,250 employees, with a 59 percent rate of return.

1998
- Work begins on the 1998–2000 strategic plan, with a review of the 1996–1998 plan and two public input opportunities. The 1998–2000 strategic plan is connected to individual division work plans and contains a national and regional trends analysis section for the first time.

Savannah Police Department*

In 1991, Savannah, Georgia had a hotly contested race for mayor in which crime, especially violent crime, was a major campaign issue. In 1991, violent

---

* Source: Adapted from Executive Summary: Comprehensive Community Crime Control Strategy, 1991, Savannah Police Department.

crime was up 17 percent over the previous year and had risen by over 66 percent since 1989. The city had experienced a large increase in homicides: from 20 in 1989 to 35 in 1990 to 59 in 1991. The increase in violence was contributed to the crack cocaine epidemic. Because of the hotly contested race, the incumbent city manager directed the police chief to develop a strategy to combat crime. In response, the police department developed a community-policing strategy called the Comprehensive Community Crime Control Strategy. The executive summary for the strategy identified six major problems with the deployment practices of the department:

1. Lack of Geographic Accountability. Currently, officers are only accountable for crime reduction efforts during their eight-hour shift. The current zone and beat boundaries are not conducive to officer accountability because officers are not consistently assigned or deployed to the same areas. Captains supervise and are responsible for an eight-hour shift. In essence no single individual is accountable for a particular problem; thus accountability is lost. In addition, current beat configurations do not square with the geographic distribution of known crime problems, that is, current boundaries do not group problem areas together.

2. Unequal Distribution of Patrol Time. Unequal distribution of patrol time is a problem because it does not permit officers sufficient time to engage in preventive patrol or problem-solving activities in areas where it is needed most. As presently structured the patrol deployment plan has an unequal distribution of the patrol time. The problem lies with the distribution of manpower by shift. The shift that operates from 4 p.m. to midnight accounts for 48.7 percent of the crimes but spends only 24 percent of available patrol time on preventive patrol. In contrast, the shift that operates between 12 midnight and 8 a.m. accounts for only 26.8 percent of the city's crimes yet spends more than 53 percent of its patrol time on preventive patrol. . . .

3. Need for Better Interaction with Residents. Research consistently shows a strong relationship between the levels of police–citizen interaction and citizen satisfaction with police services. The

unequal distribution of patrol time in Savannah shows that officers spend a disproportionate amount of time on answering calls for service, leaving little time for the kinds of activities that would enhance positive interaction between the police and neighborhood residents. . . .

4. Need for More Proactive Patrol. While responding to calls for service is the most essential service provided by patrol officers, responding to calls, by definition, is reactive. Current police services are incident-oriented rather than problem-oriented. The effect is that police are neither solving problems nor preventing crime. If patrol is limited to satisfying demands on calls for services, then patrol becomes a reactive service with little impact on crime.

5. Inadequate Police Response System. At present the police call response system does not make optimal use of available resources. . . . In essence, a mobile police response was sent to answer almost all calls for service, even though only 19 percent were calls in which immediate mobile response was needed. Nor does a rapid response affect crime rates. . . . Tying up officers on calls that could be delayed or handled by telephone detracts from an officer's time and attention to proactive activities such as problem solving and crime prevention. More important, however, it reduces the department's capacity to quickly and adequately respond to calls requiring an immediate police response. Consequently, a new method for prioritizing and managing calls-for-service workload is needed.

6. Inadequate Data Management. Accurate data are needed to adequately manage effective patrol deployment. Current data availability limits continued detailed analysis of crime and deployment conditions.

The six major problems identified by the Savannah Police Department can all be related to traditional policing. Although many aspects of traditional policing are valuable and ingrained into the police culture and our society's culture, aspects of traditional policing can be improved upon. The Savannah Police Department was a good traditional police department, but it was not responding to the crime problem of its city. The department's officers were responding to service calls, many of them trivial, when their officers could have been working on solving the problems that led to the city's high crime rate.

The same study made several keen observations concerning the limitations of the criminal justice system in the Savannah area. First, it found a lack of cooperation among the criminal justice components. For example, the community lacked a process for coordinating the flow of criminal cases. The criminal justice system consequently suffered from a case overload. Arrests, indictments, criminal trials, and probation revocations were all increasing substantially, and most offenders were repeaters. Another criminal justice problem was the lack of an integrated database for the various criminal justice components so that the criminal justice agencies could not coordinate their activities and operate effectively and efficiently.

In their transition from a traditional police department to a community-policing agency, the Savannah Police Department developed a number of strategies, both internal and external. The internal strategies included the following:

1. Command Accountability. Accountability will be geographically distributed. Each of the twelve areas will be placed in one of four zones (District Police Stations). A captain will be assigned to and be held accountable for all police services in his zone 24 hours a day. He will direct police strategies for his zone and will specify objectives, which are tied to each of the goals. To accomplish this, each captain will assign manpower for each zone and each area in the zone, specifically how this manpower will be used and when it will be used. The captain will freely schedule officers according to activity in the area. This may include staggered shifts, overlapping shifts, or hour-by-hour scheduling. In addition, the captain will maintain continuing contact with the people living in his zone. The service areas are aggregated into four zones to group crime problems into manageable sections of the city and to facilitate patrol management. . . .

2. Manpower Deployment. The new manpower deployment plan will resolve the problem of unequal distribution of patrol time. Manpower will be distributed to each of the service areas and zones on the basis of calls for service, time to provide for preventive patrol, citizen participation, and other activities. . . .

3. Community-Oriented Policing. Community-oriented policing directly addresses the need for patrol officers to interact more with residents in the neighborhoods they patrol.

4. Problem-Oriented Policing. Problem-oriented policing (POP) is a proactive approach to patrol operations that identifies, analyzes, and responds to specific programs.

5. Differential Police Response. To resolve the problem of inadequate police response and to allow patrol officers more time for problem solving, a revised differential police response system (DPR) is recommended. DPR is a deliberate stacking of certain non-emergency calls so as to not occupy too many officers at once, and to allow the dispatch to go to the neighborhood officer when he/she becomes available. . . .

6. Improved Analytical Capabilities. A planning and research director has recently been staffed to oversee data management efforts, since effective patrol deployment requires accurate and timely information.

The Savannah Police Department took an acceptable approach in their transition from traditional policing to community policing. They recognized the importance of decentralization. District police captains would now be accountable for specific areas of the city with an established number of officers under their command. They were held responsible for the crime rate in their district along with crime prevention. The patrol officers worked for one captain in the same district of the city. The department accepted problem-oriented policing and community-oriented policing as its policing strategy. In addition, it addressed differential police response and improved the department's analytical capabilities.

The Savannah Police Department, like other community-oriented police departments, recognized that crime was a community problem, not just a police problem. The department developed a plan to build trust between the police and the community. All police officers were encouraged to increase contact with citizens, share information about crime with citizens, be visible in the community, and engage in cooperative problem solving with citizens. In addition, the department made a concentrated effort to coordinate criminal justice activities with other criminal justice agencies. For example, it worked with other criminal justice agencies on jail overcrowding, recidivism, and escalating caseloads.

Wichita Police Department

In the early 1990s, the City of Wichita Police Department, with the encouragement of the mayor, established community policing in two high-crime neighborhoods. A lieutenant and several community-policing officers were assigned to perform problem-solving activities. Under the command of the two lieutenants, problem-solving activities and cooperation from the neighborhoods were successful. In 1995, the police chief resigned, and a new police chief was appointed who was committed to community policing and its implementation citywide. The new police chief, observing the success of community policing in the pilot neighborhoods, directed that a strategic plan be developed. The strategic plan, referred to as the Public Safety Initiative (Wichita Police Department 1996) was implemented in 1996. It should be noted that the newly appointed police chief had the support of the city council, the newly elected mayor, and the city manager.

The Wichita Police Department's primary aim was to improve the department's ability to deliver police services by using the community-policing philosophy. A transition from traditional policing to community policing involving the entire department was to take place. Under the Public Safety Initiative, the department was combining community officers' duties with the mission of the patrol officers and other departmental units in a policy that integrated all departmental operations.

The policy established 36 patrol beats, each of which had seven police officers assigned to it. One beat police officer would function as a community-policing officer, and the remaining officers would provide police services to the beat. Two patrol officers were assigned to each shift. The responsibilities of the community-policing officer included collecting crime analysis and staffing information and meeting with beat officers, neighborhood associations, community groups, and others to coordinate police services unique to the beat's needs. The six other beat officers were to use the information provided by the community-policing officer to implement tailored police services and assist in implementing community-policing activities. All the officers assigned to a specific beat were expected to assess problems within the beat and to work with the community to develop and implement solutions to beat problems. The beat officers and the community-policing officer were held accountable for solving problems on their beats. The Public Safety Initiative of the Wichita Police Department (January 30, 1996) had the following goals:

- Make Wichita a safer community through a reduction in crime. By developing partnerships throughout the community, the root of crime problems will be determined, and solutions to those problems will be designed and implemented in conjunction with the community. By addressing the community's public safety problems through partnerships, existing crime and the prospects for future crime will be reduced.
- Provide high-quality customer service. By providing the community with a better-staffed and equipped police force that is specially trained in the community policing philosophy, the Police Department will improve its ability to deliver police services in a more timely, customer-oriented fashion.
- Ensure timely, effective follow-up investigations. One of the major improvements provided by the Public Safety Initiative is the addition of personnel and equipment assigned to investigate crime. These improvements will allow the Police Department both to investigate more crimes in a more efficient manner and to improve communications with the community regarding the status of investigations.
- Institute accountability at all levels within the department. By assigning officers to work with citizens throughout the community, officers will be more accountable to citizens through the development of partnerships. In addition, increased numbers of front line supervisors are provided to ensure that beat teams remain focused

on community goals. The personnel evaluation process will be revised to ensure that personnel are responsible for accomplishing performance goals tailored to unique needs of the community they serve.

The Public Safety Initiative required the hiring of 24 police officers and the purchase of new portable radios, marked police vehicles, fax machines, computers, and uniforms. The initiative was to cost $3.3 million in 1996 and $5.7 million in 1997.

The Public Safety Initiative required that the field services division be reorganized. Ninety-one positions were added to this field division: one lieutenant, 19 sergeants, 69 police officers, and two clerks. The structure of the division was revamped: four patrol bureaus (precinct stations) were established, each commanded by a captain. Lieutenants supervised each shift, and sergeants supervised patrol officers in groups of beats, called sectors. The number of officers assigned to each bureau varied based on call load. However, each patrol bureau had nine community-policing officers to coordinate police services.

The investigative division was not overlooked by the Public Safety Initiative. Twenty-seven positions were added to it: one lieutenant, 18 detectives, one officer, three chemists, one photo technician, and three clerks. The division received additional personnel to allow them to investigate more crimes. The third major unit of the Wichita Police Department, the support function, also received additional personnel: three lieutenants, two administrative assistants, one planning analyst, one dispatcher, and one management intern. The Public Safety Initiative focused on crime prevention, crime analysis, and training. One lieutenant was placed in charge of crime prevention, and one lieutenant was assigned to training to improve the department's ability to hire and train officers. An administrative assistant was added to records, and an analyst was added to crime analysis.

The Public Safety Initiative that laid the foundation for the Wichita community-policing strategy is still in operation and seems to be successful. Morale of the department seems high, and most police officers seem to have accepted the concept.

Summary

The training of police officers is going through a transition. The traditional approach, or pedagogical technique, emphasizes information-based learning, primarily through the lecture-driven class. In the new approach, known as the andragogical technique, adult learners are held responsible for their own learning and the instructor functions as a facilitator who guides and assists them but does not necessarily make learning decisions for them.

In 1990, the Royal Canadian Mounted Police introduced a new approach to training that incorporated many aspects of the andragogical technique because they recognized that their introduction of community policing would require police to be innovative problem solvers with excellent people skills. All police are trained in a problem-solving model, known as CAPRA, which emphasizes understanding the client, analyzing information, working in partnerships, choosing appropriate responses, and assessing for continuous improvement.

The Savannah, Georgia Police Department recognized that all departmental members had to be trained in the community-policing philosophy before it could be implemented. Their seven training modules cover community policing, problem-oriented policing, crime in Savannah, service agencies in Savannah, city codes, working with citizens, developing trust, and conducting crime analysis.

The Los Angeles Sheriff's Department developed a six-hour training course on community policing specifically for supervisors and managers. It covers such topics as the broken windows theory, problem-oriented policing, history of policing, combining investigative and patrol functions, allowing lower-level flexibility in decision making, and permanently assigning patrol officers to neighborhoods. Other training approaches include regional community-policing training centers for both law enforcement officers and civilians, which offer courses at no cost, and citizen police academies where citizens learn about police procedures.

This chapter offered an array of examples of approaches to implementing community policing in police departments, some of which involved extensive strategic planning and others which did not. Astoria's implementation was small scale and slow and did not involve much planning because the department had few resources to spare. The Bellingham

Police Department, in contrast, developed a very extensive strategic plan that included principles of community policing, a mission statement, a values statement, and numerous goals and objectives and a time frame for achieving them.

The Madison Police Department adopted total quality management as its management philosophy and incorporated it into the Madison community-policing program under the name of quality policing. This philosophy emphasized a focus on the customer (citizen), a problem-solving orientation, a drive toward continuous quality improvement, an openness to employee input, and a commitment to teamwork.

The Portland Police Department initiated community policing in 1988. The chapter offered an outline of major accomplishments and developments in the program over the ensuing decade.

The Savannah, Georgia Police Department launched community policing in 1991 after an election-time furor over high crime rates. Its plan decentralized patrol service and held captains responsible for crime in their assigned geographical area and for the patrol officers under their command. The Wichita Police Department developed a similar plan, with the exception that they specifically assigned community-policing officers to work with patrol officers who were responsible for answering service calls. Wichita's community-policing officers were to be a resource to the patrol beat officers and to work in conjunction with beat officers to solve problems on their beats.

KEY TERMS

- andragogical approach
- CAPRA
- CIP Action Plan
- citizen police academies
- Comprehensive Community Crime
- control strategy
- COPS
- GEOCOM
- Malcolm Knowles
- pedagogical approach
- Public Safety Initiative
- quality policing

REVIEW QUESTIONS

1. Compare andragogical and pedagogical approaches to learning.

2. Discuss the Royal Canadian Mounted Police approach to police training.

3. Discuss at least one innovative community-police training program.

4. Discuss the Bellingham Police Department's community-policing strategy.

5. Discuss the eight-point action plan of the Eugene, Oregon Police Department.

6. Discuss quality policing.

7. Discuss the Public Safety Initiative of the Wichita Police Department.

12

DISTINCTIVE COMMUNITY-
POLICING PROGRAMS

CHAPTER OBJECTIVES

1. Be familiar with community-policing programs that deal with drugs and drug-related crime.
2. Be familiar with distinctive programs for juveniles.
3. Be familiar with distinctive programs that deal with domestic violence.
4. Be familiar with distinctive programs dealing with the business community.
5. Be familiar with distinctive programs that deal with homelessness.
6. Be familiar with distinctive programs that deal with hate crime.

Introduction

Although community policing has been explained as a philosophy that should permeate all aspects of policing, this chapter deals with distinctive programs for specific social problems that take a community-policing approach. One of the most influential programs, Operation Weed and Seed, was initiated by the U.S. Department of Justice. However, most community-policing programs are initiated by local police agencies and sheriff's departments. Many local police agencies have shown creativity and initiative in developing programs to solve their communities' problems.

Operation Weed and Seed

In 1992, the U.S. Department of Justice introduced Operation Weed and Seed to illustrate how comprehensive resources could be coordinated to control drugs and crime, while at the same time improving the quality of life in high-crime neighborhoods. Residents of the neighborhoods targeted were mostly at or below the poverty line. The program had a two-pronged strategy: "weed out" violent offenders, and "seed" the neighborhood with treatment, prevention, intervention, and revitalization (Roehl et al. 1996, 2, 9). The first strategy of prevention, intervention, and treatment dealt with substance abuse programs and activities such as health and nutrition, victim assistance, and community crime prevention. Also, Safe Haven Centers were established in most Weed and Seed cities. These were multiservice centers that provided a safe neighborhood facility for locating various youth and adult services. Many of the seeding activities were present when Operation Weed and Seed was implemented, but some were federally funded. These included Safe Havens, Boys and Girls Clubs, the Race Against Drugs, and Wings of Hope. Also, state and federal funding continued to support existing programs such as HUD renovation projects, DARE, the Police Athletic League, and Aid to Dependent Children.

The role of community policing in Operation Weed and Seed was that officers were assigned to targeted areas to cultivate relationships with the neighborhood residents and promote efforts to deal with residents' concerns. Community-policing officers were not assigned radio service calls so that they could concentrate on problem solving, community contacts, and youth activities, but they still performed law enforcement activities and made arrests where appropriate. Often, they had partners or worked in teams. The program placed community-policing officers in contact with prosecutors, probation and parole officers, federal law enforcement agents, neighborhood residents, and governmental and social service personnel and enabled these diverse groups to work together. Through steering committees, various agencies coordinated programs, shared resources, and solved problems.

The extent to which Operation Weed and Seed played a major part in reducing violent crime and drug-related crime has been difficult to evaluate, but it assisted in spreading the community-policing philosophy, and the community-policing strategy had a positive impact on both the communities involved and the police departments. This program demonstrated that law enforcement can be enhanced by interacting with the community and that law enforcement and community services are not incompatible police functions.

Value-Based Initiatives

The value-based initiative (VBI) is a Community-Oriented Policing Services (COPS) funded strategy with emphasis on technical assistance and training for problem solving through community initiatives that will promote the community's values. The goal of value-based initiatives is for the community to provide leadership in identifying and developing strategies that challenge the quality of life in the community (Gordon 2002). The value-based initiative can be defined as an

> innovative program that enhances collaboration by engaging early on all members of a community policing partnership in the collaborative problem solving process. It does this by focusing on something that everyone can agree on: basic values. The first step for police and their collaboration partners is to identify and mobilize around a specific community value, such as safe neighborhoods or drug-free schools. Once this is accomplished, VBI partners can begin to clarify the factors that threaten a priority community value and devise realistic intervention strategies.
>
> (Gordon 2002, 1)

VBI includes important community and neighborhood resources, which are faith-based organizations. To be specific, the religious leaders of the community will be included in the VBI. The community-policing philosophy emphasizes developing a partnership with the community and neighborhood and this should not only include social service agencies but also faith-based organizations. Clergy and faith leaders can play a pivotal role in controlling and preventing crime and in improving the quality of life for neighborhood residents. In some communities the clergy have greater influence than political and elected officials. To include faith-based organizations in the policy-making and decision-making process is important if the police, social services agencies, and neighborhood residents want to maintain order. Faith-based organizations must be on an equal footing with the police along with social service agencies and neighbor-hood residents if the VBI is to be effective and a success.

Racial Profiling

During the mid-1990s racial profiling became an issue for policing. "The phenomenon of targeting 'people of color' in traffic enforcement as a pretext to further investigation or search describes the term racial profiling" (Carrick 2000, 8).

The 2000 United States Census indicates that the color of America is changing. Approximately 12 percent of America is African American and more than 12 percent are Hispanic. At the same time the Asian population of America is continuing to increase. It must be realized that nearly one out of every four American citizens identifies themselves with a race other than Caucasian. This includes black, Asian, Native Hawaiian, American Indian, and a race characterized as two or more races (Carrick 2001, 79).

In 1999 a Gallup poll survey found that 81 percent of Americans disapprove of police use of racial profiling with 59 percent believing it was widespread police practice. The same survey reported that 42 percent of black Americans believed that they were stopped simply because of their race at one time. A 2000 Mark Penn Poll found that 75 percent of Americans believed that racial profiling was occurring, while 69 percent indicated that police should be prohibited from targeting people based on their race (Aether Systems 2001, 94).

Because "racial profiling" has caused an uproar from the public states have passed laws requiring that data be collected and classes on racial profiling be held for police officers. Traffic stop data collection can include the reason for the stop; race, sex, approximate age, and ethnicity of the individual stopped; type of search conducted, if any; rationale for the search; nature of contraband recovered, if any; and enforcement action taken during the stop (Carrick 2000, 9).

To bridge the gap that can be caused by racial profiling to the community-policing philosophy police officers must focus on eliminating racial profiling or any perception that it is occurring. The police cannot form a partnership with that segment of the community targeted for racial profiling. The Community-Oriented Policing Service (COPS) office has been deeply concerned about the effect racial profiling can have on community policing. The COPS has developed a racial profile training program for police officers. The purpose of the training is to provide police officers with an understanding of racial profiling as a violation of state and federal laws and how the practice of racial profiling can have a negative impact on community trust. The major objectives of the training are as follows (Courtney 2002, 2):

- Promote understanding and respect for racial and cultural differences and use of effective non-combative methods of carrying out law enforcement duties in a racially and culturally diverse environment.
- Discuss the concepts of Public Trust, Social Contract, and Racial Profiling as a moral issue.
- Describe the Fourth and Fourteenth Amendments relevant to traffic stops and racial profiling.

With America moving toward a more diverse society the police have as one of their primary duties the protection of the constitutional rights of all citizens. The police also have an ethical responsibility to enforce the law in a fair and just manner. At no time should the police use the law for their own prejudices and personal biases.

Business Alliance Program

The Business Alliance Program grew out of Operation Weed and Seed. Its purpose was to rebuild the economic structure of neighborhoods through community efforts by improving living and working conditions—specifically, to help businesses grow, attract new employment opportunities to neighborhoods, and increase training opportunities for neighborhood residents and the private sector through partnerships between the business community and neighborhood residents. The Business Alliance, when it is successful, can be beneficial to the police, because crime rates are down when the unemployment rate is down. Removing drugs and crime from a neighborhood will not last if the community lacks employment opportunities. Further, community policing has a role to play in Business Alliance programs, because communities and neighborhoods with high crime rates and disorder will not attract or maintain businesses. According to a U.S. Department of Justice publication on Business Alliance (Bureau of Justice Assistance 1994), "Community policing is essential for attracting economic enterprises through which the community, law enforcement, and businesses can support revitalization efforts" (2).

Citizens on Patrol

In 1991, 105 persons from 11 Ft. Worth neighborhoods attended 12 hours of training sessions at the Ft. Worth Police Academy to become members of a group called Citizens on Patrol. Classes covered legal liabilities, patrol procedures, communications, and the criminal code. Upon completing the training, each citizen graduate was given a diploma, cap, T-shirt, and windbreaker bearing the insignia Citizens on Patrol. After the training, each citizen was required to ride with a patrol officer and to meet with the officer in charge of the Citizens on Patrol program in his or her neighborhood to review regulations. All Citizens on Patrol groups selected a leader who worked the neighborhood patrolling schedule. The group was furnished with a portable radio to report suspicious persons or activities to their base station. The base station could be housed either at the local field operations division or at an individual's home. Base units notified the police dispatcher.

Citizens on Patrol interfaced with neighborhood patrol officers (NPOs). Ten NPOs were assigned to each of the four field operations divisions. Each NPO was assigned to a specific geographical neighborhood within the division to address root causes of crime. A variety of nontraditional methods could be used, each with the purpose of including and empowering the community. For example, some NPOs were in charge of sports teams that participated in the City's Youth League. Others were involved with the Explorer Scout groups. NPOs worked closely with Citizens on Patrol groups. They provided crime data and advised Citizens on Patrol groups on when and where to patrol their neighborhood. Also, NPOs worked with Citizens on Patrol to develop or expand problem-solving concepts that fit their specific neighborhood. In one neighborhood, residents were listed in a central data log, and neighbors each had a bumper sticker to identify the neighborhood to which they belonged, allowing for rapid identification of suspicious vehicles in the area. Citizens on Patrol also advised residents when they left themselves open to victimization, such as when they left their garage doors open or left expensive items in an unlocked vehicle parked on the street (Ft. Worth Police Department, n.d.).

Domestic Violence Programs

Traditional policing considers domestic violence primarily a problem for social services agencies, but community-policing agencies recognize that police have an important role to play in reducing it. Domestic violence is often unreported, and victims often lack knowledge about available services. Policing can provide an important link between victims in need of services and domestic violence service agencies in the community. Police officer resistance to domestic violence initiatives is often symptomatic of attitudinal problems.

In 1996, the Cheektowaga Police Department, located in western New York, began participating in the Community Policing to Combat Domestic Violence Program, funded by the U.S. Justice Department.* The Erie County Coalition against Family Violence had found that victims of domestic violence were not receiving readily available community services, so the police department sought to change the behavior of police officers who were ineffective in delivery of services to victims of domestic violence and to develop an organizational culture that would be responsive to the domestic violence-related needs of the community.

To combat domestic violence, the Cheektowaga Police Department entered into a partnership with Haven House, the local battered women's shelter, and the National Conference (formerly the National Conference of Christian and Jews), a human relations organization committed to diversity and to combating prejudice. The domestic violence project had the following objectives:

1. To dispel invalid mythology regarding victims of domestic violence our officers may harbor
2. To increase the interpersonal and communication skills of the responding officers
3. To reduce bias and discrimination by the officer towards victims
4. To increase the skill level of officers in the recognition of violent human dynamics in domestic scenarios

---

* Source: The next seven paragraphs are adapted from C. Rucinski, et al., Transitions, © 1997, Cheektowaga Police Department.

5. To develop data identifying areas for growth and continuous improvement

(Rucinski et al. 1997, 1)

Based on the objectives, a two-day domestic violence training program was developed that focused on combating myths about domestic violence, developing interpersonal skills, and overcoming bias and stereotypes that hamper problem solving. Training was open to all police officers, public safety dispatchers, and civilian personnel, including the community partners. Both the community partners and the police had input in selecting training topics and developing vignettes.

In the training, police officers were assisted in identifying risk factors for several types of assaultive behavior, predicting dangerousness of individuals, intervening with effective methods, thereby increasing both officer and victim safety, and working with victims in trauma and crisis situations. They were given practical tips on how to handle domestic violence situations, including defusing the anger of the victim and the aggressor, letting the victim know her options and alternatives, and letting the victim know that shelter was available. The Theater for Change, professional actors, performed three vignettes: one concerning a victim reluctant to press charges, one presenting parties with conflicting stories, and one involving repeated reconciliations between the parties. The National Conference presented a workshop on recognizing diversity, overcoming myths and stereotypes (especially those associated with victims and offenders of domestic violence) that hinder creative problem solving, understanding prejudice, and strengthening communications and interpersonal skills. Other issues addressed by the training were effects of violence on children, signs of domestic violence, resources to help victims, why women stay, and updates on law changes dealing with domestic violence and restraining order protection.

The Cheektowaga Police Department's domestic violence training program is a practical program that police officers can use when they respond to domestic violence calls. Over 300 police officers in Western New York had taken the domestic violence training course as of 1997, and, in 1997, the National League of Cities gave the Cheektowaga Police Department their project award for the program.

Other police agencies throughout America are also taking constructive action to end violence against women. The Community Police Exchange ("A Law Enforcement Checklist" 1997) delineated a number of strategies that can be used by police agencies to reduce incidents of violence against women:

- create a community roundtable
- record domestic violence
- continue to educate
- provide clear guidance on responding to domestic violence
- ensure that law enforcement is well informed
- reach out to the front lines
- improve enforcement by implementing a registry of restraining orders and a uniform order of protection
- support and pursue legislative initiatives
- conduct training
- structure courts to respond to domestic violence/create special-ized domestic violence courts

(8)

Community-police officers have a role to play in many of these recom-mendations because they involve collaboration with various community groups and agencies to prevent crime and improve the quality of life for community residents. Domestic violence is an area in which community policing can be effective.

Drug Awareness and Resistance Education

The Drug Awareness and Resistance Education (DARE) program was initiated by the Los Angeles Police Department in 1983 as an educational program to prevent drug use and violence among young people. In a short time, it made its way to police departments throughout the country. Its emphasis has always been to help students recognize and resist the pressures and influence of their peers so that they refrain from experi-menting with alcohol, marijuana, tobacco, and other drugs. Strategies focus on building self-esteem, assertiveness, interpersonal and communication skills, decision-making skills, and awareness of positive alternatives to drug use and gang involvement.

The DARE program usually has 17 sessions, with either police officers or deputy sheriffs as classroom instructors. Classes are generally taught from the fourth or fifth grade to the eighth grade. The police officers remain on campus all day to interact with students during lunch and recess.

The combining of DARE with community policing can be advantageous. It performs a service to the community, develops a potential partnership with the community's young people, and helps to prevent drug-related and other crime among young people.

Gang Resistance Education and Training Program

The Gang Resistance Education and Training (GREAT) program was designed to

- reduce the incidence of violent youth crime
- reduce gang activity and violence
- provide youth with life skills and strategies to resist gang involvement pressure
- familiarize youth with the means by which to resolve conflicts in a non-violent manner
- provide alternative activities for GREAT graduates during the summer months

(Bureau of Alcohol, Tobacco, and Firearms (BATF) 1998b, 2)

It teaches young people to establish goals for themselves, resist pressures, and resolves conflicts without violence and allows them to discover for themselves how gang and youth violence can affect the quality of their lives through structured exercises and interactive approaches to learning. GREAT began in 1992 through a partnership with the Treasury Department's Bureau of Alcohol, Tobacco, and Firearms and the Phoenix Police Department. The two agencies developed a nine-lesson middle-school curriculum that has become a national model, with more than 800 police agencies involved in it. BATF continues to fund police agencies and manages cooperative agreements and communities' interest in GREAT (BATF 1998a, 1).

Like DARE, GREAT exposes young people to specific programs that will help them stay out of trouble with legal authorities. It draws on the community-policing philosophy in that it involves police partnership with the schools, a federal agency, and the young people.

Hate Crime Programs

The federal Hate Crimes Sentencing Enhancement Act of 1994 defines hate crimes as those in which "the defendant intentionally selects a victim, or in the case of a property crime, the property that is the object of the crime, because of the actual or perceived race, religion, national origin, ethnicity, gender, disability, or sexual orientation of any person" (Leadership Conference 1998, 1). The crimes included in hate crimes are murder, forcible rape, robbery, aggravated assault, burglary, larceny, motor vehicle theft, arson, intimidation, and vandalism. Usually, hate crimes are more violent than other crimes. Generally, their intention is to murder, maim, or injure. Hate crimes are five times more likely than other crimes to involve assaults, and hate crime assaults are twice as likely as other assaults to cause injuries that will result in hospitalization. Offenders of hate crimes are likely to be marauding groups of predators searching for targets at which to direct their hatred.

The attackers or offenders of hate crimes are usually young people, mostly young men in their teens or 20s, who are primarily looking for thrills and respect from friends. Sometimes people carry out hate crimes because they feel insulted: by interracial dating, integration of their neighborhood, their battered wife's decision to leave, their competition with women for jobs, or just the existence of homosexuality, whether male or female. Fanatic ideological racist, religious, or ethnic bigots are the most common offenders (Leadership Conference 1998, 3–4).

Since data have been collected for hate crimes, victims have included whites, blacks, Hispanics, American Indians, Asian Americans, and multiracial people; Jews, Catholics, Muslims, and atheists; and gay men, lesbians, bisexuals, and heterosexuals. As the preceding list indicates, no one is left out: regardless of a person's race, ethnicity, religion, gender, or sexual orientation, there is always someone or some group who might attack him or her simply because of one of those characteristics. Anyone in America could be a victim of a hate crime, and this type of crime should be considered offensive to all Americans with a sense of fair play and justice. Groups and individuals who commit hate crimes pose a threat to our communities.

Both the federal and most state governments have taken actions to stem the tide of hate crimes. In 1990, Congress passed the Hate Crimes Statistical Act to get a handle on the extent of hate crimes occurring in our nation. This act mandates that the Attorney General of the United States obtains data on crimes that manifest evidence of prejudice based on "race, religion, ethnicity, and sexual orientation." In 1992, Congress passed the Juvenile and Delinquency Prevention Act, which requires that each state's juvenile delinquency plan include a component designed to combat hate crime. In 1994, Congress passed the Violence Against Women Act, a comprehensive federal law to address the national problem of violence against women. In 1996, Congress passed the Church Arson Prevention Act to enhance federal jurisdiction over and increase federal penalties for the destruction of houses of worship. This law was passed in response to the numerous burnings of African American churches during the 1990s. In addition, the U.S. Commission on Civil Rights has undertaken to produce radio public service announcements on discrimination and denial of equal protection of the law (Leadership Conference 1998, 11).

Most states have some form of hate crime laws. These state statutes take a variety of forms, which include requiring states to compile statistics on hate crime, holding parents liable for the actions of their children, allowing civil actions against perpetrators of hate crimes, outlawing intimidation of individuals, and outlawing vandalism against houses of worship. Also, several states have passed legislation imposing heavier criminal penalties for hate-motivated crimes. On the local level, a number of police departments have established bias units. The New York City Police Department's special bias unit has been trained to be sensitive to victims, because victims who believe the police are sympathetic to their plight are usually more encouraged to report hate crimes and to be cooperative with investigations and prosecutions. A successful police bias unit develops a working relationship with minority communities, with prosecutors, and with police officers from different law enforcement agencies (Leadership Conference 1998, 12).

Not all police agencies have reported hate crimes. Areas whose police departments report hate crimes comprise 58 percent of the United States population (Leadership Conference 1998, 1–3).

The Chicago Police Department is one department committed to community policing that has addressed hate crimes. It has established policies and procedures for handling criminal and noncriminal incidents motivated by hatred. These policies define hate crimes, outline reporting and notification procedures when an incident occurs, and provide an annual statistical report. They also describe the department's strategies for assessing community tension and responding to potential problems before they escalate. The department's response to hate crimes involves many divisions: the patrol division, the detective division, the youth division, and prevention programs (Chicago Police Department 1998, 1).

Police departments committed to the community-policing philosophy must be committed to eliminating hate crimes. A police–community partnership cannot be developed when hate crimes are occurring in a community and the police take no action to prevent them or to arrest the attackers. Police departments need to report hate crimes, encourage reporting, and develop effective intervention strategies. Community-policing officers should anticipate potential hate crime problems and engage in problem solving, with the cooperation of residents, the police, and other social and governmental agencies, before threats are put into action.

Programs for the Homeless

In the last 15–20 years, the homeless population has grown substantially. According to the National Coalition for the Homeless (NCH), two trends are responsible for homelessness: poverty and a shortage of affordable rental housing. Poverty and homelessness are intimately connected. Poor people frequently cannot afford housing, food, child and health care, and education, and, because housing consumes most of a person's income, housing is often not economically possible. Many people are only one paycheck from poverty and can easily be made homeless by an illness, an accident, or a lost job. By 1996, 14 million people in the United States were living below the poverty level. Children made up 40 percent of those living in poverty (NCH 1998, 1).

The eroding labor market, low wages, and decrease in public benefits have all been important factors in increasing poverty. Rates of both unemployment and underemployment have increased since the 1970s. Many people cannot get enough work to live on or have given up looking for work. Low-skilled and poorly educated workers are especially vulnerable as blue-collar jobs continue to disappear. The transition to a global economy has meant that many American corporations are moving their operations overseas, often to countries where workers are paid more cheaply, and are laying off their American workers.

Many poor people, including homeless people, are in the workforce but have very low wages. Many are employed as temporary workers or independent contractors. Generally, these workers receive no benefits and lack job security. Even those working full time may not make enough to get above the poverty level. Wages have not kept pace with inflation, and unions have lost much of their power to fight for higher wages (NCH 1998, 1–2). The availability of public assistance has also decreased in the last decade. Most people who receive public assistance do not receive enough funds to afford rental property. Although the welfare caseloads have decreased since the passage of welfare reform legislation during the 1990s, declining welfare rolls only mean that fewer people are receiving public assistance; they do not mean that people are better off financially. Those individuals terminated from welfare rolls may not be able to find employment or may be able to find only low-paying jobs without benefits. If this is the case, they may not be able to afford housing (NCH 1998, 2–3).

The increasing scarcity of affordable housing must also be considered a contributing factor to homelessness. There are not enough affordable housing units to meet the demands and, in many urban areas, gentrification is resulting in the eviction of low-income tenants and the demolition of low-income housing. Other factors as well have contributed to the homeless problem:

- Lack of affordable health care: For families and individuals struggling to pay the rent, a serious illness or disability can start a downward spiral into homelessness, beginning with a lost job, depletion of savings to pay for care, and eventual eviction. . . .
- Domestic violence: Battered women who live in poverty are often forced to choose between abusive relationships and homelessness. . . .

- Mental illness: Approximately 20%–25% of the single adult homeless population suffers from some form of severe and persistent mental illness. . . . [However], many mentally ill homeless people are unable to obtain access to mental health support services such as case management, treatment, and provision of housing.
- Chemical dependency: In recent years, the relationship between substance abuse and homelessness has stirred much debate. While rates of alcohol and drug abuse are disproportionately high among the homeless population, the increase in homelessness in the 1980s cannot be explained by substance abuse. During the 1980s, competition for increasingly scarce low-income housing grew so intense that those with disabilities such as chemical addiction and mental illness were more likely to lose out and find themselves on the streets.

(NCH 1998, 4–6)

The homeless problem in America is complex, and the homeless should not be blamed for their situation. Obviously, there are many circumstances that allow people to fall into poverty. In many communities, citizens have chosen to consider this social problem a police problem. But the police cannot handle the homeless problem by using the traditional approach to policing. The community-policing approach is far better suited to dealing with homelessness.

An agreement between the City of Miami and the American Civil Liberties Union (ACLU) in December 1997 may be used as a model for other cities that have a homeless population. The agreement, the result of a federal lawsuit, Pottinger v. Miami, initiated in 1988, challenged as unconstitutional the city's policy of arresting homeless people for sleeping, eating, and congregating in public and the city's policy of having police confiscate and destroy the possessions of homeless people. Under the ACLU-Miami settlement, the city was required to develop a training program to sensitize Miami police officers to the predicament of homeless people and to ensure that the police do not violate the legal rights of homeless people. The city had to develop guidelines on how the police were to deal with encounters with the homeless. If a police officer observed a homeless person engaging in a violation of a city ordinance, such as sleeping on a park bench, the homeless person would have to be informed of homeless shelters available and given transportation before an arrest could occur. The homeless person could only be arrested if he or she refused available shelter. In addition, the police would not be allowed to destroy the property of homeless people, except under very limited circumstances. Also, an advisory committee composed of homeless people and city representatives would monitor police contacts with the homeless and issue a report every six months (National Law Center 1998, 2).

In 1991, the Santa Monica, California Police Department set up a Homeless Liaison Program (HLP) that created a four-person police unit to deal directly with the community's concerns about homeless issues. The program goals were to end the cycle of homelessness and improve the quality of life for residents and business owners in the community. The HLP unit works with social service agencies to place homeless people in shelters and long-term housing and to provide basic needs for homeless people (Santa Monica Police Department 1998, 1). The new approaches to homeless problems in Miami and Santa Monica exemplify the community-policing philosophy. Both involve partnership with social service agencies, citizen input, and the use of a broad problem-solving approach.

School Resource Officers

The Arvada, Colorado Police Department started a school resource officer (SRO) program in 1995 to establish high visibility of police officers in and around schools in order to prevent disorder problems. At first, the department assigned one police officer to each of the city's three high schools. In 1996, an SRO was assigned to one middle school as well, and then, as a result of the positive feedback from the middle school, SROs were assigned to all the city's middle schools. SROs function as liaisons between the police department, the school, and the surrounding community and do classroom instruction, student mentoring, crime prevention, problem identification, problem solving, and law enforcement. They deal with issues directly related to the school and its student population and associated problems within the surrounding neighborhood. They are not expected to respond to radio service calls. They are available to students during school hours as well as for many extracurricular activities. The Arvada Police Department's SRO program does not follow rigid guidelines, because schools, students, and police officers all have different personalities. SROs are given the latitude to adapt their distinctive styles to the requirements of each specific issue (Hoffman n.d.).

Senior Liaison Officers

In 1995, the Arvada, Colorado Police Department initiated a senior liaison officer (SLO) program customized to provide services to citizens 60 years of age and older. SLOs work proactively with seniors to identify concerns and service needs, resolve problems, and obtain appropriate services. The long-range goal of the program is to reduce the fear of crime among seniors and to provide quality police service to senior citizens. The SLOs maintain a high visibility in retired senior facilities and make weekly visits to senior centers. Some of the activities of SLOs are:

1. Regular visits to senior housing facilities
2. Security at selected senior activities, such as dances and cultural events
3. Identification of seniors who are abused or neglected, or who can no longer adequately care for themselves, and facilitation in the resolution of these situations so that the best care possible can be provided for them
4. Crime prevention and personal safety classes for seniors
5. Referral to outside resources which assist seniors with concerns and problems, dispute resolution, and other personal services for senior citizens as they are identified
6. Personal contact with seniors who are victims of crime

(Hoffman, n.d., n.p.)

Substance Abuse Narcotics Education Program

The Substance Abuse Narcotics Education (SANE) program has been in existence in the Los Angeles County Sheriff's Department since the mid-1980s. SANE provides a unique approach in drug prevention that involves the Los Angeles County Sheriff's Department, school districts, schools, and municipalities throughout Los Angeles County. Currently, deputies are working with third- through eighth-grade students in all 54 public school districts of Los Angeles County, juvenile court and community schools, and many private schools. SANE uses a variety of professionally developed drug prevention education curricula to meet the diverse needs of the various schools and communities. Each curriculum has the components of building self-esteem, teaching coping and decision-making skills and skills for dealing with peer pressure, and basic substance education. Deputies and classroom teachers co-teach the program so that the drug prevention message will come from two role models. All deputies assigned to SANE receive intensive training both in general teaching methodologies and in their special curriculum. Classroom teachers are trained in drug use prevention techniques and recognition, thereby becoming valuable resources for their schools.

The SANE program introduced Curriculum Integrated Drug Abuse Prevention (CIDAP) into the schools. CIDAP is a ten-lesson program whose objectives are to develop an awareness of the effects of drugs on the individual's physical and mental health, increase knowledge of drugs, improve decision-making skills, improve self-esteem, explain peer pressure and offer easy-to-use responses to it, review the social problem of drug abuse, affect students' attitudes toward personal use of drugs, give students a better understanding of themselves, and recommend alternatives to drug abuse. The CIDAP program is very flexible and can be used to supplement an existing curriculum or can function as an independent component of the SANE program.

Because of the increase in gang violence and the connection between gangs and drugs, SANE developed a gang prevention curriculum. This curriculum includes lessons on self-esteem, media influence, alternatives, power, violence, and social values.*

Volunteer Programs**

The Delray Beach Police Department in southern Florida has several volunteer programs that have been incorporated into their community-policing strategy. The volunteer programs allow citizens of the community to be involved in policing activities and provide citizens with a better understanding of police work. Volunteers are screened and trained by the police department.

---

* This information was taken from Drug Abuse—SANE Program, a Los Angeles County Sheriff's Department brochure, 1998.

** Source: R.G. Overman, Chief, Delray Beach Police Department, personal communication, 1998.

Citizen Observer Patrol

This program consists of approximately 1,000 volunteers from 20 neighborhoods who patrol their own neighborhoods in two-hour shifts over both daytime and night-time hours. The volunteers are equipped with cellular telephones to call in suspicious activity. In some patrols, volunteers drive their own personal vehicles; in other areas, patrol members use and maintain retired police vehicles that were given to the neighborhood by the police department.

Roving Patrol

The Roving Patrol consists of 15 volunteers. It is used by the Delray Beach Police Department in areas that are experiencing property crime problems and areas that require a high-profile type of patrolling. Members use retired police department vehicles equipped with yellow light bars and spotlights. They are trained in the use of a police radio as well as a cell phone. They do three-hour shifts between 6.00 p.m. and 11.00 p.m. throughout the week. They are also used in conjunction with detectives in auto theft ring operations.

Haitian Roving Patrol

The Haitian Roving Patrol has 18 members and patrols with retired police vehicles in the Haitian community as well as on other assignments throughout the city. They assist patrol officers in translations on radio calls for service. Haitian volunteers also walk the downtown business section during the evening hours, providing extra security to merchants and shoppers alike. The Haitian volunteers are dedicated to the Roving Patrol program and the Delray Beach Police Department. Three of them hold the rank of volunteer sergeants. They are trained in the use of the cell phone and binoculars.

Downtown Walking Patrol

The Downtown Walking Patrol has eight volunteer members. They patrol in pairs and receive training in the use of the police radio and cell phone. They walk a beat in the downtown Delray Beach area and provide a sense of security to both merchants and shoppers. They give directions to tourists and answer questions for the business owners. They also watch out for suspicious activity and call the police on the radio when they are needed.

Parking Enforcement Specialist

There are 51 volunteer Parking Enforcement Specialists. These volunteers provide parking enforcement for the downtown, beach, business district, and shopping center areas throughout the city. They use retired city vehicles with a yellow flashing light and golf carts that allow them to get around easily in traffic. They receive 40 hours of instruction on traffic laws and ticket writing.

Traffic Monitoring Patrol

The Traffic Monitoring Patrol has 14 volunteers. Traffic monitors are trained in the operation and setup of the mobile radar trailer, which is used in problem areas of the city where there are speed problems. The trailer has a self-contained radar unit and a large display board that displays the speed of approaching vehicles. If these vehicles exceed the posted speed limits, the members write down the tag numbers of the suspected vehicles, and the city sends the owners of the vehicles a warning letter. The traffic monitoring program provides training and safety for citizens in the City of Delray Beach and is a good public relations tool for the police department. The volunteers also assist in the collection of data for the department's traffic unit for developing plans to resolve traffic-related problems, such as traffic facilities, accidents, and speed enforcement.

Volunteer Front Lobby

The Volunteer Front Lobby team has 16 volunteers. Volunteers are responsible for greeting all visitors who enter the police department and assisting them in contacting the appropriate police personnel. Also, the Front Lobby team assists in administrative duties.

Volunteer Administrative Support Team

The Administrative Support Team has 25 members. These volunteers help sworn and support personnel in a variety of administrative duties, such as victim services, tracking auto thefts, tracking pawn shop tickets, and filing paperwork.

Youth Programs

A joint study by the National Institute of Justice and the Carnegie Corporation of New York (Chaiken 1998) found that many popular approaches to dealing with juvenile violence have not worked. The main approach used has been that of locking up juveniles in state and local facilities. The juveniles are supervised when in custody, but once they are released nothing seems to change. Even boot camps provide only temporary supervision. Many teenage programs available after school are ineffective. Many gang prevention approaches that provide information about the wickedness of delinquency backfire, with the juveniles becoming more delinquent. The approaches that appear to be the most promising for preventing delinquency and violence are long term, continuous, and comprehensive. They involve adult tutors and mentors who instruct young people in social skills and give them opportunities to practice these skills. Many national youth organizations follow this approach. They provide a variety of activities appropriate for a young person's age and period of development.

- An environment in which kids are valued and are considered resources rather than problems for their community
- Activities that present teens with real challenges and experiences in planning, preparing for, and publicly presenting projects they and their communities truly value
- Ongoing outreach to teens and adults in the community, with messages that are understandable

(Chaiken 1998, xiv)

The National Institute of Justice study found that partnerships between the police and youth service agencies take many forms, from police officer involvement in youth advisory boards to police coaching of sports teams to youth involvement in crime prevention programs. Several youth service organizations have requested police to provide programs for young people to make them aware of dangerous situations, such as threats and pressures from gang members, violence among family members, and rape attempts. The police have devoted hours as volunteers to Boy Scouts and Girl Scouts in high-crime areas. They have also been involved in juvenile diversion programs (i.e., programs that provide sentencing alternatives to locking up offenders) (Chaiken 1998, xv). All of these are aspects of community policing.

Bristol Family Center

The Bristol Family Center in Bristol, Connecticut, is a comprehensive facility for boys and girls. The center opens at 6.30 a.m. and closes at 9.00 p.m. Its facilities have child care, swimming, gymnastics, dance classes, and other activities. The center offers special events for adolescents in specific grades: for example, there are sixth-grade Friday night socials. The Bristol Police Department and the Youth Service Bureau are leaders in the coalition that implements the juvenile offender diversion program in which the Bristol Family Center collaborates. Also involved in the coalition are the Bristol public schools, the department of probation, and agencies that provide clinical services for children.

A juvenile review board composed of representatives from the above-named agencies meets on a regular basis to review juvenile cases. The discussion at the board meeting is confidential. Initially, the meeting opens with a juvenile officer giving information concerning the incident leading to the arrest of a juvenile. The board members may provide information about the family and children involved in the incident. Because the board is composed not only of police officers and probation officers but also of school counselors, after-school activities directors, and psychological counselors, a multifaceted view of the juvenile offender can be obtained. The board explores alternative options to locking up juvenile offenders, such as having them write an essay about the consequences of their actions or perform community service. Juveniles who perform community service in the Family Center sign a contract as to the number of hours they will be working. If they fail to live up to the contract, their case is referred to the juvenile review board again for action. Family Center staff members are not made aware of why a youngster is performing community service.

In addition to serving on the juvenile review board, the Bristol Police often work directly with children on projects sponsored by youth organizations. These projects can include "antidrug poster coloring contests," at which officers have the opportunity to talk with children, and training for youth organization participants on topics such as gang awareness and dealing with babysitting emergencies. The community-policing "Walk-and-Talk" approach encourages police officers to stop at youth centers as part of community outreach (Chaiken 1998, 22–24).

Spokane Police Department

Spokane's community-policing approach has encouraged police officers to address problems involving the children and teens of Spokane, Washington, and to develop a wide variety of programs to create an environment of safety for young people. One officer developed "Every 15 Minutes," a program to prevent alcohol-related deaths of teenagers on prom nights. Also, a two-day, one-night multimedia program was developed for junior and senior high school students to alert them to the dangers of drinking and driving.

The COPS-N-Kids annual truck and car event held every August is an attempt to deal with teenagers' "cruising." The Spokane officers support cruising by teenagers if it is properly monitored and directed. Police officers have convinced automobile business owners and adults with automobile hobbies to come to the cruising area and to assist the teenagers in maintaining their vehicles. The August truck and car event, which includes free food and drinks, is promised to the teenagers if they remain trouble free.

A COPS (community-oriented policing) West Ministration, staffed by community volunteers and a neighborhood resource officer, has several programs directed at or including young people, such as McGruff safe houses, responses to calls involving conflicts between community children and teenagers, and adult patrolling of the streets before and after school to ensure children's safety and to keep older children from harassing younger children (Chaiken 1998, 35–37).

Additional Community-Policing Programs

To cover all community-policing programs in one chapter would be an impossible task. Below are listed a few more community-policing programs. Several of these have been around for several decades and were initiated for improving police–community relations or for crime prevention:

- Basic Car Plan: A city is subdivided by computer-generated crime occurrence data, and teams of nine officers are given 24-hour responsibility for a specific subdivision on permanent assignment to develop proprietary interest through formal and informal meetings with the public.

- Basic Commander System: A police sergeant is given command of 20 officers, including detectives, who only investigate crimes in the beat command area on permanent assignment and who are closely monitored for job satisfaction and efficiency at improving citizen satisfaction.
- Bilingual Programs: These include such efforts as bilingual public announcements, bilingual education programs, and incentive pay for dual-language officers.
- Compstat: Weekly community policing meetings are held. Precinct commanders and other police executives are rotated on a regular basis, and immediate accountability is required every five weeks from the executives in front of the others at staff meetings to see if crime goes down under their watch.
- Neighborhood Advisory Councils: Community leaders are invited or elected to explore community needs. They meet with assigned police officers to consider specific patrol tactics and manpower scheduling and to voice complaints and commend personnel.
- Split Force Policing: One portion of the police force is used for responding to calls regularly and another portion is assigned to directed patrol.

(North Carolina Wesleyan College 1998, 1–10)

Summary

Many police departments and federal and state law enforcement agencies have established distinctive programs that deal with specific problems and take a community-policing approach. They address a variety of issues, such as drugs, gangs, juvenile delinquency, domestic violence, hate crimes, and homelessness.

In 1992, the U.S. Department of Justice introduced Operation Weed and Seed to illustrate how comprehensive resources could be coordinated to control drugs and crime, while at the same time improving the quality of life in high-crime neighborhoods. The Weed and Seed program had a two-pronged strategy: "weed out" violent and drug offenders, and "seed" the neighborhood with treatment, prevention, intervention, and revitalization. Community-policing officers were assigned to neighborhoods to participate in both weeding and seeding strategies.

Police have an important role to play in addressing domestic violence effectively, and several police departments are initiating proactive approaches in this area. For example, the Cheektowaga, New York, Police Department entered a partnership with a local battered women's shelter and a human relations organization committed to diversity and to combating prejudice to design a comprehensive domestic violence training program that police officers could use when they responded to domestic violence calls. The program dispelled myths about domestic violence, taught effective intervention methods, helped officers to work with victims in trauma and crisis situations, and presented resources to help victims.

Drug Awareness and Resistance Education (DARE) and Gang Resistance Education and Training (GREAT) are programs to help elementary- and middle-school children stay away from drugs and gangs. These programs have police officers functioning as instructors in the classroom. This allows the police officer to be a role model for children and also gives children a chance to see the police officer as a person.

Hate crimes are crimes in which the defendant intentionally selects a victim or his or her property because of the victim's actual or perceived race, religion, national origin, ethnicity, gender, disability, or sexual orientation. Hate crimes are usually more violent than other crimes and disrupt communities by creating fear and encouraging further hostilities. Community-policing programs can assess potential hate crime problems and address them before they escalate through community cooperation.

Homelessness is a social problem created by poverty and a lack of affordable rental housing. It is frequently referred to the police to deal with by enforcing city ordinances. But tactics that force homeless people to leave a public area or that confiscate or destroy their possessions often violate homeless people's legal rights, as well as being inhumane. Community-policing programs have found more constructive approaches to dealing with homelessness that involve cooperation with social service agencies.

Volunteer programs have played a big role in community policing. These programs can involve citizens in neighborhood patrols, traffic monitoring, parking enforcement, or receptionist or administrative support services to the police department. Because of tight budgets, police departments cannot provide all the services that the citizens of the community may want. The use of citizen volunteers can assist the police in providing resources that they normally could not provide. Community-policing departments have found a valuable community resource.

KEY TERMS

- Business Alliance
- Citizens on Patrol
- DARE
- GREAT
- hate crimes

- juvenile diversion programs
- Operation Weed and Seed
- SANE
- school resource officers
- senior liaison officers

REVIEW QUESTIONS

1. What role should the police play in the homeless problem?
2. Why should local police agencies be involved in efforts to reduce hate crimes?
3. How can community policing be involved in the Business Alliance?
4. What are the major advantages of Operation Weed and Seed to community policing?
5. Why should police officers be involved in DARE and GREAT?

13

THE FUTURE OF
COMMUNITY POLICING

CHAPTER OBJECTIVES

1. Have an understanding of the challenges to community policing that Taylor et al. (1998) describe.

2. Be familiar with Taylor et al.'s (1998) list of five questions that indicate whether a department is doing community policing.

3. Be familiar with the Community Policing Strategies Conference's recommendations for community policing.

4. Be familiar with possible future trends in community policing.

Introduction

In the latter part of the twentieth century, police practitioners realized that the professional or traditional policing approach was not working to solve and prevent crimes and that a new strategy would be necessary. The new approach became known as "community policing." It was based on the recognition that police could be successful in solving crimes only when the public fully cooperated with them by providing information that could lead to the arrest of law violators.

Community-oriented policing grew out of earlier experiments, such as team policing, ministations, programs to improve police–community relations, directed patrol, and foot patrols that had been conducted in the 1960s and 1970s. One especially important concept to the development of community policing was problem-oriented policing, first described by Herman Goldstein, a noted police scholar. It involved encouraging police officers to take a proactive approach to solving recurrent problems on their beat rather than merely having them respond to 911 calls and do random patrol. Community policing builds on problem-oriented policing by adding the crucial ingredient of community participation in both problem identification and problem solving.

One driving force behind "community policing" has been citizens' desire to improve and maintain the quality of life in their neighborhoods. Average citizens have indicated their concern about disorderly behavior that, if unchecked, can lead to neighborhood deterioration. Because quality of life can only be improved or maintained when the neighborhood residents play a major role, the role of police has been to assist the community in this endeavor. As policing has evolved more and more toward a service orientation, police departments have focused more on addressing crime problems and enforcement priorities as the community defines them.

Community Policing and Homeland Security*

The role of state and local law enforcement has taken on additional responsibilities after the terrorist attacks of September 11, 2001. The federal government has announced that there are simply not enough resources available at the national level to ensure protection of our communities from the threat of terrorism. State and local police officials understand the importance of protecting our communities from not only the criminal element, but also foreign and domestic terrorist organizations that wish to do harm and cause destruction. Although the federal government has provided millions of dollars to communities in Homeland Security Grants, the amounts received by local governments are truly insignificant when the funding is dispersed amongst all deserving and eligible agencies. State and local police agencies must look for ways to utilize resources already in place to better safeguard their neighborhoods.

Foreign terrorism has been a major concern of the American government and its citizens and is an issue that received significant media attention since the first attack on the World Trade Center in 1993. Media headlines from around the world are packed with information about terrorist activities. To the average American citizen, the threat of terrorism becoming a major problem within our own country is now being perceived

---

* The information for this section was provided by Joe A. Dessenberger of the Wichita Police Department.

as a realistic concern. Historically, Americans have liked to think that terrorist activities occur in other countries, and occasionally target United States interests overseas, but are not a major concern to our country. However, recent Congressional hearings on the September 11th attacks and detailed information from Jama Ahmed al-Fadl, a former top lieutenant to Osama bin Laden (Griset and Mahan 2003, 53) have begun to paint a picture that Americans have been a target, within our own country, since the 1993 World Trade Center attack. We are facing an enemy that is highly organized, well financed, and patient. Due in large part to our free and open society, persons from abroad wishing to do harm within America had been entering the United States routinely before September 11, 2001.

Even after increased border protection and passport screening began taking effect post September 11, 2001 foreign terrorists have continued to enter the United States. Porous areas along the southwest border with Mexico have allowed foreign terrorists to enter by intermingling with the large illegal immigrant population that crosses into America on a daily basis. Commercial seaports have reported finding containers offloaded from cargo vessels that have been turned into makeshift apartments for persons to smuggle themselves and weapons into the country. Homeland Security authorities have informed the American people that foreign terrorists will plague America for decades to come.

Although America faces terrorist threats from foreign terrorists, local governments must also be aware of the dangers faced from within our own society and communities. Domestic terrorism has not been in the media spotlight nearly as much as foreign terrorism. No American born before 1990 will soon forget the attack on the Murrah Federal Building in Oklahoma City that occurred in 1995. Timothy McVeigh and Terry Nichols were both convicted in the attack, with McVeigh receiving the death penalty for his role. McVeigh was a homegrown domestic terrorist who had once been a member of the U. S. Army. He became a follower of Dr. William Pierce, founder of the Aryan National Alliance and followed the teachings outlined by a book written by Pierce, *The Turner Diaries*. The domestic terrorist threat has become a very serious problem for law enforcement, as the number of terrorist organizations within America continues to grow. The level of violence that terrorists' organizations are willing to use continues to increase. Organizations such as the

Earth Liberation Front (ELF) and the Animal Liberation Front (ALF) have taken credit for millions of dollars in damages to places such as car dealerships, resort buildings, and universities.

Law enforcement agencies that have fostered extended relationships through the use of community-policing strategies are well positioned to use these relationships for protecting communities from the terrorist threat. Programs such as Neighborhood Watch and Business Watch are good examples of avenues that can be used by law enforcement agencies to extend existing community programs into a free exchange of information between police and the community, on suspicious behavior that goes beyond the typical criminal threat.

Homeland Security initiatives have been developed for the city of Wichita, Kansas. A committee of industrial and corporate private security officials has begun working closely with the City of Wichita Police Department and the Sedgwick County Sheriff Office. Established with the support of the Wichita Police Chief and the County Sheriff, the Homeland Security Industrial Committee has resulted in meeting on a quarterly basis. Formal communication in the Homeland Security Industrial Committee sessions allows all members and participants to share information on resources, response strategies, and interoperability issues. Guest speakers routinely provide education on how resources from outside the community will be integrated into the local response strategy should the need ever arise. Common threat information can be routinely shared as a result of key corporate partnerships. Benefits include the integration of patrol commanders and representatives from the FBI Joint Terrorism Task Force into this group of business professionals so that relationships can be allowed to develop that will better prepare the community as a whole.

Additional initiatives in the Wichita community include the creation of a new position in the Wichita Police Department. The position of Coordinator of Emergency Planning and Security is a commissioned officer of supervisory rank. Responsibilities include the coordination of emergency planning efforts within the police department and establishing relationships and plans with other first responders and public safety agencies, as well as educating employees of the City of Wichita in recognizing threats to the community. Efforts include being the liaison between all City employees and the FBI Joint Terrorism Task Force (JTTF). This position is also expected to assist in educating the public about possible threats to the community and how to be active in protecting neighborhoods and reporting suspicious behavior. Venues for educating the public include the annual Neighborhood Watch Block Leaders Seminar.

While the process of integrating Homeland Security initiatives into community policing seems rather simplistic, results have already been observed. Two recent examples of close relationships between police and the community that they serve can serve as reminders of just how effective such strategies can be.

In the spring of 2004, a vendor near a large transportation center observed the presence of a middle-aged male every morning for a period of a few hours. The male was lingering near terminal passengers and asking specific questions about transportation activities and crowds. The vendor offered the male a potential job and requested a contact name and number so that he could call if the job came open. The vendor passed information on to transportation administration who forwarded it on to local police officials whom they had become acquainted with through joint training and education efforts. Once the police received the information, it was forwarded directly to the local JTTF. Within hours, JTTF had identified the male as being illegally in the United States and a former member of a hostile army that had fought against U.S. forces in the Gulf War. The male was quickly picked up and deported because of the risk he posed to the safety and security of the United States.

In the summer of 2004, as a result of community contacts, a citizen reported to local police that she was concerned about the activities of her neighbor. While reporting that she did not believe the neighbor to be a serious threat, she did feel that police should be aware of his activities. It was reported that the neighbor was known to send his family out of country anytime there was an imminent threat of a terrorist act occurring inside the United States. When local police reported the neighbor's information to the federal authorities, it was determined that this neighbor had connections with a known terrorist organization that had operatives inside the United States. Thanks to the alert and conscientious citizen, local and federal authorities were able to identify a new potential threat to America.

Through the initiatives and examples described within this section, it is easy to see just how effective open communication and proactive partnerships between the police and the community can become. Expanding upon the principles of community policing to provide the community with additional education on how individual citizens can be effective in the defense of the United States is a key concept in the safety and security of our society. Citizens will feel the duty to report seemingly insignificant information through established local police relationships. The reporting of suspicious behaviors or peculiar occurrences is critical in identifying a threat and providing intervention before a terrorist act can occur. The police and the citizens that they serve must be fully aware of the benefits of established communication channels and proactive reporting of suspicious behaviors through the foundation of community-policing principles.

The increase in funding for Homeland Security has come at the expense of community policing. In New York City the Federal Budget had a substantial impact on community policing for that city. The Federal Budget decrease caused the elimination of the hiring component of the Community-Oriented Policing Services (COPS) program, which has put 7,000 new police officers on the beat in New York City (Weiner 2004, 1). In addition to funding Homeland Security the war in Iraq has led to a cut in funds for community policing. In the first year of the war municipal leaders said they faced cuts of nearly one billion dollars of annual federal monies for community policing (Detroit Free Press 2003). In the years ahead community policing may see further decrease in funding because of Homeland Security or because of military engagements America may be involved in.

Community Policing and Space

Space is an important element of community policing. Space can be referred to as a location, neighborhood, census tract, a police sector, or a crime reporting area. This term refers to police and space. Place may include a classroom or street corner while space includes a census tract or a neighbourhood. Space is a larger area than place (Lersch 2004, 5). The notion of space can be divided into numerous categories; this can include a police force that can divide the city into zones, beats, districts or neighborhoods.

Community-policing philosophy holds that controlling space is important to maintaining order. Community policing suggests that the police should operate under a decentralized structure. Police working under a centralized structure defeats the philosophy of community policing. Decentralized community policing provides the police with an opportunity to work out of a decentralized location closer to the neighborhoods they police. The police are closer to neighborhood problems and concerns and are in a better position for problem solving and decision making. When officers are directly involved in the neighborhood they are in a position to be more in tune to the problems, cares, and concerns of the neighborhood and are in an excellent position to solve problems and implement solutions (Palmiotto 2005, 175–177).

One of the goals of community policing has been to get the police closer to the neighborhoods they police. For decades, big cities such as New York and Chicago had precincts in neighborhoods but with the implementation of community policing midsized cities and smaller cities are establishing district stations to get the police closer to the people. It is a trend that will continue into the foreseeable future. When the police get closer to the people they gain greater control of space for specific neighborhoods. The police need to be aware of the importance of space and how it is applied to community policing. Community-policing officers need to understand space and its importance to the success of community policing. A study of space should be incorporated to community-policing training (Palmiotto and Kingshott 2010, 48).

An important aspect of space is territoriality. Generally, the police are oriented toward territoriality, which means they are maintaining order. Territoriality means the police are controlling space. The major distinction between private and public space could be the most critical spatial delimitation that controls police activities. Private space may have barriers that cannot be easily overcome. For example, police cannot walk freely on private property. The police may need a warrant to search private space. The lines of demarcation between the public space and private space may be clear and limit the ability of the police to intervene (Palmiotto and Kingshott 2010, 49–50). Palmiotto and Kingshott wrote the following:

> Along with territoriality, crime mapping, surveying, and geography have all played a part in spatial analysis. Spatial analysis focuses on computer-based techniques because of a large amount

of statistical and geographical information. Police departments that have adopted the community policing philosophy should apply analytical techniques associated with geographical phenomena together with their spatial dimensions. This is a process of examining the locations, attributes, and relationships of features in spatial information through overlay and analytical techniques to obtain valuable knowledge. Spatial analysis creates new information from spatial information. This information can be effectively used in crime detection and assist in target hardening and crime prevention strategies.

(Palmiotto and Kingshott 2010, 49–50)

Police Community Support Officers

A new development of policing which has been developed in Great Britain is the Police Community Support Officer (PCSO). The American police may want to review what the British police are doing with PCSOs to determine if the concept should be incorporated into American policing. PCSOs are not police officers who have the task of supporting and complementing sworn police officers. They provide a visible and accessible presence in the neighborhood to improve the quality of life in the sectors they patrol. The PCSOs handle assignments that do not require experience or powers held by police officers. The PCSOs are given training that enables them to take needed action in the event of difficult encounters. They are supervised by police officers and have radio access that allows them to call for assistance if needed. The primary purpose of the PCSO program is to improve the neighborhood and provide public confidence and to support police officers within targeted patrol targets. PCSOs will address anti-social behavior, the fear of crime, environmental issues, and other factors that may affect the quality of people's lives (www.police communitysupportofficer.com/welcome.html, accessed April 2, 2010). The offenses that PCSOs have the authority to deal with include the following (www.homeoffice.gov.uk/anti-social-behaviour/penalities/penalty-notices/index.html, accessed April 2, 2010):

- Littering
- Graffiting or fly posting
- Causing so much loud noise that neighbors complain

- Intentionally harassing or scaring people
- Being drunk and disorderly in public
- Destroying or damaging property
- Petty shoplifting
- Selling alcohol to underage customers
- Selling alcohol to someone who is drunk
- Using fireworks after curfew

Challenges to Community Policing

In 1998, Robert Taylor and colleagues authored an article that assesses where community policing is today. Their insight is as valid in the first decade of the twenty-first century as it was in the latter part of the twentieth century. Taylor et al. stated that problems with community policing lie not so much with the concept itself as with the definition and implementation of the concept. It would be foolish to debate an approach that emphasizes development of a working relationship between the police and the community. But given how much federal money is available to police departments that wish to do community policing, everyone is claiming to be doing it—even when the changes made are superficial. Taylor et al. list five questions, all of which police departments should be able to say yes to if they are truly doing community policing:

1. Do we really see implemented most of the changes that community-policing advocates have recommended?
2. Have the entrance requirements for new officers been changed to reflect changes in the police role?
3. Has the department changed recruit training from a military-oriented academy to curriculum more in tune with the new role demanded by community policing?
4. Has the department flattened its organizational pyramid and placed more decision making in the hands of the officer? Has it implemented these structural changes on a citywide basis?
5. Has the chief turned the organization "upside down" and become committed to participatory dialogue with officers as a major part of his management style?

(3)

According to Taylor et al., community policing faces the following challenges:

1. Community policing has been insufficiently evaluated. Research has mostly focused on specific programs and not on the holistic implementation of the community-policing concept.
2. Community policing requires system change in all of city government.
3. Community policing is often not fully implemented and exists more in plans on paper than in actual policy.
4. Community policing has become too "politicized." It has been shielded from criticism in the departments that adopt it and the agencies that promote it.
5. Nationally, the rates of crime in general and violent crime in particular are declining. But the effect, if any, of community policing on this trend is difficult to disentangle from the effects of other factors, such as an increasingly aging population. Community policing may be claiming successes for which it is not responsible.

(3–5)

Recommendations

The following are recommendations for improving community policing. They came out of the Community Policing Strategies Conference sponsored by the Southwestern Law Enforcement Institute, in the latter part of the twentieth century:

1. Police departments should sustain community involvement in the community-policing effort.
2. Organizational structure must change if community policing is to be sustained. It must be decentralized, flattened, and streamlined.
3. Police departments, in their effort to sustain community policing, need to learn how to harness the power of new technology.
4. Management styles should emphasize motivation and coaching and deemphasize control over employees.

5. Policing strategies should change in response to the changing dynamics of the community.
6. Police agencies should see a community as a group of neighborhoods that are different.
7. Supervisors should be trained on how to evaluate community-policing officers.
8. Training should focus on diversity issues.
9. Separate community-policing units must be abolished. Every police officer is a community-policing officer.
10. All the criminal justice components—courts, probations, prosecution, corrections—should become community oriented.
11. Community-oriented policing should evolve into community-oriented government. Other governmental agencies should implement the tenets of the community-policing philosophy and help take control of the neighborhoods.
12. Police agencies should develop strategies to sustain community partnerships.

Prospects of Community Policing

The outlook for community policing is positive. Insightful police chiefs are questioning and searching for ways to improve community policing. The twelve recommendations will eventually become a reality. Already, many police departments have made great strides in implementing them. Further, the intellectual quality of police executives and line personnel is much superior collectively today than at any time in the past, and we can expect this trend to continue. Police recruits will be better educated, with most having a college degree, and their training will be expanded to include problem solving as well as law enforcement.

We can expect that in the future the community will play a larger role in the community-policing effort. The community will decide which problems and crimes have priority and will be involved in the decisions on who gets hired as a police officer to work in their community. They will take on more responsibilities in crime prevention and take control not only of crime and disorder problems but also of other problems affecting the community, such as those involving streets and zoning.

Community advisory councils will have a larger role in community policing. They will meet on a regular basis and work with operational commanders and police department policy makers to decrease the crime rate, disorder, and the fear of crime. They will identify and prioritize problems that a majority of residents want solved, will devise strategies to solve them, and will evaluate the success of the solutions devised. They will print a newsletter to inform residents of recent crime trends and provide crime prevention techniques to help citizens avoid becoming victims. They will also organize citizen patrols with the supervision of the police department. Working with the police, they will have graffiti and abandoned cars removed and will strive to clear the neighborhood of any appearance of disorganization.

Eventually, community-oriented policing will evolve into community-oriented government. Realistically, the police are not equipped to handle all of a community's problems, and all too often they have been saddled with problems caused by the incompetence or inefficiency of other government agencies. In the future, all the components of the criminal justice system—courts, probation, parole, prosecution, and corrections—are community oriented.

By now, community policing is so incorporated into police departments' operations that it is unlikely to disappear. Further, once communities have bought into the concept, they are unlikely to endorse a return to the traditional model of policing. When residents and business owners feel empowered to safeguard their communities, it will be difficult to turn the clock back.

Community policing will survive if it changes as society changes. Its concepts and strategies must continue to evolve.

When community policing becomes fully implemented in all the ways that Taylor et al. described, the term community policing will no longer be used because all policing will be based on the assumption that the community has a crucial role in crime prevention and crime solving.

Summary

In the latter part of the twentieth century, police practitioners realized that the professional policing approach was not working and that the public needed to play a larger role in solving and preventing crime. They began to experiment with a new approach that emphasized community participation in identifying, preventing, and solving crime and disorder problems. The new strategy became known as "community policing." The approach addressed not only law enforcement issues but also broader issues of improving and maintaining neighborhoods' quality of life.

The outlook for community policing is positive. We can expect that police training will be expanded to include community problem solving and that educational requirements for recruits will rise. Also, the community will play a larger role in making decisions about the policing they want for their neighborhood and the problems that have priority. They will do more in crime prevention and will take control of not only crime and disorder problems but also other problems affecting the community.

In the first decade of the twenty-first century community policing is becoming the foundation in the prevention of terrorist acts not only by foreigners but also by homegrown terrorists.

REVIEW QUESTIONS

1. Describe the changes that Taylor et al. consider necessary for the full implementation of community policing.

2. Describe the five "core challenges" that community policing faces, according to Taylor et al.

3. What does the future hold for community policing?

REFERENCES

1 Police History Relevant to Community Policing

Appier, J. 1992. Preventing justice: The campaign for women police, 1910–1940. *Women and Criminal Justice* 4(1): 5–7, 11–12.

Bopp, W.J. and D.O. Schultz. 1972. *A short history of American law enforcement*. Springfield, IL: Charles C. Thomas.

Carte, G.E. and E.H. Carte. 1975. *Police reform in the United States: The era of August Vollmer, 1905–1932*. Berkeley: University of California Press.

Connolly, V. 1944. Job for a lady. *Collier's*, June 10, p. 19.

Eck, J.E. and W. Spelman. 1987. *Problem-solving: Problem-oriented policing in Newport News*. Washington, DC: Police Executive Research Forum.

Federal Bureau of Investigation. 1970. *Uniform crime reports 1969*. Washington, DC: Government Printing Office.

Fogelson, R.M. 1977. *Big-city police*. Cambridge, MA: Harvard University Press.

Fosdick, R.B. 1920. *American police systems*. New York: Century.

Goldstein, H. 1979. Improving policing: A problem-oriented approach. *Crime and Delinquency* 25: 236–258.

Johnson, D.R. 1981. *American law enforcement: A history*. Saint Louis, MO: Forum Press.

Kelling, G.L. and M.H. Moore. 1988. The evolving strategy of policing. *Perspectives on Policing* 4: 1–15.

National Advisory Commission on Civil Disorders. 1970. *Report of the National Advisory Commission on Civil Disorders*. 90th Congress, June. Washington, DC: Government Printing Office.

National Advisory Commission on Criminal Justice Standards and Goals. 1973. *Task force report: The police*. Washington, DC: Government Printing Office.

National Advisory Commission on Intergovernmental Relations. 1970. *Making the Safe Streets Act work: An intergovernmental challenge*. Washington, DC: Government Printing Office.

President's Commission on Law Enforcement and Administration of Justice. 1967. *The challenge of crime in a free society*. Washington, DC: Government Printing Office.

Strecher, V.G. 1991. Histories and future of policing: Readings and misreadings of a pivotal present. *Police Forum* 1(1): 2.

Trojanowicz, R. and B. Bucqueroux. 1994. *Community policing: How to get started.* Cincinnati, OH: Anderson.

U.S. Code, Title 18, Part 1, Chapter 113B, $2331.

Walker, S. 1977. *A critical history of police reform.* Lexington, MA: Lexington.

———. 1992. *The police in America.* 2nd ed. New York: McGraw-Hill.

Williams, H. and P.V. Murphy. 1990. The evolving strategy of policing: A minority view. *Perspectives on Policing* 13: 1–15.

Wilson, J.Q. 1978. *Varieties of police behavior: The management of law and order in eight communities.* Cambridge, MA: Harvard University Press.

2 Understanding Police Culture

Baldwin, J. 1962. *Nobody knows my name.* New York: Dell.

Bayley, D.H. 1994. *Police for the future.* New York: Oxford University Press.

Brinkerhoff, D.B. et al. 1997. *Sociology.* 4th ed. Albany, NY: Wadsworth.

Crank, J.P. 1998. *Understanding police culture.* Cincinnati, OH: Anderson.

Downs, Raymond L. 2007. Less lethal weapons: A technologist's perspective. *Policing: An International Journal of Police Sciences and Management* 30(2).

Durkheim, E. 1966. *The sociological tradition,* trans. R.A. Nisbet. New York: Basic Books.

Fischler, G.L. 2005. *The psychological examination of peace officer applicants: Theory and practice.* www.psycheval.com/preemployment_screening.htm.

Ford, R.L. 1988. *Work, organization, and power: Introduction to industrial sociology.* Needham Heights, MA: Allyn & Bacon.

Fyfe, J.J. 1997. The split-second syndrome and other determinants of police violence. In *Critical issues in policing: Contemporary readings,* 3rd ed., ed. R. Durham and G.P. Albert. Prospect Heights, IL: Waveland.

Harris, R.H. 1973. *The police academy: An inside view.* New York: John Wiley.

Hellriegel, D. et al. 1983. *Organizational behavior.* 3rd ed. St. Paul, MN: West.

Janowitz, M. 1964. *The professional soldier: A social and political portrait.* New York: Free Press of Glencoe.

Kappeler, V.E. et al. 1995. Breeding deviant conformity: Police ideology and culture. In *The police and society: Touchstone readings,* ed. V.E. Kappeler. Prospect Heights, IL: Waveland.

———. 1998. *Forces of deviance.* 2nd ed. Prospect Heights, IL: Waveland.

Manning, P.K. 1997. *Police work: The social organization of policing.* 2nd ed. Prospect Heights, IL: Waveland.

McNall, S. and S. McNall. 1992. *Sociology.* Englewood Cliffs, NJ: Prentice-Hall.

Onnen, J. 1993. Oeoresin capsicum. *Police Chief* 60(5): 1–2.

Reuss-Ianni, E. 1983. *Two cultures of policing: Street cops and management cops.* New Brunswick, NJ: Transaction.

Rostow, C.D. and R.D. Davis. 2004. *A handbook for psychological fitness-for-duty evaluations in law enforcement.* New York: The Haworth Clinical Practice Press.

Rothman, R.A. 1987. *Working: Sociological perspectives.* Englewood Cliffs, NJ: Prentice-Hall.

Rubinstein, J. 1973. *City police.* New York: Farrar Straus Giroux.

Skolnick, J. 1994. *Justice without trial: Law enforcement in democratic society.* 3rd ed. New York: Macmillan.

Van Maanen, J. 1978. Observations on the making of policemen. In *Policing: A view from the street*, ed. P.K. Manning and J. Van Maanen. Santa Monica, CA: Goodyear.

Vilke, G.M. and T.C. Chan. 2007. Less lethal technology: Medical issues. *Policing: An International Journal of Police Strategies & Management* 30(2).

Wesley, W.A. 1951. *The police: A sociological study of law, custom and morality.* Unpublished doctoral dissertation, University of Chicago.

3 Police Discretion, Police Misconduct, and Mechanisms to Control Police Misconduct

Aaronson, D.E. et al. 1984. *Public policy and police discretion: Processes of decriminalization.* New York: Clark Boardman.

American Bar Association. 1974. *The urban police function.* Gaithersburg, MD: International Association of Chiefs of Police.

Barker, T. 1977. Peer group support for police occupational deviance. *Criminology* 15(2): 356.

———. 1986. An empirical study of police deviance other than corruption. In *Police deviance* ed. T. Barker and D.L. Carter. Cincinnati, OH: Anderson.

Barker, T. and R.O. Wells. 1981. Police administrators' attitudes toward the definition and control of police deviance. Paper presented at the Academy of Criminal Justice Sciences, Philadelphia.

Bopp, W.J. and D.O. Schultz. 1972. *A short history of American law enforcement.* Springfield, IL: Charles C. Thomas.

Brown, M.K. 1988. *Working the streets: Police discretion and the dilemmas of reform.* New York: Russell Sage Foundation.

Cox, S.M. and W.P. McCamey. 2008. *Introduction to criminal justice*, 5th ed., Durham, NC: Carolina Academic Press.

Davis, K.C. 1971. *Discretionary justice: A preliminary inquiry.* Urbana: University of Illinois Press.

Farley, C.J. 1997. A beating in Brooklyn. *Time*, August 22, p. 38.

Goldstein, J. 1960. Police discretion not to invoke the criminal process: Low-visibility decisions in the administration of justice. *Yale Journal* 69: 543–561.

Hyatt, W.D. 2001. Parameters of police misconduct. In *Police misconduct* ed. M.J. Palmiotto, Upper Saddle River, NJ: Prentice-Hall.

Klockars, C.B. 1986. Street justice: Some micro-moral reservations: Comments on Sykes. *Justice Quarterly* 3(4): 515–516.

Nahmond, S.H. 1986. *Civil rights and civil liberties litigation.* New York: McGraw-Hill.

National Advisory Commission on Criminal Justice Standards and Goals. 1973. *Police.* Washington, DC: Government Printing Office.

Palmiotto, M.J. 2001. Police misconduct: What is it? In *Police misconduct* ed. M.J. Palmiotto, Upper Saddle River: NJ: Prentice-Hall.

Policing the police [editorial] 1994. *New York Times*, May 1, section 4, p. 16.

President's Commission on Law Enforcement and Administration of Justice. 1967. *The challenge of crime in a free society.* Washington, DC: Government Printing Office.

Reiss, A.J. 1984. Consequences of compliance and deterrence models of law enforcement for the exercise of police discretion. *Law and Contemporary Problems* 47 (Autumn): 89.

Snow, R. 1992. Civilian oversight: Plus or minus. *Law and Order* 40(12): 51.

Stoddard, E.R. 1995. The informal "code" of police deviancy: A group approach to "bluecoat crime." In *The police and society: Touchstone readings*, ed. V.K. Kappeler. Prospects Heights, IL: Waveland.

Sweeney, Joan, n.d. "Use of Force Issues in a Community Policing Environment," U.S. Department of Justice: COPS.

Sykes, G. 1986. Street justice: A moral defense of order maintenance policing. *Justice Quarterly* 3: 498–507.

Terrill, R.J. 1990. Alternative perceptions of independence in civilian oversight. *Journal of Police Science and Administration* 17(2): 80.

Walker, S. 1986. Controlling the cops: A legislative approach to police rulemaking. *University of Detroit Law Review* 63: 362–389.

——. 1993. *Taming the system: The control of discretion in criminal justice 1950–1990*. New York: Oxford University Press.

4 Concepts, Strategies, Experiments, and Research Findings That Have Influenced Community Policing

Albright, E.J. and L. Siegel. 1979. *Team policing: Recommended approaches*. Washington, DC: Government Printing Office.

Attunes, G. and E.J. Scott. 1981. Calling the cops: Police telephone operators and citizens calling the police. *Journal of Criminal Justice* 9: 165–179.

Blank, M., S. Rollins and C. Ingacio. 1999. *Building effective community partnerships*. Washington, DC: Institutional Leadership, Office of Juvenile Justice and Delinquency Prevention, Office of Justice Programs, U.S. Department of Justice.

Brown, S.E. and J.H. Curtis. 1967. *Fundamentals in criminal justice research*. Cincinnati, OH: Anderson.

Courtney, B. 2002. *Collaborative problem solving as a catalyst for community policing*. Unpublished Master thesis, Washburn University, Topeka, Kansas.

Directed Patrol Project: Kansas City, Missouri. 1979. Washington, DC: Law Enforcement Assistance Administration.

Gay, W.G. et al. 1977a. *Improving patrol productivity: Vol. 1. Routine patrol*. Washington, DC: National Institute of Law Enforcement and Criminal Justice.

——. 1977b. *Issues in team policing: A review of the literature*. Washington, DC: Government Printing Office.

Gregory, E. and P. Turner. 1968. Unit beat policing in England. *Police Chief* 35(7): 42.

International City Managers' Association. 1967. *Police community relations programs*. Washington, DC: Management Information Service Report no. 286.

Kelling, G.L. and C.M. Coles. 1996. *Fixing broken windows*. New York: Free Press.

Kelling, G.L. et al. 1974. *The Kansas City Preventive Patrol Experiment*. Washington, DC: Police Foundation.

Momboisse, R.M. 1967. *Community relations and riot prevention*. Springfield, IL: Charles C. Thomas.

National Advisory Commission on Criminal Justice Standards and Goals. 1973. *Taskforce: The police*. Washington, DC: Government Printing Office.

Niederhoffer, A. and A.B. Smith. 1974. *New directions in police community relations*. San Francisco: Holt, Rinehart, & Winston.

Palmiotto, M.J. 1998. A study of residents' perceptions of fear of crime in public housing. *Justice Professional* 10(4).

President's Commission on Law Enforcement and Administration of Justice. 1967a. *The challenge of crime in a free society*. Washington, DC: Government Printing Office.

——— . 1967b. *Taskforce: The police*. Washington, DC: Government Printing Office.

Sherman, L.W. et al. 1973. *Team policing: Seven case studies*. Washington, DC: Police Foundation.

Skolnick, J. and D.H. Bayley. 1986. *The new blue line: Police innovations in six American cities*. New York: Free Press.

Spelman, W. and D.K. Brown. 1980. *Calling the police: Citizen reporting of serious crime*. Washington, DC: Government Printing Office.

Szynkowski, L.J. 1981. Preventive patrol: Traditional versus specialized. *Journal of Police Science and Administration* 9(2): 169.

The Newark foot patrol experiment. 1981. Washington, DC: Police Foundation.

Trojanowicz, R.C. 1984. Foot patrol: Some problem areas. *Police Chief* 49.

Van Kirk, M. 1977. *Response time analysis: Executive summary*. Washington, DC: Law Enforcement Assistance Administration.

Wilson, O.W. and R.C. McLaren. 1977. *Police administration*. 4th ed. New York: McGraw-Hill.

Wilson, J.Q. and G.L. Kelling. 1982. Broken windows. *Atlantic Monthly*, March.

——— . 1989. Making neighborhoods safe. *Atlantic Monthly*, February, 31–48.

Wycoff, M.A. 1988. The benefits of community policing: Evidence and conjecture. In *Community policing: Rhetoric or reality*, ed. J.R. Greene and S.D. Mastrosfski. New York: Praeger.

5 Communities and Neighborhoods

Austin, M.D. 1991. Neighborhood attributes and crime prevention activities. *Criminal Justice Review* 16(1): 18.

Brislin, R.W. 1981. *Cross cultural encounters: Face to face interaction*. New York: Pergamon.

Brown, L.P. and M.A. Wycoff. 1987. Policing Houston: Reducing fear and improving service. *Crime and Delinquency* 33(1): 71.

Bursik, R.M., Jr. and H.G. Grasmick. 1993. *Neighborhoods and crime: The dimensions of effective community control*. New York: Lexington.

Chideya, F. 1995. *Don't believe the hype: Fighting cultural misinformation about African Americans*. New York: Penguin.

Davidson, W.B. and P.R. Cotter. 1991. The relationship between sense of community and subjective well-being: A first look. *Journal of Community Psychology* 19 (July): 251.

Gusfield, J. 1975. *Community: A critical response*. New York: Harper & Row.

Heskin, A.D. 1991. *The struggle for community*. San Francisco: Westview.

Jason, L.A. 1997. *Community building: Values for a sustained future*. Westport, CT: Praeger.

MacIver, R.M. 1936. *Community: A sociological study*. London: Macmillan.

McMillan, D.W. and D.M. Chavis. 1986. Sense of community: A definition and theory. *Journal of Community Psychology* 14 (January): 9–16.

McNall, S. and S.A. McNall. 1992. *Sociology.* Englewood Cliffs, NJ: Prentice-Hall.

Mott, A.H. 1992. The decades ahead for community organizations. *Social Policy* 16(4): 12.

National Conference of Christians and Jews. 1994. Taking America's pulse: The National Survey on Inter-Group Relations.

Nisbet, R. 1966. *The sociological tradition.* New York: Basic Books.

Pearlman, J. 1979. Neighborhood research: A proposed methodology. *South Atlantic Urban Studies* 4: 43–63.

Peterson, M. 2003. *Intelligence-led policing: The new intelligence architecture.*

Ratcliffe, J.H. 2003. Intelligence-led policing. *Australian Institute of Criminology: Trends and Issues in Criminal Justice* (April).

Silverman, E. 1999. *NYPD Battles Crime: Innovative Strategies in Policing.* Northeastern University Press.

Wandersman, A. 1981. A framework of participation in community organizations. *Journal of Applied Behavioral Sciences* 17(1): 43–53.

Wellman, B. and B. Leighton. 1988. Networks, neighborhoods, and communities: Approaches to the study of the community question. In *New perspectives on the American community*, 5th ed., ed. R.L. Warren and L. Lyon. Chicago: Dorsey.

Williams, M.R. 1985. *Neighborhood organizations: Seeds of a new urban life.* Westport, CT: Greenwood.

Wilson, J.Q. and G.L. Kelling. 1982. Broken windows. *Atlantic Monthly* 249(3): 30.

6 Multiculturalism and Organizational Change

Administration on Aging. 2008. *A profile of older Americans: 2008.* Washington, DC: Department of Health and Human Services.

Brislin, R.W. 1981. *Cross cultural encounters: Face to face interactions.* New York: Pergamon.

Buhler, P. 1997. Managing in the 1990s. *Supervision* (September).

Caudron, S. 1997. The search for meaning at work. *Training and Development*, September, 24–27.

Chideya, F. 1995. *Don't believe the hype: Fighting cultural misinformation about African-Americans.* New York: Penguin.

Couper, D.C. and S. Lobitz. 1993. Leadership for change: A national agenda. *Police Chief*, December, 15–19.

Gergen, K. 1997. The significance of skin color in international relations. *Daedalus* 96: 397.

Gray, K. et al. 1997. Community policing and organizational dynamics. In *Community policing in a rural setting*, ed. Q.C. Thurman and E.F. McGarrel, Cincinnati, OH: Anderson.

Green, J. 2009. *Multicultural policing: The role of executive leadership*, www.fbinaa.org, retrieved February 2010 (July–August edition).

Henry, W.A., III. 1990. The browning of America. *Time*, 137(4): 4.

Holmes, M. and B.W. Smith. 2008. *Race and police brutality: Roots of an urban dilemma.* Albany, NY: SUNY Press.

Jackson, M. 2006. *Policing in a diverse society: Another American dilemma*. Durham, NC: Carolina Academic Press.

Klineberg, O. 1964. *The human dimension in international relations*. New York: Holt, Rinehart & Winston.

National Conference of Christian and Jews. 1994. *Taking America's pulse. The National Survey on Inter-Group Relations*. New York: NCCJ.

Osgood, M.W. and M.M. Osgood. 1975. *Cross-cultural universals of affective meaning*. Urbana: University of Illinois Press.

Principles of Good Policing: Avoiding violence between the police and citizens. 2003.

Schaefer, R. 2006. *Racial and ethnic groups*, 10th ed., Upper Saddle River, NJ: Pearson/Prentice-Hall.

Shusta, R.M., D.R. Levine, H.Z. Wong, A.T. Olson, and P.R. Harris. 1995. *Multiculturalism nationalism*. Englewood Cliffs, NJ: Prentice-Hall.

——. 2008. *Multicultural law enforcement: Strategies for peacekeeping in a diverse society*. Upper Saddle River, NJ: Pearson/Prentice-Hall.

Skogan, W.G. and S.M. Hartnett. 1997. *Community policing; Chicago style*. New York: Oxford Press.

Stephan, W. and D. Rosenfield. 1978. Effects of desegregation on racial attitudes. *Journal of Personality and Social Psychology* 36: 802.

Strecher,V. 1997. *Planning community policing: Goal specific cases and exercises*. Prospect Heights, IL: Waveland.

U.S. schools teach racism, educator tells conference. 1992. *Wichita Eagle*, September 11, pp. 1D, 3D.

Watson, E.M. et al. 1998. *Strategies for community policing*. Upper Saddle River, NJ: Prentice-Hall.

Webster's II. 1984. *New Riverside university dictionary*. Boston: Houghton Mifflin.

Weitzer, R. and S.A. Tuch. 2006. *Race and policing in America: Conflict and reform*. New York: Cambridge University Press.

7 Crime Prevention and Community Policing

Bayley, D.H. 1994. *Police for the future*. New York: Oxford University Press.

Bouza, A. V. 1990. *The police mystique*. New York: Plenum.

Brantingham, P.L. and P.J. Brantingham. 1990. Situational crime prevention in practice. *Canadian Journal of Criminology* 32(1): 25.

Bursik, R.J., Jr. and H.G. Grasmick. 1993. *Neighborhood and crime*. New York: Lexington.

Cantrell, B. 1988. A commitment to crime prevention. *FBI Law Enforcement Bulletin* 57(10): 3.

Chuda, T.J. 1990. *Basic crime prevention curriculum*. Columbus, OH: International Society of Crime Prevention Practitioners.

Clark, R.V. 1992. *Situational crime prevention: Successful case studies*. New York: Harrow & Heston.

Crime prevention and community policing: A vital partnership, part I. 1996a. *Washington Crime News Service* 2(1).

Crime prevention and community policing: A vital partnership, part II. 1996b. *Washington Crime News Service* 2(1).

Crime prevention and community policing: A vital partnership, part III. 1996c. *Washington Crime News Service* 2(4).

Crowe, T.D. 1991. *Crime prevention through environmental design: Application of architectural design and space management concepts.* Boston: Butterworth-Heinemann.

Ellison, S.L. 1995. *The Dade County (Miami, Florida) Neighborhood Cellular Watch Project: Evaluation of an innovative approach.* Unpublished report, Florida International University, College of Urban and Public Affairs.

Garofalo, J. and M. McLeod. 1988. *Improving the use and effectiveness of Neighborhood Watch programs.* Washington, DC: National Institute of Justice.

GMability. 2004. OnStar helps police locate, recover stolen vehicles. *General Motors: News and Issues* (October).

Hatler, R.W. 1990. Operation CLEAN: Reclaiming city neighborhoods. *FBI Law Enforcement Bulletin* 59(9): 22–23.

Hoffmann, J.W. 1994. Crime prevention officers can improve retail security. *Law and Order* 46(6): 94–96.

Jefferies, C.R. 1977. *Crime prevention through environmental design.* Beverly Hills, CA: Sage.

Kelling, G. et al. 1974. *The Kansas City preventive patrol experiment: A summary report.* Washington, DC: Police Foundation.

Lab, S.P. 1997. *Crime prevention: Approaches, practices, and evaluations.* 3rd ed. Cincinnati, OH: Anderson.

Lindsay, B. and D. McGillis. 1986. Citywide community crime prevention: An assessment of the Seattle program. In *Community crime prevention: Does it work?* ed. D. Rosenbaum. Beverly Hills, CA: Sage.

National Advisory Commission on Criminal Justice Standards and Goals. 1973. *Police.* Washington, DC: Government Printing Office.

National Crime Prevention Council. 1989. The success of community crime prevention. *Canadian Journal of Criminology* 31(4): 488.

——— . 1992. *Creating a climate of hope: Ten neighborhoods tackle the drug crisis.* Washington, DC: National Crime Prevention Council.

National Crime Prevention Institute. 1986. *Understanding crime prevention.* Boston: Butterworth.

Newman, O. 1973a. *Architectural design for crime prevention.* Washington, DC: U.S. Department of Justice.

——— . 1973b. *Defensible space: Crime prevention through urban design.* New York: Collier.

O'Keefe, G. et al. 1996. *Taking a bite out of crime: The impact of the National Citizens' Crime Prevention Media Campaign.* Thousand Oaks, CA: Sage Publications.

Perry, T. 1994. *Basic patrol procedures.* Salem, WI: Sheffield.

Rechenmacker, D.I. 1991. Telemarketing crime prevention. *FBI Law Enforcement Bulletin* 60(10): 8–9.

Rich, T.F. 1988. *The use of computerized mapping in crime control and prevention programs.* National Institute of Justice Research in Action. Washington, DC: Government Printing Office.

Rosenbaum, D.P. et al. 1986. *Crime stoppers: A national evaluation.* Washington, DC: National Institute of Justice.

Street Smarts: A guide to protecting your vehicle from auto theft. LOJACK Corporation, n.d.

Sherman, L.W. et al. 1997. *Preventing crime: What works, what doesn't, what's promising.* www.ncjrs.gov/works.

Walker, S. 1989. *Sense and nonsense about crime.* 2nd ed. Pacific Grove, CA: Brooks/Cole.

Whisenand, P.M. 1977. *Crime prevention.* Boston: Holbrook.

8 Problem-Oriented Policing

Boba, Rachel. 2003. *Problem analysis in policing.* Washington, DC: Police Foundation.

Bynum, T.S. 2002. *Using analysis for problem-solving: A guidebook for law enforcement.* Washington, DC: U.S. Department of Justice, Office of Community Oriented Policing Services.

Eck, J.E. and W. Spelman. 1988. *Problem solving: Problem-oriented policing in Newport News.* Washington, DC: National Institute of Justice.

Goldstein, H. 1979. Improving policing: A problem-oriented approach. *Crime and Delinquency* 25(2): 238–241.

———. 1990. *Problem-oriented policing.* New York: McGraw-Hill.

Moore, M.H. and R.C. Trojanowicz. 1988. *Corporate strategies for policing.* Washington, DC: National Institute of Justice.

Savannah Police Department. 1994. *Community policing and problem solving workshop: Participants' handbook.* Washington, DC: National Institute of Justice.

Taft, P.B., Jr. 1986. *Fighting fear: The Baltimore County COPE Project.* Washington, DC: Police Executive Research Forum.

Vaughn, M.S. 1992. Problem-oriented policing: A philosophy of policing in the 21st century. *Crime and Justice* 19(3): 345.

9 Community-Oriented Policing

Bayley, D.H. 1988. Community policing: A report from the devil's advocate. In *Community policing: Rhetoric or reality,* ed. J.R. Green and S.D. Mastrofski. New York: Praeger.

———. 1994. *Police for the future.* New York: Oxford University Press.

Brown, L.P. 1989. Community policing: A practical guide for police officials. *Perspectives on Policing* 12. Washington, DC: National Institute of Justice.

Cordner, G. 2005. Community policing elements and effects. In *Critical issues in policing: Contemporary readings,* ed. R.G. Dunham and G.P. Alpert, Long Grove, IL: Waveland.

Farrell, M.J. 1988. The development of the Community Patrol Officer Program: Community-oriented policing in the New York City Police Department. In *Community policing: Rhetoric or reality,* ed. J.R. Green and S.D. Mastrofski. New York: Praeger.

Goldstein, H. 1979. Improving policing: A problem-oriented approach. *Crime and Delinquency* 25(2): 238–241.

Grinc, R. 1994. Angels in marble: Problems in stimulating community involvement in community policing. *Crime and Delinquency* 40(3): 437–442.

Holland, M. 1994. Gellatly: Two programs help cut city crime. *Savannah Evening Press,* January 26, p. 12.

Klockars, C.B. 1985. *The idea of police.* Newbury Park, CA: Sage.

MacCulloch, C. 1915. *Outlook*, February 10.

Manning, P.K. 1997. *Police work: The social organization of policing*. 2nd ed. Prospect Heights, IL: Waveland.

McElroy, J. et al. 1993. *Community policing: The CPOP in New York*. Newbury Park, CA: Sage.

Moore, M.H. et al. 1988. *Crime and policing. Perspectives on policing*. Washington, DC: National Institute of Justice.

National Advisory Commission on Civil Disorders. 1968. *Report of the National Advisory Commission on Civil Disorders*. New York: E.P. Dutton.

National Institute of Justice. 1992. Community policing in Seattle: A model partnership between citizens and police. *National Institute of Justice Research in Brief*, August, 7–9.

New York City Police Department. 1987. *The Community Patrol Officers Program: Orientation guide*. New York: NYPD.

President's Commission on Law Enforcement and Administration of Justice. 1967. *The challenge of crime in a free society*. Washington, DC: Government Printing Office.

Skogan, W.G. 1996. The community's role in community policing. *National Institute of Justice Journal*, August, 31–34.

Skolnick, J. and D. Bayley. 1986. *The new blue line*. New York: Free Press.

———. 1988. *Community policing: Issues and practices throughout the world*. Washington, DC: National Institute of Justice.

Stipak, B. 1994. Are you really doing community policing? *Police Chief*, October, 115.

Trojanowicz, R. 1994. *Community policing: A survey of police departments in the United States*. Washington, DC: U.S. Department of Justice.

Trojanowicz, R. and B. Bucqueroux. 1990. *Community policing: A contemporary perspective*. Cincinnati, OH: Anderson.

———. 1994. *Community policing: How to get started*. Cincinnati, OH: Anderson.

Watson, E.M. et al. 1998. *Strategies for community policing*. Upper Saddle River, NJ: Prentice Hall.

Weisburd, D. and J.E. McElroy. 1988. Enacting the CPO role: Findings from the New York City Pilot Program in Community Policing. In *Community policing: Rhetoric or reality*, ed. J.R. Green and S.D. Mastrofski. New York: Praeger.

Wilson, J.Q. and G.L. Kelling. 1982. Broken windows. *Atlantic Monthly* 249(3): 30.

Wycoff, M.A. 1988. The benefits of community policing: Evidence and conjecture. In *Community policing: Rhetoric or reality*, ed. J.R. Green and S.D. Mastrofski. New York: Praeger.

10 Planning the Implementation of Community Policing

Adams, R.E., W.M. Rohe and T.A. Arcury. 2002. Implementing Community-Oriented Policing: Organizational Change and Street Officer Attitudes. *Crime and Delinquency* 48(3): 399–430.

Bureau of Justice Assistance. 1994a. *Neighborhood-oriented policing in rural communities: A program planning guide*. Washington, DC: U.S. Justice Department.

———. 1994b. *Understanding community policing: A framework for action*. Washington, DC: U.S. Justice Department.

Fyfe, J.J. et al. 1997. *Police administration*. 5th ed. New York: McGraw-Hill.

Koontz, H. et al. 1986. *Essentials of management*. New York: McGraw-Hill.

Kuykendall, J.L. and P.C. Unsinger. 1979. *Community policing administration*. Chicago: Nelson-Hall.

McKee, A.J. 2001. The Community Policing Evaluation Survey: Reliability, validity, and structure. *American Journal of Criminal Justice* 25(2).

Meese, E., III. 1991. *Community policing and the police officer. Perspectives on policing*. Washington, DC: National Institute of Justice.

Mottley, C. 1972. Strategy in planning. In *Planning, programming, budgeting: A systems approach to management*, 2nd ed., ed. J.F. Lyden and E.S. Miller. Chicago: Markham.

National Center for State, Local and International Law Enforcement. 1997. *Strategic planning and implementation*. Glynco, GA: Federal Law Enforcement Training Center.

Rossi, P.H., M.W. Lipsey, and H.E. Freeman. 2004. *Evaluation: A systematic approach*, 7th ed., Thousand Oaks, CA: Sage Publications.

Roth, J. and J.F. Ryan. 2000. *The COPS Program after 4 Years—National Evaluation*. Washington, DC: National Institute of Justice.

Rush, G. 1992. Community policing: Overcoming the obstacles. *Police Chief*, October, 50–55.

Sadd, S. and R.M. Grinc. 1996. *Implementation challenges in community policing: Innovative neighborhood-oriented policing in eight cities*. Washington, DC: National Institute of Justice.

Silverman, E. 1995. Community policing: The implementation gap. In *Issues in community policing*, ed. P.C. Kratcoski and D. Dukes. Cincinnati, OH: Anderson.

Sparrow, M. 1982. *Implementing community policing. Perspectives on policing*. Washington, DC: National Institute of Justice.

Tansik, D.A. and J. Elliott. 1981. *Managing police organizations*. Belmont, CA: Duxbury.

Ward, K., S. Chibnall, and R. Harris. 2007. *Measuring effectiveness: Planning and managing evaluations of law*. Washington, DC: Office of Community Oriented Policing.

Whisenand, P.M. and F. Ferguson. 1989. *The managing of police organizations*. Englewood Cliffs, NJ: Prentice-Hall.

11 Selected Approaches to Training and Planning

Couper, D.C. and S.H. Lobitz. 1991. *Quality policing: The Madison experience*. Washington, DC: Police Executive Research Forum.

Cross, P.F. 1981. *Adults as learners*. San Francisco: Jossey-Bass.

Eugene Police Department. 1997. *Community Involved Policing (CIP) Action Plan*. Eugene, OR: Eugene Police Department.

———. 1998. *Discussion paper on the formation of police/citizen/council committees*. Eugene, OR: Eugene Police Department.

Himelfarb, F. 1997. RCMP learning and renewal: Building on strengths. In *Community policing in a rural setting*, ed. Q. Thunnan and E. McGarrel. Cincinnati, OH: Anderson.

Illinois State Police, n.d. *Illinois State Police: Community-oriented policing*. Unpublished document, Springfield, IL.

Knowles, M. 1990a. *The adult learner: A neglected species*. Houston, TX: Gulf.

——. 1990b. The field of human resource development. In *Handbook of human resource development*, 2nd ed., ed. L. Nadler and Z. Nadler. New York: John Wiley.

Meese, E., III. 1991. *Community policing and the police officer. Perspectives on Policing*. Washington, DC: National Institute of Justice.

Palmiotto, M.J. et al. 1998. *A model curriculum for police recruit training in community policing*. Paper presented at the Academy of Criminal Justice Sciences, March 10–14, Albuquerque, NM.

Portland Police Bureau. 1990. *Community policing transition plan*. Portland, OR: Portland Police Bureau.

Royal Canadian Mounted Police, n.d. *CAPRA problem solving model*.

Wichita Police Department. 1996. *Public Safety Initiative*. Wichita, KS: Wichita Police Department.

12 Distinctive Community-Policing Programs

Aether Systems. 2001. Overcoming the perception of racial profiling. *Law and Order*, April.

Bureau of Alcohol, Tobacco, and Firearms. 1998a. GREAT National Policy Board. www.atf.treas.gov/greatiphisosy.htm. Accessed July 27.

——. 1998b. GREAT (Gang Resistance Education and Training). www.great-online.org. Accessed July 27.

Bureau of Justice Assistance. 1994. *Business Alliance: Planning for business and community partnerships*. Washington, DC: U.S. Department of Justice.

Carrick, G. 2000. Professional police traffic stops: strategies to address racial profiling. *FBI Law Enforcement Bulletin*, November.

——. 2001. A police response to racial profiling. www.lawandordermag.com.

Chaiken, M.R. 1998. *Kids, cops, and communities*. Washington, DC: National Institute of Justice.

Chicago Police Department. 1998. How does the Chicago Police Department respond to hate crimes? www.adl.org/issue_government/hate_crime_sentencing_act.asp Accessed July 30.

Courtney, B. 2002. *Racial profiling: Curriculum design and development*. Unpublished manuscript, Missouri Regional Community Policing Institute.

Ft. Worth Police Department, n.d. *Citizens on Patrol. Blue Code*. Ft. Worth, TX: Ft. Worth Police Department.

Gordon, M.B. 2002. *Making the match: Law enforcement, the faith community and the value-based initiative*. U.S. Department of Justice, Office of Community Oriented Policing Services.

Hoffman, D., n.d. *Community Service Unit information*. Arvada, CO: Arvada Police Department.

A law enforcement checklist: Important steps to end violence against women. 1997. Community Policing Exchange. November/December, p. 8.

Leadership Conference Education Fund Online. 1998. Cause for Concern: Hate crime in America. http:/civilrights.org/lcef/hate. Accessed July 29.

National Coalition for the Homeless. 1998. *Why are people homeless?* NCH Fact Sheet no. 1. www.nationalhomeless.org. Accessed May.

National Law Center on Homelessness and Poverty. 1998. Recent Legal Development. www.nlchp.org. Accessed March.

North Carolina Wesleyan College. 1998. List of community policing programs. www.ncwc.edu/~toconnor/comlist.htm.

Roehl, J.A. et al. 1996. *National Process of Operation Weed and Seed*. Washington, DC: National Institute of Justice.

Rucinski, C., et al. 1997. *Transitions*. Cheektowaga, NY: Cheektowaga Police Department.

Santa Monica Police Department. 1998. Homeless Liaison Program. www01.smgov. net/hsd/articles/1hhomelessfaqs.htmhip_team/hipteam.htm. Accessed July 26.

13 The Future of Community Policing

Detroit Free Press. 2003. *Iraq war, security cut funds for cops*. October 25, www.freep. com/new/nw/nat25_20031025htm.

Griset, P.L. and S. Mahan. 2003. *Terrorism in perspective*. Thousand Oaks, CA: Sage Publications.

Lersch, K.M. 2004. *Space, time, and crime*. Durham, NC: Carolina Academic Press.

Palmiotto, M.J. 2005. *Policing: Concepts, strateges and current issues in American police forces*. 2nd ed. Durham, NC: Carolina Academic Press.

Palmiotto, M.J. and B. Kingshott. 2010. Community policing and spatial analysis. In *Spatial Policing* ed. C.E. Crawford. Durham, NC: Carolina Academic Press.

Taylor, R.W. et al. 1998. Core challenges facing community policing: The emperor still has no clothes. *Academy of Criminal Justice Services Today* 17(1): 1–5.

Weiner, A.D. 2004. *Impact of the Bush Budget on New York City FY 2005*. Prepared by Congressmen Anthony D. Weiner, February 4.

www.homeoffice.gov.uk/anti-social-behaviour/penalties/penalty-notices/index.html (2010) Anti-Social Behaviour. Accessed April 2.

www.policecommunitysupportofficer.com/welcome.html (2010) What is PSCO? Accessed April 2.

INDEX